Studies in Australian Federation

THE EMERGENT COMMONWEALTH

THE EMERGENT COMMONWEALTH

Australian Federation: Expectations and Fulfilment 1889-1910

R. Norris

Lecturer in History
University of Adelaide

MELBOURNE UNIVERSITY PRESS

1975

First published 1975
Printed in Australia by
Wilke and Co. Ltd, Clayton, Victoria 3168, for
Melbourne University Press, Carlton, Victoria 3053
USA and Canada: ISBS Inc.,
10300 S. W. Allen Boulevard, Beaverton, Oregon 97005
Great Britain, Europe, the Middle East, Africa and the Caribbean:
International Book Distributors Ltd (Prentice-Hall International)
66 Wood Lane End, Hemel Hempstead,
Hertfordshire HP2 4RG, England

National Library of Australia Cataloguing in Publication data:
Norris, Ronald
    The emergent Commonwealth: Australian federation, expectations and fulfilment, 1889–1910/ [by] R. Norris.— Carlton, Vic.: Melbourne University Press, 1975.— (Studies in Australian federation).
    Index.
    Bibliography.
    ISBN 0 522 84090 6.
    1. Australia—History—1889–1910. I. Title. (Series)
994

To Mo

PREFACE

The Commonwealth of Australia came into being on the first day of the twentieth century. The Constitution, the formal document under which the new creation was to operate, empowered the Commonwealth Parliament to legislate on a number of subjects. The legislation of early federation in part embodied the expectations of the founding fathers. But in several notable ways it deviated from, or indeed moved beyond, anything the founders seemed to have contemplated.

This book defines some of the expectations of the makers of the Constitution and supporters of the Commonwealth Bill, and it plots some of the deviations in the first decade of federation. It tests assumptions about the new governmental machine against the evolution of three of the most important areas of policy: White Australia, defence, and socio-industrial welfare. It reappraises traditional interpretations for the origin of Commonwealth legislation on these subjects.

I owe much to many people for their assistance and advice. I thank the staffs of Commonwealth and State libraries, especially those of the National Library of Australia, the Menzies Library, and the Mitchell Library; the staffs of Commonwealth and State Archives, especially Dr K. Penny and Miss T. M. Exley of the Australian Archives; Mr L. F. Fitzhardinge, Mr H. J. Gibbney, and Mr Bede Nairn of the Australian National University; Dr J. Playford and Mrs D. Denholm of the University of Adelaide; the staff of Melbourne University Press, especially Ms J. Mackenzie; my wife, Muriel, and daughters, Jackie and Lee. I am most deeply indebted to Professor J. A. La Nauze and Dr F. B. Smith, who supervised the thesis from which this book emerged.

For permission to consult or quote manuscripts I am grateful to Mr E. G. Whitlam, and to the appropriate authorities of the Australian Archives, the New South Wales Government Archives, the National Library of Australia, and the Mitchell Library.

For the illustrations I acknowledge the permission or assistance of the National Library of Australia for those numbered 3, 8, 10, 11; of the State Library of Victoria for 1, and 4 and 6 from the La Trobe Collection; of the same, and the *Daily Telegraph*, Sydney, for 2; of the State Library of South Australia for 5 and 7; and of the Australian Archives for 9.

R. NORRIS

University of Adelaide

CONTENTS

ILLUSTRATIONS

1

FEDERATION: DESIGNS AND EXPECTATIONS

On the final day of the second Federal Convention Edmund Barton declared the Constitution Bill 'so clearly drawn that every man of ordinary intelligence . . . will be able to readily grasp its meaning'.[1] The satisfaction of the chief draftsman is understandable. In three sessions and seventeen weeks delegates had revised the Draft Bill of 1891 and replaced the 'simple and sometimes stately general language' of Sir Samuel Griffith with 'more elaborate and technical phraseology in order to render the intention more precise'.[2] Barton's remarks were a climax to a long history of conferences, conventions, and debates, designed to further the federation of the Australian colonies. Ahead loomed federation referenda, which would submit the issue of union under the Bill to electors in at least four colonies, and new problems, which Barton perhaps could not reasonably foresee in 1898.

The Bill may well have been, as Josiah Symon claimed, the 'finest instrument of government' ever framed.[3] Gifted draftsmen and lawyers such as Griffith, Barton, Inglis Clark, Charles Kingston, and Richard O'Connor had incorporated in it what delegates believed were the better features of the American, Canadian, Swiss, Norwegian, British, and Australian colonial Constitutions. Nonetheless, despite Barton's confidence, delegates themselves were not always clear what they intended and they left several contentious issues unresolved. Within a few years Griffith, O'Connor, and Barton himself were to disagree with former delegates and fellow Justices of the High Court, Isaac Isaacs and Henry Bournes Higgins, as to the meaning of sections of the Constitution. The revised version possibly used more 'technical phraseology', but its framers also resorted to 'vague or ambiguous' phrases to cover disagreements and they 'inadequately prepared and investigated' some questions.[4]

In fact, it is not easy to determine the intentions of the 'founding fathers' behind the formal (and perhaps on occasions deliberately obscure) language of a legal document. In the first place, while there are full reports of the general debates in the Conventions and the Committees of the Whole, the special Committees met in secret and their records do not report discussion. Secondly, all delegates at the first Convention, and the great majority at the second, were colonial parliamentarians.* Naturally, therefore, they were subject to local pressures, and, being uncertain of the prospects for federation and their own political careers, they were wary of committing themselves to specific policies. Delegates appeared reluctant to say what the proposed federal parliament should actually do, and how it would, or should, use and develop its powers. They were more concerned to devise a blueprint for a governmental machine, and arrange the working of its parts one with the other, than to predict precisely what its output would be.

However, despite the inherent difficulties, it is still possible to gain some idea of the intentions and expectations of the founders. For this purpose we shall consider aspects of the work at the Conventions: the principal resolutions; the system of dividing the powers between the Commonwealth and the States; the scope of the delegated powers; the status of the Senate and High Court. Finally we shall examine the federation referenda, when 'Billites' and 'anti-Billites' fought their public campaigns.

The first of the four resolutions to 'establish and secure an enduring foundation for the structure of a Federal Government' reflected the strength of State-rights sentiments in 1891. Sir Henry Parkes moved that

the powers and privileges and territorial rights of the several existing colonies shall remain intact, except in respect to such surrenders as may be agreed upon as necessary and incidental to the power and authority of the National Federal Government.[5]

Although Parkes, as instigator and president of the Convention, necessarily moved the resolution, this prime principle was not his. At a preliminary meeting of New South Wales delegates, Parkes had suggested four resolutions dealing with intercolonial free trade, federal customs power, defence forces, and public lands. His colleagues accepted the first three without objection, and subsequently

---

* See Appendices 1 and 2 for biographical notes on delegates.

resolutions embraced these subjects at the Convention. But they rejected the fourth, which instead of guaranteeing territorial rights, stated that a High Commission should 'enquire into, consider, and recommend for adoption an equitable scheme for the distribution of public lands.' Parkes explained that he had in mind the 'Northern part of Queensland, the Northern Territory of South Australia, and the enormous tracts of land within the boundaries of Western Australia, which never can be turned to proper account by the Government of Perth.'[6] The new resolution, which affirmed the powers and rights of the existing colonies, almost certainly resulted from a small informal meeting of Premiers and some other delegates in Parkes' office on the opening day of the Convention. Griffith, Clark, and Kingston were probably its co-authors, as all three had included a sentence to this effect in their own draft resolutions or constitutions.[7]

Whatever its origin this first principle of federation, which ran counter to the centralist tendencies of Parkes, received an enthusiastic reception at the Convention proper. Sir Thomas McIlwraith, Treasurer of Queensland, in a reaction typical of many delegates, termed it the 'cream of the resolutions'. Philip Fysh, Premier of Tasmania, expressed pleasure at the use of the word 'surrender'. This clearly indicated to the people of Australia that the Convention was 'unlikely to try their patience, to try their spirit of justice, in asking them to surrender any rights which they consider to be of vital importance to their local autonomies.' The purpose of the Convention was 'to continue in all its harmony, in all its prestige, the position of the local parliaments'. Alfred Deakin felt obliged to assert that delegates would fail in their duty if they did not embody in the Bill 'such a distinct limitation of federal powers as would put the preservation of state rights beyond the possibility of doubt'. Parkes rapidly sensed the mood of the assembly. He hastened to reassure the colonies that

neither their territorial rights nor their powers of legislation for the well-being of their own country will be interfered with in any way that can impair the security of those rights, and the efficiency of their legislative powers.[8]

Sentiments in favour of a maximum safeguard for the privileges of the States and a minimum surrender of powers to the central authority were still dominant at the Convention of 1897-8. The resolutions of 1891, Barton explained, had been altered only 'in the direction of brevity and simplicity'. On this occasion Barton moved resolutions intended to 'enlarge the powers of self-government of the people of Australia'. The first of the 'principal conditions' of federation read:

That the powers, privileges, and territories of the several existing colonies shall remain intact, except in respect of such surrenders as may be agreed upon to secure uniformity of law and administration in matters of common concern.[9]

Delegates sought to implement this basic principle by adopting a particular method of distributing powers between the Commonwealth and the States and by limiting the functions 'surrendered' to the federal parliament. The question of which authority, the central or local, should retain the residual powers was settled before the first Convention at the Australasian Federation Conference in Melbourne in 1890. Representatives of the colonial governments firmly rejected the Canadian model, which delegated powers to the Provinces and left the residue to the national parliament, in favour of the American, which delegated powers to Congress and left the residue to the States. Thomas Playford announced that South Australia would 'never agree' to union on Canadian lines. Inglis Clark, an admirer of the American Constitution, regarded the Dominion of Canada as 'an instance of amalgamation rather than of federation'; the colonies did not want this.[10] Convention delegates accepted, Barton acknowledged in 1891, that federal powers could not embrace the large range provided by constitutions which gave residuary powers to the central government. Kingston believed that the American system commended itself to every delegate and colony.[11] At Adelaide in 1897 Simon Fraser, a prominent Victorian MLC, claimed that Canada had made a great mistake in abridging the powers and privileges of the local parliaments.[12]

While the method of dividing the powers was never in doubt, members said little about the specific powers the central parliament should actually receive. Many delegates were well read in constitutional history and thoroughly versed in the precedents of existing federal constitutions. In 1890 Griffith submitted the first list of legislative powers (derived largely from the American Constitution, and the British North America and Federal Council Acts) and comparatively few substantive additions or alterations were made later.[13] Delegates apparently assumed that federal constitutions necessarily contained such powers, and most were content to leave questions of this nature to the experts. They seldom challenged the desirability of the presence of the great majority of Commonwealth legislative powers (or the absence of others) which eventually found their way mainly into sections 51 and 52 of the Australian Constitution. The handful of powers that delegates debated tended, therefore, to be those which they considered the most important, the more contentious, the new additions, and the obscure.

Two of the most important—taxation and defence—became closely connected in the Conventions. The founders conferred a concurrent power of taxation on the central parliament, and they provided for the exclusive control of defence.[14] The grant of full rights of taxation, together with the superiority of Commonwealth law whenever it conflicted with State, might seem to have infringed the spirit of the opening resolutions and the principle of distributing the powers. Delegates, however, ceded this broad power for two main reasons. First, it was an essential concession to free-traders. The founding fathers were not prepared to jeopardize federation, especially in New South Wales, by writing in the Constitution that for all time the federal government would have to rely solely for revenue on its share of customs and excise. Secondly, members considered it a reserve power to provide, if the need ever arose, for increased defence forces in times of national emergency.

Anxiety for the defence of the continent, prompted by the report and memorandum of Major-General Bevan Edwards on the individual colonial forces, is commonly thought to have caused Parkes to promote federation in 1889.[15] At the Conventions of 1891 and 1897–8 delegates generally endorsed central control of defence forces and policy. In 1891 Richard Chaffey Baker, an extreme States-righter, approved the taxation clause because 'We may have to spend our last shilling or to sacrifice our last man in our own defence'.[16] Deakin immediately made a similar statement. But though support for the defence power was near unanimous, few members appeared to expect that an actual need could arise for heavy expenditure. Australia could have no foreign policy of her own, and she was protected by her 'mighty moat'[17] and the power of the British Empire. Rather, they expected greater efficiency (Deakin argued that the very size of the existing forces warranted central control) and greater economy as a result of the amalgamation of separate forces and administrations into a common system. The practical danger to be guarded against was less a hypothetical enemy than possible federal folly in squandering surplus revenue on unnecessary naval and military expenditure.

Frederick Holder, Treasurer of South Australia and an influential delegate on financial questions, warned of this possibility and welcomed the Braddon clause as a check to federal extravagance.[18]

Delegates quickly dismissed the likelihood of a clash between the Commonwealth and States in the field of taxation. Deakin, a strong advocate of unlimited central powers of taxation, argued that if the States resorted one day to direct taxation (e.g. land tax) then they would thereby gain the 'priority in time' over the Commonwealth. He brushed aside the handful of objections on the wisdom of an unqualified right of taxation. Abuse of the power could be discounted. Electors who returned members to their local parliaments would be the same people who would return members to the House of Representatives. Therefore, not only would the States pre-empt the Commonwealth (which in any event was unlikely to venture beyond customs revenue), but people having once taxed themselves through their several legislatures would not wish to impose further taxes 'for the mere pleasure of taxing'. Andrew Thynne, a conservative Queensland MLC, pointed out that when central and local laws were inconsistent, the former prevailed. It was 'quite possible, and of course, in theory . . . quite feasible' that the Commonwealth would have the 'first helping hand' in funds for land taxation.[19] Deakin lightly conceded the point, which disturbed only Thynne, a delegate of minor rank. The question was not mentioned again in either Convention.

Several clauses fell within the contentious category. One of these, the proposed federal control of 'Postal, telegraphic, telephonic, and other like services' might reasonably have been expected to pass without dispute into the Constitution in the manner of others dealing with uniform administration. Some South Australians, however, opposed the transfer of the power. In 1891 Baker postulated that federal members representing the large States* would control the House of Representatives:

It would only be necessary for them to put a line in the estimates to enable them in making postal contracts to ensure that their states should be the only termini of the ocean steamers, and they would have thus placed in their hands the sole control of trade and commerce.[20]

At Adelaide in 1897, John Hannah Gordon, a liberal MLC, saw no advantage in handing over the services. The benefit of having the

* The terms 'large' and 'small' States (or colonies) referred to relative populations, not to areas: the large ones were New South Wales and Victoria.

same Queen's head upon all the stamps did not compensate for the disadvantages of a less effective administration and a large body of federal servants in each State. Holder feared 'undue centralisation', and moved to restrict central jurisdiction to beyond the boundaries of the Commonwealth. At Sydney the Convention dealt with an amendment proposed by the South Australia House of Assembly to confine the power to 'outside the limits of the Commonwealth'.[21] Presumably the earlier arguments of Barton and Deakin prevailed. Commercial interests wanted federal control of communications, which would be cheaper: America regretted the lack of a national telegraphic system.

A second proposed power not found in the American Constitution —marriage and divorce—also met with some opposition. Patrick McMahon Glynn, a Roman Catholic, spoke in support of an amendment of the South Australian Assembly to omit the sub-clause. Many South Australians strongly objected to the idea of the marriage tie being 'dragged down' to the level of New South Wales and Victoria. Divorce rates had soared in these colonies since their new divorce legislation of the early nineties, and they compared unfavourably with colonies which kept to the 'old notions' of marriage. However O'Connor, the second Catholic in the Convention, termed the absence of uniform laws in the United States a 'blot' which had led to deplorable social evils. Sir John Downer, a South Australian MHA, referred to the anomaly of a colonial marriage between a man and his deceased wife's sister being invalid in the United Kingdom: this was a 'highly proper' power which would 'probably be exercised at the earliest possible moment'.[22]

Delegates advanced fuller reasons than usual for two significant powers added to the original list proposed by Griffith. These were the sub-clauses dealing with the social questions of conciliation and arbitration, and old-age pensions. Professor Crisp's influential explanation for the limited legislative functions of the Commonwealth depicts the allocation of powers as a victory for 'Conservative Men of Property' over 'Liberal Men of Progressive Reform'.[23] Considerable debate took place at the Conventions on attempts to introduce these particular novel provisions. But the history of these attempts reveals division and confusion, rather than solidarity and order, between conservatives such as Griffith, Braddon, Downer, McMillan, and Zeal on the one hand, and radicals such as Kingston, Deakin, Higgins, Trenwith, and Cockburn on the other.

Kingston, who in 1891 first suggested a 'federal tribunal' to settle industrial disputes, was evidently motivated by the inability of the

South Australian Parliament to deal with the local effects of strikes originating in the eastern colonies. Capital and labour had federated: strikes called in New South Wales were obeyed in South Australia. His motion for 'courts of conciliation and arbitration' received little backing. Deakin gave it reluctant approval. He failed to see how this could possibly become a proper subject for federal legislation. On the contrary, he feared that

if this power were given to the federal legislature, it might be exercised less satisfactorily than it would be by the individual colonies. There must be in such a matter as this, a certain amount of experimental legislation. The colonies, left to themselves, may take different, and, to some extent diverse paths; and from the knowledge then gained, the federal parliament may legislate in the future.

Griffith promptly quashed the amendment with a potent argument. The proposal interfered with the rightful functions of the States: 'property and civil rights are left to the states!'[24] At the Adelaide session in 1897 Higgins and Kingston tried to give federal parliament a conciliation and arbitration power: delegates were not persuaded by their references to the shearers', maritime, and Broken Hill strikes. They met with success at Melbourne. William Trenwith, the only Labor Party representative at the Conventions, confessed that his views had 'undergone some change'; he now approved the sub-clause. Deakin now argued: 'Wherever we can detect a federal interest or power we should provide for it in advance', but predicted that this power, like many others, was 'not likely to be exercised by the Federal Parliament for many years to come'.[25] Conservatives such as Abbott, Forrest, and Lee Steere supported the amendment: without their votes it would have been lost.

The first Convention did not consider a federal pension power. James Howe, a conservative South Australian MLC, raised the issue at Adelaide and twice proposed sub-clauses at Melbourne in sessions of the second. Howe was inspired by the humanity of the old world, and disturbed by the inhumanity of the new. He spoke eloquently of the enlightened attitudes of Charles Booth, Canon Blackley, and the Bismarckian German Empire. Workers everywhere feared dependence in their old age 'upon the cold charity of the State'.[26] Experience as a member of the Royal Commission on the subject had convinced him that it was not a proper state matter as the population was 'too migratory'. The hard-earned lifetime savings of many thrifty people had recently been swept away like 'snow before the noonday sun'. Because of reckless and corrupt management

men who thought they had provided for their old and declining age found themselves stranded on the cheerless shores of charity, and many of them have had to accept even amongst ourselves the pauper's lot . . . one of the saddest and darkest blots on our civilization.[27]

At Adelaide, Higgins opposed the idea: the subject was 'a matter for the State Parliament and not the Federal Parliament'.[28] At Melbourne, Trenwith sympathized with the intention but considered a federal power 'extremely undesirable': it would be better 'to leave this matter as it is—a matter of domestic legislation—until under the powers of the Constitution the various states choose voluntarily subsequently to hand them over'.[29] Members defeated the motion, a mixture of conservatives and liberals voting both for and against the provision. Braddon, Forrest, and Solomon joined Kingston, Deakin, and Cockburn in support: Downer, Zeal, McMillan, and Symon allied with Higgins and Trenwith in opposition. Probably Trenwith's change of attitude encouraged Howe to re-submit the sub-clause and delegates to approve it. The Labor man had consulted a 'large number of people'. Though he himself still favoured leaving the subject to the States, he had now resolved to vote for the provision in order to induce the workers to accept the Constitution Bill at the referenda. Higgins also recanted 'with much misgiving'.[30] The Convention, in a clear example of enlightened self-interest, endorsed the amendment.

One of the late attempts to give the Commonwealth Parliament a new power resulted in confusion, and called into question the whole status of the central body. John Henry, a Tasmanian, proposed a clause which would enable the federal parliament to render financial aid to States during the period of transition or at times of natural disaster. The proposal provoked a variety of reactions, but a basic disagreement emerged in the course of debate. One group of delegates argued that an implied power already existed by virtue of clause 51 (iv) 'Borrowing money on the public credit of the Commonwealth', and in the 'very fact of the Union'.[31] Another contended that the Constitution strictly confined federal expenditure to its enumerated powers: O'Connor, Reid, Glynn, and Isaacs relied on the distinction between the terms 'Commonwealth' and 'States' in the Constitution. The preamble to clause 51 (the concurrent list of delegated powers) referred to the 'good government of the Commonwealth', as distinct from the *States*. Clause 81 (covering the appropriation of federal revenue) alluded to appropriations for 'the purposes of the Commonwealth', again as distinct from the States. Therefore, O'Connor asserted, he had no hesitation in denying the existence of any such implied power.

Here, then, in the final session of the second Convention serious doubts arose about an important power of the Commonwealth Parliament. The borrowing power, and its possible use, had never been fully debated. In 1891 delegates discussed not the clause itself, but whether having approved it they should 'insist' on the Commonwealth consolidating the debts of the colonies. Only Thynne observed that no provision existed in the Bill to limit the objects for which the Commonwealth could borrow money.[32] Members accepted the sub-clause without comment at Adelaide and Sydney in 1897. Now, at the last session in Melbourne, they reached no decision on a fundamental issue, the powers of borrowing and appropriation of the federal parliament.

A similar situation arose on the vaguely worded and obscure federal power to make laws respecting 'Trade and commerce with other countries, and among the States'. Inglis Clark, aware of American precedents, advised that this could be one of the widest powers. Barton regarded the clause as the natural corollary of intercolonial free trade (which many delegates termed the supreme motive for federating). Delegates readily accepted the clause, but they were uncertain as to its meaning. The provision became inextricably bound up with the vexed questions of preferential railway rates and gauges, and irrigation and navigation on inland rivers. Victorians hopefully interpreted this and related clauses as implying readier access to the Riverina. South Australians construed it to safeguard their rights to the Murray traffic and Broken Hill trade. New South Welshmen defended their interests and found comfort in ambiguity. In the end at Melbourne, their differences still unresolved, they agreed to disagree.[33]

Nonetheless, while the founders thought reasons for including most of the individual powers were self-evident and they made few predictions on their use, their opinion of the enumerated list as a whole became apparent. Griffith, when he first detailed the powers, challenged any member who believed the scheme took too much from the local parliaments to 'take up any volume of the statutes of the state legislatures, and see how few of those statutes deal with subjects with respect to which powers are taken from the states.'[34] It was impossible to enumerate the residual powers, he explained, but he would mention some for the benefit of those who suspected that the Convention had some 'sinister object' to deprive State parliaments of their autonomy:

Their constitutions, the borrowing of money, the complete control of the government of the state, all laws relating to property and civil rights, the whole subject of public lands and mines, registration of titles, education, criminal law and its enforcement, municipal institutions, imposition of licenses, the administration of justice, both criminal and civil, and the establishment of courts, and an absolute power to dispose of their revenue in any way they think fit . . .[35]

Cockburn pleaded that no attempt be made to define the powers retained by the States because to define meant to limit and

the advance in the future will be in the direction of the state taking upon itself many functions which are at present performed by private individuals. . . . Many things which are now entirely conducted by private enterprise . . . will before no long interval of time elapses, be undertaken by state governments.[36]

Deakin claimed that the division of powers guarded State rights: 'The states will retain full powers over the greater part of the domain in which they at present enjoy those powers, and will retain them intact for all time'. In 1897 he discounted the possibility of the central government becoming so powerful as to 'overshadow and dwarf' the States. On the contrary the States would probably 'over-awe' the Commonwealth: it appeared 'certain' that the federal government 'with its limited scope and its authority chiefly on the seaboard, will be a comparatively feeble power when opposed to the great States growing up in this continent'.[37] Reid surveyed the list, observed that functions not expressly handed over remained with the States, and commented: 'the question of State rights ceases to press so seriously'. At Sydney he read out the powers of federal parliament and added that the sphere of the 'socialistic agitator' was absent.[38]

The Constitution provided two inbuilt impediments to the freedom of action of the central government within its own limited area of legislation. These were the Senate and the High Court.

The question of the status and role of the Senate provoked the sharpest debates at the Conventions. In 1891 a combination of conservatives and small-State liberals such as Abbott, Baker, Barton, Clark, Downer, Griffith, Thynne, Cockburn, Gordon, and Kingston advocated a strong 'States House': the States must, Griffith believed, 'concur by a majority in every proposal'. This large group admired the powerful American Senate and despised the degenerate House of Lords. Members denied the analogy between a Second Chamber in a federal system and an Upper House in a unitary one: 'council of the states', Baker claimed, better described the Senate's constitution and functions. Some even doubted the efficacy of responsible government and the party system: 'Has not the very existence of responsible government', Clark asked, 'very often lowered the character and quality of legislation? . . . Party government [was] played out'. A second combination headed by the Victorian MLAs—Deakin, Gillies, Munro, Wrixon, Smith—Parkes, and Macrossan advocated a weak Senate. This smaller group disapproved of the American Senate as a model for the Australian, and approved of the House of Lords. Members saw some similarity between the functions of the proposed Senate and those of colonial Legislative Councils (especially the Victorian) and they endorsed the familiar system of responsible government: Parkes sought a ministry 'as similar as it can be to the ministry of England'.[39]

The conflict centred on the crucial question of the power of the Senate to veto proposed legislation, especially money Bills. Thomas Playford first alluded to the method (based on the practice in South Australia) which eventually solved the conundrum, though Kingston had incorporated the idea in his own Draft Bill. The first Convention empowered the Senate to veto *in globo* or in detail all Bills except those dealing with taxation and appropriation. These it could either reject outright or return with 'suggestions' for amendment to the House of Representatives. The second Convention reopened the question. The financial clause introduced into the Committee of the Whole abandoned the 'compromise of 1891' and strengthened the 'States Assembly' by permitting it to amend proposed taxation laws. Delegates narrowly carried Reid's amendment to revert to the earlier compromise. The 'defection' of two South Australians (Kingston, Glynn) and three Tasmanians (Brown, Lewis, Henry) in a small versus large States division, averted a possible collapse of the Convention.[40]

Several changes affecting the Senate resulted from the greater faith in the notions of popular democracy and parliamentary sovereignty evident at the second Convention. Delegates introduced provisions to resolve deadlocks between the Chambers at joint sittings (the Nor-wegian system) and to establish a fixed ratio of 1:2 between the number of Senators and Representatives. Direct election of Senators replaced their indirect nomination by State parliaments, and the responsible cabinet system was now assured by the provision that ministers must be members of parliament within three months of the first general election. These alterations in the Draft Bill of 1891 un-doubtedly reflected the less conservative character of the later Con-vention, most of whose members were elected by popular vote in 1897.[41] Progressive delegates such as Higgins, Deakin, Kingston, and Cockburn succeeded in making the revised Bill more democratic, which, rather than expanding the delegated powers of the Common-wealth Parliament was surely their intention ('since what time', Cockburn once asked, 'have centralisation and democracy been associated?').[42]

Nonetheless, the 'liberalized' Constitution was not necessarily expected, or intended, to weaken the Senate as a States House (or perhaps even to reduce its potentially conservative role as an Upper House of review). The Drafting Committee—Barton, O'Connor, Downer—introduced the 'nexus' to prevent the Senate from being 'confined to some small number, with the result of seriously diminish-ing its importance and its consequence in the eyes of the federa-tion'.[43] Isaacs suspected that the provision was intended to preserve the strength of the Second Chamber at joint sittings on deadlocks. O'Connor and Downer, a staunch conservative and States-righter, supported direct election to make the Senate stronger. Baker endorsed the change for the same reason. Besides, as Forrest pointed out, dele-gates expected the system of voting with the State as the whole electorate, to return Senators of a similar character to themselves.[44]

Taken in all, therefore, the advocates of a powerful Senate in either of its dual roles in checking the federal government were thought to have gained the better of the compromises. In 1891 Sir John Bray, Chief Secretary of South Australia, believed that the system operating in the colony 'really in effect [amounted] to giving the power to the Legislative Council' to alter money Bills.[45] Kingston, who made a 'concession' in 1897 by supporting the return to the compromise of 1891, had, as Premier of South Australia, good reason to know the strength of an Upper House clothed with such powers. Henry, the Tasmanian defector, saw practically no difference between the powers of suggestion and amendment. Isaacs regretted that the Senate was protected in money matters like no other Upper Chamber.

Lyne anticipated that only men of means who commanded wealth could become Senators. Trenwith predicted that the Senate would be 'prejudicial and baneful' in resisting legislation that the people desired: a large number of delegates expected it to be the 'dominant' House. At the end of the Melbourne session Baker, who as Chairman of Committees had been unable to enter debate, took the opportunity to give his verdict. He considered the changes since 1891 and weighed the strengths and weaknesses of the Senate. It would be the 'sheet-anchor' of small States: he could 'safely recommend' the Bill to the people who had sent him to the Convention.[46]

Whereas the intentions of the founding fathers of the American Constitution concerning judicial interpretation remain controversial, there can be no doubt that their Australian counterparts deliberately incorporated the doctrine of judicial review in their Constitution. The framers took the American Supreme Court, as it appeared in the last decade of the nineteenth century, as their model. They expected the High Court to function as an independent brake on the central parliament and government, stopping any possible excesses. In 1897 Barton saw the Court as 'one of the strongest' guarantees of indestructibility of federation: its chief value would be to prevent the federal government being the arbitrator and to forestall the secession of States denied justice. Trenwith sought a 'strong and dignified custodian of the Constitution' because otherwise people might suspect that the Commonwealth Parliament would exceed the powers 'intended by the Constitution, and thereby curtail the State rights about which [they were] all so anxious'. Symon, a conservative States-righter, declared that the High Court would 'safeguard the liberties of the subject and the rights of the individual States against the encroachment of the Legislature'. The Draft Bill of 1891 provided for the creation of the Court by an Act of parliament, the Bill of 1897–8 by sections of the Constitution itself. The object of the change, Bernhard Wise explained, was to 'make the High Court in all essential parts independent of Parliament'.[47]

Before turning to the federation referenda campaigns we may first briefly assess some of the expectations of the framers of the Constitution. The nature of the principal resolutions and the method of distributing the powers reflected the strength of State-rights sentiments in 1891 and 1897–8. Delegates believed that the scope of the delegated powers had to be, and indeed was, severely restricted. They planned a strong Senate, a sort of cuckoo in the federal nest, to check any excesses of an ambitious central government. They provided for the establishment of an independent High Court to safeguard the Constitution and the States against federal aggrandizement.

Statements by delegates on two important questions—the financial requirements of the Commonwealth and the work of the central parliament—illustrate their belief in the limited potential of the new machine. Wise asserted that it would be 'exceedingly difficult, if not impossible, for the Federal Government to levy direct taxation'. McMillan claimed 'they will never go beyond Customs; nobody dreams of such a thing'. Deakin was 'absolutely certain' that whatever the fiscal policy 'the whole sum required will be raised by means of the Custom-house'. Downer wanted to know 'where, in this Constitution, any great expenditure can come in, either in the first five, seven, or eight years, or at any subsequent time except, possibly, it may be in regard to defence?' Baker ('our last man . . . our last shilling') believed that 'for a considerable time—perhaps for ever— the Federal Government will rely on taxes raised through the Customs'. Barton predicted that any tariff, free trade or protectionist, would 'for the sake of the states, result in a considerable surplus'.[48] The greatest financial problem of the Convention was how to devise a just and equitable distribution of the surplus.

The great tasks of the Commonwealth Parliament would be to arrange a uniform tariff and to serve as a central customs agency: thereafter there would be little of consequence for it to do. Braddon had no doubt that the first sitting would be long because of the tariff: transactions after that would be 'of an exceedingly simple character, and occupy a very small amount of time'. Glynn believed the tariff would take up the whole session and

during the first ten or fifteen years very few of the matters delegated to the Federal Parliament will become the subject of legislation. If there were such expedition . . . the functions of the Federal Parliament would be exhausted in 25 or 30 years.

Holder claimed parliament would sit for five months a year at the very most: Turner forecast three months. Higgins expected the Commonwealth Parliament to have

much less to do than the ordinary local Parliaments after the first Parliament. . . . the work done in the States Parliaments [would take] far more time than will the work in the Federal Parliament, after its first meeting. It is not likely, indeed, that the Federal Parliament will sit more than two months in the year.[49]

In short, the founding fathers apparently did not conceive that the federal union of their single colonies could beget an offspring which might one day outstrip the States.

The Convention delegates, having persuaded themselves that the proposed Constitution embraced the most perfect instrument of government yet devised, had now to convert colonial electors to this view and to persuade them to vote for union under the Bill. The colonies which had sent elected representatives to the second Convention—New South Wales, Victoria, South Australia and Tasmania—held referenda on 3 and 4 June 1898. The Bill received majorities in all four colonies. But in New South Wales the affirmative vote fell 8405 short of the 80 000 minimum imposed by the local parliament. This 'defeat' in the mother colony led to a conference of all six colonial Premiers in Melbourne early in 1899, from which emerged seven amendments to the Bill.[50] Second federation referenda carried the amended Bill in South Australia, New South Wales, Victoria, and Tasmania between April and July 1899. Queensland, unrepresented at the Convention of 1897–8, eventually passed an Enabling Bill for its referendum and submitted the Constitution Bill to the popular test on 2 September 1899. Western Australia, whose delegation had been elected by parliament, stood out until the eleventh hour; finally it held its required referendum on 31 July 1900. Thus from the breakup of the Federal Convention in March 1898 to mid-1900 there were ten federation referenda in the six colonies. Never before had such campaigning taken place on any issue.

Detailed accounts of the campaigns require, but still await, exhaustive studies of events in the separate colonies. Nonetheless, some insights into aspects of the federation movement can still be gained from a more cursory survey of the public campaigns. The issues Billites stressed or neglected, the nature of counter-appeals made by anti-Billites, and the composition of the two opposing groups provide some indication of what federalists and anti-federalists expected from federation, of what they led the public at large to believe, and perhaps even what people did expect and believe. In this way, and by examining the voting in the referenda, the influence of political, economic, and other factors may also be assessed.

The referenda of 1898 were unquestionably the decisive ones. Although the Bill narrowly failed to get the statutory 'Yes' vote in New South Wales, its moral victory there, together with the clear victories in the other three colonies, ensured that a federation embracing at least some of the Australian colonies would be formed. By the time of the second referenda in 1899 the anti-Billites, except for a desperate last stand in New South Wales, had virtually conceded defeat and the result was a foregone conclusion.

The most active campaigners were the Convention delegates, prominent parliamentarians, representatives of vested interests, and the major newspapers. The delegates were near unanimous in their support of the federal Bill; only Higgins in Victoria, and Lyne and Brunker in New South Wales declared against the measure, though 'Yes-No' Reid, then Premier, gave it a qualified approval in a mere four speeches. In New South Wales parliamentary and business opinion was sharply divided. In Victoria, South Australia, and Tasmania the governments backed the Bill, while a few politicians and businessmen, together with the majority of Labor members, opposed it. The Sydney *Daily Telegraph*—violently anti-federal—the Adelaide *Advertiser*—'academically critical'—the Hobart *Mercury* and the Labor papers were the outstanding exceptions to the massive news and editorial support of metropolitan and country newspapers. As the polling days drew near the opposing camps marshalled their forces until finally Federation and Commonwealth Leagues openly faced Anti-Commonwealth Bill Leagues in each colony.

One of the more persistent appeals Billites used to disarm the opposition and arouse the apathetic was that of the progressive character of the proposed Constitution. The qualifications of electors of the House of Representatives were those applying to electors of 'the more numerous House of Parliament of the State'. The Senate, in contrast to its American namesake, would be directly elected: its franchise, in contrast to colonial practice, would be the same as that for the Lower House. The amending process rendered the Australian Constitution more flexible, more amenable to the popular will than any existing federal compact. Baker, the Chairman of Committees, on his return from the Melbourne Session remarked: 'Never in the history of the world has a more democratic Constitution been submitted for the approval of any people'. Kingston, Convention president, at the opening of his campaign recommended the Constitution as an 'advance' upon their own, the best in Australia: it was the 'most democratic measure ever framed by the chosen representatives of a free people'. Deakin, leader of the Victorian Billites, at the close of his campaign, confessed he was astounded and delighted with 'the radical constitution they had obtained'.[51]

Federalists also referred to the benefits which would result from the uniformity of certain laws and administration. Uniform commercial laws would simplify business procedure. Centrally administered departments of posts, telegraphs, telephones, defence, lighthouses, and quarantine would increase efficiency and decrease running costs. Campaigners occasionally alluded to the advantages of common systems of old-age pensions, immigration control, marriage and divorce.

Besides these particular claims there were a number of important basic appeals about the economic advantages of federation. Union would restore the confidence of British investors and revive the flow of investment. Consolidation of loans and conversion of debts would reduce interest payments and secure cheaper loans. The construction of north–south and east–west transcontinental railways, and a uniform rail gauge, would further the development of remote regions and facilitate trade. Above all intercolonial free trade promised to open up vast unrestricted markets for primary and secondary produce, stimulate the economy, decrease unemployment, and restore prosperity to the depressed colonies.

Barton advised electors in New South Wales to accept the Bill because intercolonial free trade was 'absolutely necessary to the full development of Australian resources'; O'Connor declared that the main object of union was to sweep away 'all obstacles to freedom of trade and intercourse between the States'.[52] Turner, at a public meeting convened by the Australian Natives Association in the Melbourne Town Hall, pointed out that federation would overcome the great drawback to the full success of their policy of protection— the restricted market for Victorian products:

This fact in itself ought to be quite sufficient to commend the proposals contained in the bill to the favourable consideration of every man, woman, and child in Victoria. (Cheers) . . . Intercolonial free trade was embedded in the constitution. He had always regarded that as the keystone of federation.[53]

The manifesto of the Victorian Federation League (chairman, Alfred Deakin) concluded:'An Australian union is certain to promote industrial development, an increase of profitable production for our farmers, and general prosperity among all classes of the community'.[54] The South Australian delegates, in their joint manifesto which accompanied copies of the Bill distributed to electors, stressed that union would open up an unrestricted market of nearly four million con-

sumers—independent of the 'goodwill or caprice' of their neighbours
—and would thereby secure 'for ever the immense commercial advantages to which the unrivalled geographical position of South Australia' entitled the colony. The appeal of the Commonwealth League,
a list of benefits heavily biased towards economic factors, placed at its
head the promotion of 'the prosperity of Australia in general and
South Australia in particular. Without Federation South Australia
never can become great or populous. She is now stationary and
depressed.'[55]

The counter-campaigns in defence of the *status quo* sought mainly
to discredit the claims of the Billites and expose the flaws in their
appeals. Thus anti-Billites directed one of their major challenges at
the alleged democratic nature of the Constitution. The Bill did not
eliminate plural voting or end property qualifications of electors of
colonial legislatures; these voters would return the federal parliament. It failed to provide for electorates of equal size. According to
S. A. Rosa, a radical, this would lead to 'jerrymandering'.[56] Equal
representation of unequal States in the Senate would be, claimed the
manifesto of the Colonists' Anti-Convention Bill League, the 'Death-
knell of Majority Rule'. The Senate's so-called power of 'suggestions'
was a denial of responsible government. The High Court, a second
likely conservative institution, infringed the traditional sovereignty of
British parliaments, and would prove an 'oppression to the people'.[57]
The amending process was only marginally more liberal than the
American, where, anti-Billites noted, the few important amendments
since the Bill of Rights had only come about after a Civil War over
State rights. The deadlock provision was a farce. In all, the un-
democratic 'cast-iron' Constitution, a 'slavish copy' of the American,
placed a 'dead hand' on future generations of Australians.

Anti-Billites also challenged the extent of the economic benefits of
union. Centrally administered departments would not necessarily be
more economical or efficient. Locally controlled ones like posts and
telegraphs were more sensitive to local needs, and possibly cheaper.
The additional expense of yet another system of government with its
paraphernalia of a Governor-General, legislature, and bureaucracy,
was bound to fall on taxpayers over-burdened with similar trappings
in their own colonies. The cost of new federal machinery, estimated
by Billites as a mere £300 000 a year, was absurdly low. George Reid
had so completely dominated the Convention that, the Hobart
Mercury alleged, 'nobody dared to mention a tariff higher than six
millions'. Internal free trade was all well and good, but the abolition

of border duties threatened State treasuries. This would be a 'step towards insolvency or additional taxation',[58] warned Hugh R. Dixson (later Sir Hugh Denison), chairman of the South Australian Anti-Bill League. The loss in revenue together with the extra cost of an expensive new government would necessitate a high federal tariff. This socially unjust form of indirect taxation would fall heavily on the working classes.

These widespread attacks on the 'financial' aspects of federation were particularly dangerous to the Billite cause. If the colonies were to reap the full benefits of intercolonial free trade—and relatively few outside New South Wales disputed the desirability of this prime aim—then clearly the gains must not be offset by losses incurred by either a costly federal system or depleted State treasuries. Hence the greatest battles of the campaigns raged over the cost of federation and the effectiveness of the financial provisions.

Federalists everywhere reassured electors. Turner, Premier and Treasurer since 1894, advised Melburnians

there need be no great fear of any extra expenditure or increased taxation. When we recognised that he [the future Commonwealth Treasurer] would be carefully watched in his expenditure, not only by the State Treasurers but by the State representatives, there need be no fear whatever that the federal Treasurer would be able to enter upon any unnecessary or extravagant expenditure.

The Melbourne *Argus* boldly put the 'Cost of Nationhood' at 'A HALFPENNY PER WEEK'. Holder, South Australian Treasurer since 1894, declared four 'dividends' to set against his colony's share of the cost, and thereby converted an apparent deficit into a potential asset.[59] The Commonwealth League predicted that federal union would cost South Australia nothing.

The conflict on the financial question was fiercest in New South Wales. There the implications of a uniform external tariff were not uniformly welcomed, especially in the metropolis. Anti-Billites charged that revenue raised by this means would inevitably tax New South Welshmen unfairly because their colony relied less upon duties and more upon the alienation of land for public finance than other colonies. A common tariff would place the ports of Sydney and Melbourne on an equal footing. Trade might be diverted to the southern rival. Sydney could lose its commanding position. A high tariff would inevitably reduce the total value of imports and speed the doom of the previously free port. The *Daily Telegraph* ranted:

'We should be VOLUNTARILY PLACING A BAR ACROSS SYDNEY HAR-
BOUR . . .'; the 'Braddon blot' was 'THE WORST, MOST UNWORKABLE
CLAUSE IN THE CONVENTION BILL'.[60] Barton implored Holder to
appear before the three-man Committee appointed by the government to investigate the financial issue so as to counter attempts by
Coghlan and others to 'swell' the new expenditure: 'The FINANCIAL
question has become all-important to us, as public opinion seems to
turn entirely upon it'.[61] The Committee's report failed to settle the
controversy as both camps claimed they had been vindicated. The
limitation of the Braddon clause to ten years 'and thereafter until the
Parliament otherwise provides' by the Premiers' Conference in 1899
took some of the sting out of attacks but did not silence all critics.
Dr Normand MacLaurin, leader of the anti-federalists in the Legislative Council, alleged that the amended clause was intended 'to keep
the Federal Treasurer in leading strings on behalf of the smaller
colonies'. Another member of the Colonists' Anti-Convention Bill
League derided Reid, who had insisted on the change, as 'a baby in
the hands of the other Premiers'. The new clause was 'a fatal disease
to the whole Constitution'. It saved the 'necessitous States', which
would not permit its repeal.[62]

It is difficult to determine what the targets of this flood of propaganda—the electors of New South Wales and the other colonies—
made of the bland assertions and counter-assertions. Interpreting the
results of an election or referendum, attempting to explain why
electors voted as they did and what they hoped to achieve, is only
less hazardous than trying to predict the actual outcome by virtue of
it being impossible to be proved wrong. Patricia Hewett, in a contribution to the debate between Professor Parker and Geoffrey Blainey
on the role of political, economic, and other possible factors in the
referenda, investigated fourteen electorates in south-eastern New
South Wales.[63] Hewett's research produced a negative result. The
lack of statistical data, the inability to identify the active electors, the
difficulty of weighting particular issues, and the overwhelming sense
of confusion produced by contradictory appeals make it impossible
to draw any positive conclusions.

These are indeed severe difficulties. But the problems are perhaps
not quite as insuperable as they may appear. A hard core of experienced politicians led the campaigning and set its tone. As such they
must be credited with knowledge of what would attract people to
their cause in 1898 and 1899. But, of course, the opposing sides made
conflicting appeals on a variety of issues. Basically, therefore, it would

seem to come down to which group of campaigners voters were prepared to trust and which of their appeals appeared the more credible and prominent. As the Billites defeated their opponents one must assume that the majority were readier to believe in them than in the anti-Billites.

It seems highly unlikely that Billite pleas for the Bill as a democratic advance could have made much impact. Support for the measure cut completely across normal political allegiances and persuasions and produced some very strange alliances. In New South Wales J. H. Want resigned from the Reid ministry in order to fight the Bill more freely. The Labor Party opposed the Bill, though a few members campaigned for it. The Colonists' Anti-Convention League included Labor men such as William Morris Hughes and staunch conservatives such as MacLaurin. Rosa, a radical republican, wrote one of the League's pamphlets. Anti-socialists such as Bruce Smith and MacLaurin found themselves on opposite sides.

In Victoria the Turner ministry, together with most parliamentarians of all persuasions, announced full support. The opponents were a less powerful combination than in New South Wales. Higgins gave the most intelligent radical criticism in any colony. But the Labor Party was hopelessly divided. Trenwith, and some others strongly approved the Bill. Bromley, Party secretary, found it necessary to explain in a letter to the *Age* that a 'majority' was actually against it.[64]

Great confusion of traditional party lines also existed in South Australia. On the one hand Kingston, radical idol of the colony, and most of his liberal colleagues, were allied with their political enemies. Baker, president of the Legislative Council (the conservative bastion which Kingston was attempting to storm), Downer and Solomon (leaders of a disorganized opposition in the Lower House) and Symon all approved the Bill. In 1893 Kingston had been bound over to keep the peace after challenging Baker to a duel and parading in Victoria Square with a loaded pistol; his public correspondence with Symon 'would have justified half a dozen duels'.[65] On the other hand T. H. Brooker, whom Kingston appointed government whip in April 1898 during the course of the campaign, actually campaigned against the measure. So too did a unanimous United Labor Party, whose active aid had enabled Kingston to govern since 1893. The honourable John Warren, a reactionary MLC known as the Longwool Conservative, lent his support to the anti-Billite cause.

Thus if any issue was nullified by utter confusion, then it was the plea to federate because of the progressive character of the Bill, not simply because of the contradictory appeals but also because of the very composition of the bodies making them. The joint advocacy of diehard conservatives such as Baker, McMillan, and Zeal with radical liberals such as Kingston, Deakin, and Isaacs on this score scarcely inspired confidence. They were, as one cartoon depicted, 'Strange Bedfellows'. Nor, surely, for the same reasons, could the converse arguments have swayed many voters. Moreover the efforts of anti-Billite radicals were prejudiced by some of their own sympathizers. For instance the Adelaide *Advertiser*, then a radical paper, opposed the Bill but admitted that it was 'beyond all question . . . a great victory for democratic opinion'. The *Age*, a reluctant and critical supporter, regarded the proposed Constitution as a 'fair instalment of democracy'; but it could not refrain from commenting on the extraordinary attitude of the Victorian Legislative Council: 'The amazing thing is that the most zealous eulogists of the Bill come from the very body which has resisted every effort to enlarge its franchise and widen the choice of candidates for its seats.'[66] No doubt electors, like the *Age*, were also incredulous.

The issues of federal finance and intercolonial free trade dominated the campaign. Appeals on these issues, unlike the political, were given some coherence and credibility by the semblance of unanimity within the ranks of the protagonists. The interests of Baker in the Wallaroo and Moonta Mining and Smelting Company possibly made it easier for him to sacrifice certain political principles. In May 1898 shareholders approved the decision of the company to borrow £100 000 to extend its works at Wallaroo to smelt lead concentrates from Broken Hill and to construct a sulphuric-acid plant. Baker, a director with, as he modestly put it 'comparatively to my means a large stake in this company', trumpeted his personal interest and pointed to the employment new works would bring, provided federation guaranteed the supply of ores.[67] Holder also developed the theme which 'could not be done without intercolonial free trade'.[68] Symon, a passionate free-trader, owned a vineyard in Adelaide: winemakers, Billites and anti-Billites agreed, had much to gain from federation. The secretary of the Vinegrowers Association in a circular to members stressed that intercolonial free trade would create fresh outlets for wines, brandies, raisins, and currants. He instructed each on his 'duty' not only to vote for federation 'but to endeavour to induce all in his power—and more especially those employed by him—to record their votes in its favour and to afford them every facility in so doing.'[69] Thomas Hardy, a pioneer vigneron, thoughtfully informed two apprehensive factory owners at a meeting of the Chamber of Manufactures that the enormous expansion in the wine industry 'would make up for all their tobacco factories'.[70] Symon and Hardy had campaigned together throughout the nineties for intercolonial free trade; the former was president of the Federation and Commonwealth Leagues, the latter a foundation executive member of the Federation League. The *Age* explained that Legislative Councillors could 'expiate' political sacrifices and display such complacency and satisfaction because of 'the prospects of increased trade and profits which they behold as within their grasp. . . . Conservatives and free-traders may need to cover the abandonment of their principles and conceal their retreat and mortification by such demonstrations.'[71] In 1900 mine managers and mine workers on the West Australian gold-fields presented a united front for federation, partly to alleviate local political and economic grievances, and partly to achieve intercolonial free trade.[72]

Conversely, the hostility of MacLaurin to federation possibly owed something to the fact that he was a director of the Colonial Sugar Refining Company. A second director, H. E. Kater, strongly backed MacLaurin's attempt to defeat the Federal Enabling Bill in the New South Wales Legislative Council.[73] The company was Sydney based but expanding rapidly into Queensland.[74] If New South Wales federated and Queensland did not (and at this time Queensland was boycotting the affair) then imports of raw and refined Queensland sugars for refining and marketing in Sydney would be subject to the Commonwealth's external tariff. At a meeting of the Chamber of Manufactures, J. Muir, the company's spokesman, ridiculed the 'very nice picture' painted by another member of the enormous benefits of intercolonial free trade. This 'rosy account' was possible 'if they lived long enough' but in reality it was 'a gilded pill to induce them to swallow Federation without regard to the cost'. MacLaurin, in his final appeal to electors, stressed that the federal tariff would inevitably be high, and warned of a proposal to impose '£7 a ton Customs duty on Sugar from Queensland, and £7 excise on our own sugar.'[75]

Similarly, Hugh R. Dixson, chairman of South Australia's Anti-Commonwealth Bill League, owned one of the largest tobacco factories in Adelaide. At a meeting of the Chamber of Manufactures, and in letters to newspapers, he predicted a drift of employers and employees to the eastern States and threatened to close his factory.

Newspapers rumoured that he had actually given notice to his men, to take effect if federation was achieved. The Tobacco Twisters' Union prophesied the ruin of the industry and declared that federation under the Bill was 'detrimental' to the workers of South Australia. Alexander Dowie, proprietor of the largest tannery and boot factory, feared the disastrous effects of cheap Victorian imports of footwear and declared himself an 'uncompromising' opponent.[76] Tanners in the Trades and Labor Council, and the West Torrens Working Men's Association, decided to urge the government to place export duties on raw hides so as to 'keep the work of handling hides in the colony'.[77] The local town councils opposed federation because it would 'crush' local industries and their ratepayers were 'dead against it'.[78] Brooker, Kingston's wayward whip, represented West Torrens, as did F. J. Hourigan, a leading anti-Billite and president of the Tanners' Union. The opposition to intercolonial free trade by Tobacco Twisters', Saddlers', and Operative Bootmakers' Unions in Western Australia in 1900 split the Coastal Trades and Labor Council, which then decided to go no further in advocating federation.[79]

Thus when political enemies such as Baker and Holder advanced common political reasons for federating, then electors might be expected to be sceptical or bewildered; but when political enemies advanced common economic reasons, then electors could well be justified in thinking that there might indeed be something in these appeals. Similarly, when political foes such as MacLaurin and Hughes used common political arguments against federation, then electors could scarcely have been impressed; but when they used common economic arguments, namely higher taxation all round and detrimental effects on trade, commerce, and industry, then these appeals were likely to have some impact. In a like manner, when capital and labour in particular industries agreed on either the beneficial or the adverse effects of federation, then workers in these and dependent or related occupations, and residents where they were located, had good reason to find their appeals credible. For instance, local traders, shopkeepers, and ratepayers in West Adelaide, where Dixson had his factory and where he and tobacco workers campaigned, could hardly have been pleased with Dixson's declared intention to close down. Their counterparts on the West Australian goldfields must surely have been impressed by the rare unity of employers and employees.

W. G. McMinn, in a study of the first referendum in the Newcastle district, emphasized the public apathy to federation reflected in the low polling in the region.[80] This poor response resulted from the lack of clear leadership in the area, the confusion of issues, and the hostility of coal miners to federation. The mining electorates suspected a cunning Victorian plot to undermine the coal industry of New South Wales and strongly opposed federation. Electors of the city of Newcastle, which as an entrepôt stood to gain considerably by the abolition of restrictions on intercolonial trade, voted for the Bill.

John Bastin, in an account of the federation movement in Western Australia, suggested that federation in the west was virtually decided on the goldfields and at Albany.[81] The remote, underprivileged, and under-represented goldfields sought political and economic reforms denied by the government in Perth; federation meant a 'burst up of Forrestism' and intercolonial free trade promised to end exorbitant railway tariffs and heavy duties on food imports, and thereby to reduce the high cost of living on the fields and to raise wage levels. Albany, also inspired by an 'intense hatred' of Forrest's government, fought the centralization of Perth with its preferential treatment of its rival, Fremantle; federation and intercolonial free trade promised to retain the mail-steamer traffic, abolish the differential tariff on imports unloaded at Albany, and to develop the district as a centre of trade, commerce, and manufacture. Voting patterns in the old settled coastal districts are more difficult to explain. In these agricultural areas there was a conflict between continuing to protect local farm produce from cheap eastern imports by not federating, and retaining important markets for food on the goldfields which might be lost if federation failed and the fields separated as they threatened. Some variations in polling in the region can be explained in terms of 'divergent economic interests', others defy analysis.

In South Australia there was a clear correlation between regional economic interests expressed at the Royal Commission on Inter-colonial Free Trade in 1891 and in the federation campaign, with actual voting in the referendum of 1898.[82] Wheat, wine, and border regions eager for new markets or the return of the old, districts and towns seeking to retain or regain the Barrier traffic and River Murray trade had great expectations of federation and intercolonial free trade. In the event they proved overwhelmingly pro-federal. The electorates of West Adelaide and West Torrens, the threatened centres of expendable 'exotic' industries which the Royal Commission termed 'features of dissent' to its call for free trade, and anxious market gardeners and orchardists in the Adelaide Hills, were anti-federal.

Probably, therefore, at least many, perhaps even most, of the extremes in voting—the peaks and troughs—can be accounted for in terms of divergent economic interests, with reactions to intercolonial free trade the greatest single determinant. Can this hypothesis be extended to explain the voting in colonies as a whole and to cover the 'grey' areas where no direct gain or loss was apparent?

The stress on capturing new and safeguarding old intercolonial markets was only in part aimed at the regions and places directly involved. Appeals of this nature had a wider application to the colony at large because of the great *revenue* derived from the traffic and the cumulative indirect gains—the multiplier effect—to the colony in general. In 1897–8, for example, revenue from the Barrier rail traffic represented over 40 per cent of South Australia's rail returns and about 12 per cent of the colony's entire revenue. In this sense then each colony was a separate economic entity. Primary producers and others who sought government aid in times of distress, and taxpayers who ultimately had to pay the bills, had a vested interest in the financial viability of the colony. Further, when prominent anti-Billites in New South Wales implied that other colonies were 'a pack of swindlers, conspirators, or thieves'[83] they strengthened the hand of Billites elsewhere. The more they protested that their colony would bear the brunt of the cost and suffer under the Bill's rail, rivers, and harbour provisions, the more credible appeals on these issues appeared in the other colonies. The greater the challenges on the 'advantages' of a 'natural' flow of trade for a Sydney more remote from some of its greatest natural assets than its rivals, the greater the delight of observant Billites outside New South Wales in claiming that their own colony was striking a good bargain. Where no clear purely local threat was evident, such appeals emanating from the large majority of experienced politicians of the other colonies—the Premiers and Treasurers past and present—must surely have carried great weight with electors who identified themselves closely with their own particular colony. Paradoxically, as already noted, their bitter political animosity strengthened their claims to be acting for the welfare of the colony as a whole. They were 'diametrically opposed to each other in politics, some being democrats and some conservatives, and yet they all recommended the adoption of the Bill.'[84]

Moreover, while New South Wales debated whether it could afford to federate, the choice for South Australia, Tasmania, and later Queensland and Western Australia was more critical. The small colonies in fact were in a dangerous position. On the one hand should federation not come about, then New South Wales could well go protectionist under William Lyne and thereby deprive them of the one remaining free market on the continent. On the other, should a small colony reject the Bill and the others accept, then under the federal tariff the self-isolated colony would be treated as a 'foreign' state and thereby rendered destitute. Hence the vital question for the small colonies became not could they afford to federate, but rather could they afford not to.

Billites made great play on the theme of committing economic suicide by spurning the opportunity of joining richer partners and going it alone. Symon warned South Australians that their colony would suffer the fate of bankrupt Newfoundland which had foolishly chosen to remain aloof from the Dominion of Canada. In Tasmania Wise invoked the same spectre of the doomed Newfoundland which had been 'unable to meet its engagements'. At a public meeting convened by the Southern Tasmanian Federal League C. H. Grant, a Convention delegate, forecast that Tasmanians would soon live to regret a veto on the Bill and Archdeacon Whitington asked 'could they afford to stand out?'[85]

The decision of the four south-eastern colonies to federate gave even greater force to the argument when applied to the dilatory colonies in the north and west. E. B. Forrest, MLA for North Brisbane and a managing partner in a merchant-pastoralist company, aired a common opinion in the *Courier*'s federation supplement

The acceptance of the Commonwealth Bill by New South Wales, Victoria, South Australia, and Tasmania, leaves Queenslanders very little room for hesitation. . . . Isolation under the altered conditions of trade, which will follow the federation of the Southern colonies, can never be justified by anybody.[86]

Federalists in the east exploited the possibility of Western Australia as a solitary foreign colony in the continent in attempts to encourage the federation movement in the west. Queensland, Deakin informed Walter James in 1899, would probably come in though perhaps after a delay: 'Can Western Australia afford isolation from Australia?'[87] On the eve of the referendum, George Leake, president of the Federation League, urged West Australians to federate 'not only on account of the many political and commercial advantages which will follow, but more especially because of the danger and disadvantages of standing out'.[88]

Therefore, it seems no mere coincidence that the broader trends of voting between one colony and another, or between large divisions within a colony, closely parallel the expected economic effects of federation. No colony was as aggressively self-confident of enormous profits from intercolonial free trade as Victoria. The *Age* explained the 'amazing' performance of Legislative Councillors in terms of them gloating at the prospect of waxing fat and reluctantly admitted: 'He would be a bold man who would say that a Customs-Union of the colonies must not be a great gain to Victoria'.[89] Significantly, the Victorian anti-Billites under Higgins—the 'Mahdi of the anti-federal dervishes'—confined their attacks almost exclusively to the constitutional defects of the Bill. As it happens no colony proved more staunchly pro-federal in the referenda than Victoria. The 'impecunious' small colonies of South Australia and Tasmania, anxious to refurbish the public and private purse and fearful of the consequences of isolation from larger and richer neighbours, also seized their opportunity to federate.

In direct contrast the economic benefits of federation were most open to dispute in New South Wales. There an important minority charged that not only would they pay the lion's share of the exorbitant cost but also that they had less to gain by, or would suffer from, a possible redirection of trade to its 'natural' outlets. As it happens New South Wales proved the least pro-federal in the 1898 referendum. Even after concessions to Reid and with his full support in 1899, some 46 out of 125 electorates defeated the amended Bill in the second referendum.[90]

Again, a broad pattern of polling emerged in Queensland. The northern and central districts, the great sugar-producing areas, carried the Bill.[91] Sugar growers such as Angus Gibson—owner of the largest plantation in Queensland—were among the most ardent supporters of federal union. Gibson, spokesmen for the industry in the *Courier*'s federation supplement, enlarged upon the fact that under federation the other States would have to purchase all their sugar from Queensland, which would be protected against foreign imports; this was 'the dream of many interested in the sugar industry'. The *Courier* warned local growers that if they rejected the Bill they 'must face the same economic conditions of production as the Javanese and Fijians and Mauritians. It [meant] the extinction of, or a vital blow at, the industry'.[92] Conversely, the Bill met its greatest opposition in Brisbane and the south. One opponent gloomily predicted that the Darling Downs would revert to a 'sheep walk'. The *Courier*, before the referendum, reported that the Downs expected to be 'swamped' by produce of other colonies and wanted to preserve Queensland markets for Queensland farmers. Quick and Garran, after the referendum, explained the situation in the following terms:

> In Brisbane and throughout the southern district the opposition to the Bill was very strong. Farmers, merchants, and manufacturers feared the competition of their New South Wales neighbours under a system of intercolonial freetrade. . . . Brisbane feared the competition of Sydney, just as Sydney had feared the competition of Melbourne. . . . It was a war of vested interests and intercolonial protection against commercial unity.[93]

Nonetheless, the influence of any one particular issue, no matter how important, cannot, of course, fully explain a complex phenomenon like the federation movement. Clearly many factors, both local and general, were at work. Australian nationalism has been suggested as a decisive motive. Bastin, for example, revived Fred Alexander's idea of applying Turner's frontier thesis to the goldfields. He asserted that a 'national feeling' in Western Australia, developed under the influence of thousands of 'T'othersiders', played an important part in the success of the movement. McMinn acknowledged that city electors in Newcastle had more to gain from intercolonial free trade than city electors in Sydney, and were indeed more pro-federal, but concluded that this explanation alone was unsatisfactory: 'Patriotic motives must have played a strong part'. Hewett suggested that for many electors 'a burning spirit of patriotism' overrode rational analysis of the federal scheme. 'National sentiment', which the 'ill-informed yet enthusiastic elector' could share, inspired a spate of anthems, prayers, and songs.[94]

It is tempting to regard the federation movement and the victory for the Commonwealth Bill as triumphs for Australian nationalism in a decade when native-born outnumbered immigrants. Leading federalists such as Parkes, Barton, and Deakin no doubt were inspired by, amongst other things, visions of a 'Nation for a Continent, and a Continent for a Nation'. Campaigners did make use of, and did evoke, patriotic demonstrations. The Billites, amongst whom numbered brilliant exponents of nineteenth-century rhetoric, addressed large, enthusiastic audiences who flourished flags and sang songs; patriotic poems proliferated. At a public meeting convened by the Australian Natives Association Deakin boasted: 'Against the measure, was not to be found one Australian born person of note in the community'.[95] Prominent federalists such as Deakin, Wise, and Garran subsequently portrayed the movement as carried forward on the crest of an irresistible wave of national enthusiasm, and the Commonwealth as launched on a high tide of popular approval.

But at the Corowa Federation Conference, which in 1893 marked an important stage in the 'popular' revival of federation, Edward Dowling, secretary of the Sydney Australian Natives Association, complained of the apathy of the public, especially of young colonials (presumably mostly native born). He had noticed in his tour of the United States that

Even the girls in schools were well up in matters of a constitutional nature. He regretted very much that the same could not be said of the Australian rising generation, who paid very little attention to the principle of self government . . .[96]

And Quick, a major figure in the new federation movement, saw federation less as a manifestation of Australian nationalism outgrowing provincialism and more as a means of reversing growing colonial separatism. In 1894 in the first edition of the *Commonwealth*, organ of the Australasian Federation League, he argued:

At the present time it is an undoubted fact that notwithstanding our community of origin, language, and religion, a feeling of alienism is rapidly developing in each colony against persons coming from other colonies. Such new-comers are often regarded as strangers and intruders. Now, this fatal tendency would be checked, if not destroyed by Federation.[97]

Anti-Billites also conducted emotional and, in their own way, patriotic campaigns. They identified themselves with their particular colony of birth or adoption, directed their efforts to protecting and preserving their existing 'nation'. Billites had no monopoly of flags, songs, or verse. The secretary of the Victorian Anti-Bill League penned in the *Age*:

> Up with the people's flag, boys,
> And warn the Billites 'Nay',
> We'll never let them drag, boys,
> Our hard won rights away.
> Ours is our children's cause, boys,
> Ours is old freedom's cause, boys,
> Ours is Australia's cause, boys,
> 'Australia'.[98]

(Perhaps it was poetic justice that anti-Billites suffered their heaviest defeat in Victoria.)

It is also difficult to avoid the impression that some federal leaders tempered idealism with political ambition. Their renewed interest in federation in 1893–4 was possibly partly inspired by a reaction to the shocks and scandals of the financial and bank crashes in which some of them were personally involved. They talked frequently of 'a higher plane of political life' and seem to have sought fresh political fields in which to gambol. Garran, again in the first edition of the *Commonwealth*, explained:

The leading statesmen in each colony now feel that what each colony wants for its development, commercially and politically, is the formation of a large political State. Provincialism, which at one time was a liberating force, has now begun to forge its own fetters. Each colony is 'cabin'd, cribb'd, confined' by its political isolation from its neighbours. The border Customs are doing more harm to inland production than they are doing good to revenue. The want of commercial interchange is a large annual waste of wealth, and the political life of each colony is kept in and narrowed for want of its natural expansion.

Apparently, too, the 'burning spirit of patriotism', even if it smouldered within the breasts of federal leaders, fired, at best, a minority of electors. The efforts of Convention delegates, Federation Leagues, Australian Natives Associations, demonstrably failed to inspire the general public. The first opportunity for an expression of public interest in federation came with the election of the Convention delegates in March 1897. Polling of qualified electors ranged from a mere 25.0 per cent in Tasmania to a grand 51.2 per cent in New South Wales. The second chance for an indication of popular approval came with the federation referenda. Although political and economic appeals possibly confused electors, at the simplest level— the one which the 'ill-informed yet enthusiastic' could share—they had a clear opportunity of founding an Australian nation. But in the crucial first referenda on which the fate of federation hinged less than half the electors in every colony troubled to vote. As expected, Victorians proved the most pro-federal, but only 39.8 per cent of them formally approved the Bill: overall 30.1 per cent of the electors in the four colonies voted 'Yes'. Public interest was greater in the second referenda, but only once in ten referenda—Victoria in 1899— was the Bill endorsed by a majority of qualified electors.[99] The Bill enticed considerably fewer voters to the polling booth than colonial elections in the same period.

Even so, it would be absurd to deny altogether the existence and influence of a spirit of nationalism. But if trying to assess the impact of tangible issues is a difficult task, then gauging the influence of an intangible one is doubly difficult. Still, Bastin's suggestion sounds plausible. For self-exiled easterners in the west there was a sharp choice between joining an Australian Commonwealth that their compatriots back home had already decided upon or declaring themselves foreign citizens cut adrift from their kith and kin. Therefore 'national feeling' among emigrants—the 'new Australians'—who retained their affinities for the east probably did reinforce their more concrete reasons for federating. However, it is not immediately clear why Newcastle electors should be more patriotic than their Sydney counterparts. Nor is it clear why Tasmanians, South Australians, and Victorians, who carried the Bill handsomely, should be more nationalistic as a whole than New South Welshmen, who only narrowly supported it. It would seem reasonable to expect that national sentiment, with the possible exception of T'othersiders in Western Australia, would be generally a fairly constant factor. But wide variations in voting existed between colonies, electorates within colonies, and polling places within electorates. Possibly patriotism did help to swell support for union, but it cannot account for the variations and it seems to have been a subordinate sentiment with electors who did not let patriotism stand in the way of self-interest or who did not vote. W. Harrison Moore, an ardent federalist, noted that the response was lower than in general elections in the colonies and explained:

it is hard indeed for any single public question to compete with the varied attractions of a general election. . . . It is 'men not measures' that in ordinary times give to politics their interest for the mass of mankind.[1]

Apparently then these were just 'ordinary times'. And whatever idealism may have inspired and motivated prominent federalists, the fact remains that the question of federation did not catch the public imagination.

Possibly some of the widespread indifference to federation, and some of the opposition, resulted, as McMinn suggested, from the confusion of issues in the campaigns. But they can probably also be attributed to State-rights sentiments, which were at the heart of much anti-Billite propaganda. State-rights arguments took two forms: protests at the powers ceded to the Commonwealth and predictions of how it would use them. Anti-Billites in small colonies denounced the 'impotent' Senate because they feared it would be unable to safeguard the vital interests of the small States against the actions of representatives of the large in the House of Representatives. Criticism of the Senate in the large colonies was only partly a democratic argument; in part it was also a State-rights argument of large States. The Lower House, where *their* representatives were in a majority, would be frustrated by the Upper House, where because of equal representation they were in a minority. Secondly, anti-Billites in both large and small colonies criticized the proposed Constitution because it gave the central government too many functions, too great a potential to interfere with the power and privileges of the States. In all the inability of small States to protect themselves, the inability of large ones to exert an influence commensurate with their size, and the infringement of the power of each, formed a major part of the counter-campaigns.

Attacks of this nature were only to be expected, as the anti-Billites were mainly defending the *status quo*. Naturally Billites in large and small colonies denied the contradictory allegations of their adversaries about the Senate with contradictory assertions of their own in their respective colonies. Paradoxically, however, they repulsed the united anti-Billite charge of interference with the States with the reply that the Commonwealth government would not impair the power of State governments. And their major position in the face of other strong challenges, namely that federation would entail a low additional cost and a low federal tariff, implied not only that the Commonwealth would require little revenue for the exercise of its functions, but also that the functions it was to have would be of little consequence. In fact this is precisely what federal leaders maintained in the federation campaigns, and indeed what they had maintained from the very outset. In 1891 Barton stood up to a hostile audience which cried: 'You are a traitor to your country. . . . Toby, you're a traitor.' Young Toby replied with spirit to the claim that the States would be robbed of their autonomy by reciting a list of powers reserved for the States. In addition residual powers remained with the States, and as for the enumerated powers of the Commonwealth

if they took the whole history of New South Wales they would not find one case in which a Government had gone out upon those questions. Of so little importance were they—so small was the 'surrender' involved in them—that they had never been the cause of a change of Government in any of the colonies.[2]

In 1896 Griffith argued that, although the list appeared a long one,

it does not include subjects which specially concern the domestic affairs of the separate States. Their powers with relation to the Constitution of their Legislatures, the disposition of Crown lands and mines, contracts and transactions between individuals, local government, the regulation of trades, joint stock companies, succession, criminal law, the administration of justice, education, police, direct taxation, public health, public works, and the infinite variety of subjects which fall within the words of their several Constitution Acts, 'the peace, order, and good government' of the colony, are left unaffected and unabridged . . .[3]

State functions included 'almost all the matters which have a direct bearing upon the social and material welfare of the people'. In 1897 Baker urged Labor Party members and local politicians who feared a loss of prestige to examine the federal powers and they will see that 'very few of such powers are of any importance, from either a Democratic, Socialistic, or Radical point of view'.[4] In 1898 Forrest tried to disabuse West Australians of a 'common misapprehension'.

It is generally supposed that all the important matters connected with the government of the colonies will be handed over to the Federal Government, and that we in this Colony—and all the other colonies—will have very little to do, or very little to control, and that we will become nothing more than a vestry board or municipal council. There is nothing further from the fact than that. (Applause) . . . We are not going to give up any of the great sources of revenue, leaving out the Customs, of which we get three-fourths back. . . . We have all the powers of self-government which are material to us. . . . All the powers necessary for our material growth and prosperity are still ours in the same way as at the present time.[5]

In 1899 the *Brisbane Courier*, a vociferous supporter of federation, appealed for a vote of 'Yes' because union under the Bill meant 'No Surrender of Existing Rights'. Even a Labor campaigner for the Bill, W. G. Higgs, defended the Constitution against talk of 'giving up powers to the Federal Parliament': if Queenslanders studied clause 51 'they would find that we were giving up nothing in the way of rights and privileges'.[6]

In short, anti-Billites confidently attacked the Bill on the grounds that it infringed State rights, and Billites stoutly defended it on the grounds that it did not. Such was the strength of State-rights sentiments, such was their assessment of the public mood, that *both* sides campaigned on what were essentially State-rights platforms.

We can now fit the legislation and functions of the early Commonwealth Parliament within the context of expectations established during the Federal Conventions and the federation campaigns.

At the Conventions, while blueprints for the federal machine were being designed, the future Senate had given delegates the most difficulty; in the referenda, campaigners used much energy in saying how they believed the new creation would work. There is little doubt that the Senate was expected to be a powerful body which would act chiefly in the interests of the States, and also a conservative House of Review. At the close of the second Convention Deakin had disputed Baker's claim that it was 'the pivot on which the whole Federal Constitution revolves', but admitted that the great growth in dignity, importance, and power of the Federal Senate as compared with our own Upper Chambers is indisputable'.[7] In the 1899 campaign Higgins, an honest and intelligent radical, anticipated that the Senate would be more powerful than the House of Representatives:

There is every reason for predicting that this 'states' house' will control the finances of Australia, and thereby control the executive, make and unmake ministries. It will have equal authority with the people's house, but a stronger position, and more power. The senators are to have a longer tenure, more secure seats, greater prestige as being elected by a whole colony, instead of by districts in a colony. The senate will be enabled to pursue a policy more steadily and continuously than the other house. True, the senate is not to originate money bills, but the senate in the United States does not originate money bills, and yet it is by far the stronger house in financial matters. So it will be here; and to the stronger house in financial matters ministers will gravitate and ministries must bow. The tremendous initiating and guiding power which ministries have will be wielded by the house of the minority, the senate . . .[8]

Much of the argument both for and against the expected role of the Senate, and attacks on the 'rigidity' of the Constitution under its amending process, presupposed that the work of federal parliament would be undertaken by members representing their particular States, rather than political parties. In 1891 Macrossan had been alone in suggesting that both Houses would divide on party lines, not State. By the end of the decade the conviction still prevailed that the Senate would serve as a States House, with the major conflicts there being between large and small. As Downer put it, the 'greatest radical in each colony will become the biggest conservative when the rights of his own colony are at stake as against those of another'. The belief that political parties would control the Lower House had gained ground. Deakin, Kingston, and Carruthers were certain that as soon as the federation was formed parties in the different States would 'coalesce and throw in their lot with each other . . . irrespective of state boundaries altogether'. But this was by no means universally accepted. Cockburn derided it as 'the most arrant nonsense possible' and defied anyone to say 'which is the liberal and which is the conservative party in America today'.[9] Responsible government was assured, but this did not necessarily entail the existence of political parties: colonial cabinets had existed for years without them.

To the extent that political parties would manipulate the new machine, it was agreed that there would be room for only *two*. The probability that the fledgling Labor parties would be excluded from the Commonwealth Parliament, especially from the Senate, was based largely on the results of the election of the Convention delegates in 1897. Then only one representative of Labor had been selected, despite the use of the popular referendum, the very device on which radicals lavished much praise. In 1899 Rosa, to whom most non-Labor politicians were by definition 'conservative', asserted

That the *Senators will* be conservative is shown not only by the fact that the 1897 elections resulted in the return of conservatives to the Convention, but also by the fact that in at least two of the colonies there is a property qualification for electors.[10]

Deakin and others confidently forecast that from the first day of federation people will align themselves into two parties 'divided by the line of "more progress and faster", and "less progress and slower", in other words Liberals and Conservatives'.[11] Some years later Hughes explained that politicians of older vintages thought that despite the success of Labor in colonial politics the party 'would altogether fail in the wider sphere of the Commonwealth. In particular, it was thought that they would not be able to secure election to the Senate. This view was generally shared by the Labor Party itself.'[12]

As to the output of the machine, it was reasonable to assume that the Commonwealth would soon take over the departments of posts, telegraphs, and telephones from the States. Lighthouses, lightships, beacons, buoys, and quarantine might also be transferred to central control in the near future. Uniform laws, like those relating to census and statistics, banking and insurance other than State, and bankruptcy, could well follow at an early date. This standardization and rationalization—'all in the common interests of facilitating trade'[13] should result in greater efficiency and economy. These were services and functions which the States were not unhappy to surrender because most operated at a loss.

The character of future policy legislation, as distinct from machinery measures, was obscure. The conservative influence of Senate, High Court, and amending process; the presence of few subjects of importance to 'Democratic, Socialistic, or Radical' viewpoints in the Commonwealth's list of powers; and the presumed absence of any strong Labor ginger group in federal parliament, suggested that probably little legislation of great social consequence could be expected. The first electoral Act—when parliament saw fit to pass one—would possibly extend the federal franchise to women in all States for the sake of uniformity with South Australia and Western Australia. Perhaps one day the Commonwealth might institute a system of old-age pensions and introduce the penny post, but these would depend upon financial resources which themselves were problematical. South Australians certainly hoped that they would be relieved of the Northern Territory, their expensive 'white elephant'. West Australians certainly expected that promises of a transcontinental railway would be honoured without delay.

Perhaps the federal government would assume full control of British New Guinea, but this possibility was not widely canvassed in the federation movement of the nineties. Convention delegates and other Billites also placed little emphasis on the issue of uniform immigration control and a White Australia. More was said about the advantages of unified defence, but still not a great deal in comparison with other subjects. Australia, of course, would be defended as one. Legal impediments to the employment of troops beyond the borders of their own States would disappear. The continent would be 'freed from any prospect of internecine war, and consequently released from any necessity for enormous expenditure for defence purposes against neighbouring states'.[14] But how Australia was to be defended, and who or what the nation had to be defended against, was not made apparent. In fact federalists had difficulty in nominating a credible potential aggressor. The Spanish-American War, which in 1898 took much of the limelight off the federation campaigns, had to serve as a warning: 'those who flattered themselves that peace was assured had but to look to America'. Deakin found it necessary to remind fellow-colonists of the seriousness of matters such as these: 'There were some things in our history, small, perhaps, but menacing, which we should not forget—the New Guinea troubles, the New Hebrides, the criminals of New Caledonia, the influx of foreign nations.'[15] Australia would present one face to the world at large, but, of course, she could have no independent foreign policy as such: rather the prestige and authority of federation would secure the Commonwealth 'a recognition in the councils of Empire'.[16]

Australia was indeed to become a nation, but it would be a nation within a nation. Founding the Commonwealth was a step towards closer and better cooperation with Britain, rather like—and the analogy was often used—a sturdy son attaining manhood yet remaining within the family fold. Rarely was the innovation regarded as a move towards cutting the apron strings with mother and those who led the federation movement were the very first to deny any such intention. Rather, more people saw Australian federation as a tentative first step towards some ill-defined form of imperial federation, or even, in wilder flights of fancy, a federation of the 'whole English-speaking race'.[17] As foundation day approached, and with the referenda battles fought and won, a national sentiment—which was possibly part cause and part effect of the movement—perhaps came more to the fore. But it was a special kind of nationalism, a nationalism held by what Deakin aptly termed 'Australian Britons'. Billite audiences sang patriotic songs, but they also rendered 'God Save the Queen' and gave three cheers for Her Majesty. The strains of 'Rule Britannia' frequently shook the rafters.

Even so, apparently relatively few Australians had much interest in, or affection for, the coming Commonwealth. Federation appears to have been widely regarded as a business merger, arranged mainly by businessmen, largely in the interests of businessmen. And for every Parkes or Barton inspired by idealism there seem to have been many more Hardys and Gibsons who dreamed less lofty dreams—the profits of federation and intercolonial free trade. The *Register*, a vociferous promoter of federation, declared:

The oratorical fripperies ought to be as the mere trimmings are to the substantial dish. Federation has come down out of the air, and federal orators should descend from the clouds. The people are invited to make a business bargain.[18]

A Presbyterian minister at Mount Gambier preached that the Bill was 'the outcome of the brightest brains of some of the best businessmen of Australia'.[19] Forrest described Western Australia as 'one of the three junior partners in the great firm'. The first question often asked of him was: ' "What will we lose by it in pounds, shillings, and pence?" Then the next question [was], "What will we gain by it in pounds, shillings, and pence?" '[20] Turner, at a meeting in Melbourne under the auspices of the Australian Natives Association, said 'he felt perfectly certain we were not going to accept the Bill on the mere ground of sentiment'.[21] Deakin believed that his Australian-born Premier and Treasurer—this 'average man', this 'ideal bourgeois'— had 'no enthusiasms except for economy and to him the Commonwealth Bill appealed no more on the emotional side than a measure for municipal rating. He had taken it up because it was part of his business to do so.'[22]

In fact the Constitution itself reflected this prime motive and preoccupation. Australians could be certain of only one major piece of legislation. Because of sections 88 and 92 they could be absolutely sure that within two years the Commonwealth would impose a uniform federal tariff and that thereafter the trade, commerce, and intercourse among the States would be 'absolutely free'. Intercolonial free trade, as Turner pointed out, was 'embedded' in the Constitution. The abhorrent border Custom houses, which had once served Victoria well, would be swept away forever. The character of the federal tariff would depend upon the outcome of an inevitable battle between free-traders and protectionists in the first session of federal parliament. In effect the framers of the Constitution took a detour around what James Service had called 'the lion in the path' of federation. The actual effects of intercolonial free trade were open to some dispute, and a few had nightmares, not dreams. But whatever the effects they would be outside the control and interference of State and Commonwealth governments.

In a sense, therefore, the federation movement was essentially negative in that its paramount aim and achievement—the one which the Constitution guaranteed—was to abolish intercolonial duties. Once politicians accomplished this supreme task, there would be little else of great moment to do. After a prolonged session on the tariff, the Commonwealth Parliament could meet for short periods. Parliamentarians could sit back and proceed leisurely lest, Glynn cautioned, the federal functions be rapidly 'exhausted'.[23] Of course Australia was destined to be a great nation, greater than the sum of its parts, but somehow the Commonwealth government was not going to need much revenue or do much with it. Precisely what it would do was uncertain. 'None of us can predict', Deakin confided to James, what would happen after federation.[24] Symon compared the six States to 'six persons who have united or agreed to unite in partnership, with no staff, no hands, no machinery, no equipment, and no clear understanding as to the distribution of immediate gains.'[25] In fact George Dibbs had been right all along: federation was indeed a 'leap in the dark'.

But it was a leap that Australians made with some confidence for the night held few terrors. The central government could have little direct impact on the average citizen. The States were protected by the Senate, the High Court, and the limited extent of surrendered powers and functions. In 1908, when calls for the amendment of the Constitution were being made, A. W. Jose, the Australian correspondent of *The Times*, described the 'lubricants' which greased the skids for launching as those that recognized 'the existing States as permanent and sovereign within their existing boundaries, except so far as a few out of the many subjects of pan-Australian concern are entrusted to the handling of the Federal Parliament.'[26] Commonwealth-State financial relations had not been placed on a permanent basis, but the arrangement was fair, even if cumbersome. The amendment of the Braddon clause was commonly perceived as a concession to New South Wales, rather than as a retrograde step that strengthened the Commonwealth's hand against the States as a whole. The new government would not be an 'alien' administration that cared nothing for them.[27] If some federalists knew better they had the good sense to keep quiet. Newspaper editorials greeted the dawn of the new century and the new federation with uniform optimism. Australia was involved in an armed conflict in South Africa, but this had enabled Australians to demonstrate their 'deep pride' in the British Empire by rallying round the Union Jack. Symon explained to Americans that

The Transvaal war now proceeding has given opportunity for irrefragable proof on this point. The sentiment was spontaneously translated into effective action. This war has beyond all controversy made the Empire one. Such a result was worth a war.[28]

Besides, the disasters of earlier years had been reversed and victory was assured. Mafeking had been relieved. Britannia ruled the waves.

Therefore potential federal politicians and aspiring Australian Statesmen had good reason to be satisfied that the good ship Commonwealth was at last about to be launched. But as they plotted their course and devised schemes to secure their safe passage into parliament, some warning signals were evident. The widespread indifference to federation, the entrenched parochialism and close identity of citizens with their own 'country', the apparently few ways in which the central parliament could act directly on the average elector —to whom federal politicians would have to appeal for support and election—and the overwhelming expectations of federal economy, could not have fully pleased men of ambition.

2

THE GENESIS OF THE COMMONWEALTH'S
WHITE AUSTRALIA POLICY

On 17 December 1901 the Pacific Island Labourers Bill received the Royal assent. Six days later the Immigration Restriction Act passed into law and history. The former regulated, reduced, and finally ended the traffic in Kanaka labour. It licensed a limited entry of Pacific Islanders to March 1904, banned their introduction thereafter, and provided for the deportation of any found in Australia after December 1906. It affected the internal political, social, and economic affairs of a founder State, Queensland, and hence involved the new Commonwealth in the sensitive and complex question of State rights. The latter Act determined the wider issue of non-Caucasian immigration. It involved the new Commonwealth in what A. T. Yarwood called 'its first essays in imperial and external relations'.[1] Moreover to the world at large the racial policy has become, in the fullness of time, synonymous with Australia. It has, as it were, along with the unique flora and fauna, the sportsmen and the soldiers, placed the island continent on the map. Together the two Acts embodied a principle which their proponents were then proud to proclaim, that of a 'White Australia'.

The fact that the first policy legislation of federal parliament embraced the question of immigration has been commonly regarded as a matter of course. Indeed the priority given to this subject really requires no explanation. The desire for uniform control of immigration and a White Australia was a major force, perhaps *the* major force, which nurtured, sustained, and ultimately ensured the triumph of the federation movement itself.

This traditional interpretation of events was best expressed by Myra Willard in her pioneer work, *History of the White Australia Policy to 1920*. Willard devoted a chapter to the Commonwealth's adoption of the policy. Under the sub-title *The Policy and Federation* it began: 'The desire to guard themselves effectively against the dangers of Asiatic immigration was one of the most powerful influences which drew the Colonies together'.[2] In support, Deakin's famous statement in the House of Representatives was quoted:

No motive power operated more universally on this continent or in the beautiful island of Tasmania, and certainly no motive operated more powerfully in dissolving the technical and arbitrary political divisions which previously separated us than the desire that we should be one people and remain one people without the admixture of other races.[3]

'Accordingly', wrote Miss Willard,

Australians decided that the Federal Parliament should have the power, subject to the Constitution, to make laws for the 'peace, order and good government' of the Commonwealth with respect to immigration and emigration; . . . the people of any race . . . for whom it was deemed necessary to make special laws.[4]

A White Australia was a much discussed question in the first federal election. J. B. Ronald, a Labor MHR, said it was the foremost plank of the party first entrusted with the government of the Commonwealth. (In fact Deakin, not Ronald, made this statement.) 'Accordingly, during the first year of its existence, the Federal Parliament dealt with the Immigration Restriction Bill which embodied this principle'.

The curious thing about this influential account is that it fails even to mention, let alone discuss, the very event—the federation movement—with which the whole question is supposed to be so intimately connected. All that is offered is the unquestioned acceptance of Deakin's statement made during the second reading of the Bill.

Other historical accounts are essentially derivatives of this thesis. For example, W. K. Hancock, in the 1933 edition of the *Cambridge History of the British Empire*, closely followed Willard's work and then wrote:

But State legislation was not enough: even when, in the nineties, the States legislated in concert, they found it difficult to close every gap through which unwelcome immigrants might squeeze. Australians decided they must speak with a single voice on this matter. No other aspiration or interest, asserted Deakin, so wrought for federation as 'the desire that we should be one people and remain one people without the admixture of other races'.[5]

Here once again the telling evidence is Deakin's speech. General histories of Australia perpetuate these views, and some elaborate. A 'genuine indigenous move towards federation' began in the 1880s and ripened in the 1890s: 'There were now two powerful issues that drew Australians together. One was defence, the other was immigration'. Although without the White Australia policy Australia must some day have federated—'it was logical, it was inevitable'—there 'had to be some one issue that appealed to the average citizen in all colonies to bring it about'.[6]

In short, to sum up the traditional school of thought, the desire for federal control of immigration was the compelling force for federation. In a sense the proof of the pudding is in the eating. One of the leading chefs said the basic ingredient of the recipe was good white stock and the legislation duly appeared at the head of the federal menu.

Despite the lack of real evidence—the lacuna between the federation movement and immigration—it is possible that this view is nonetheless valid. If so, it would seem reasonable to expect to find that the question of immigration control was a dominant theme, or at least a prominent one, at important stages of the federation movement. If what Deakin said after federation was achieved is correct, then it should be possible to verify the claim by reference to events which led up to federation.

The series of official conferences and conventions began in Melbourne in 1890 with the Australasian Federation Conference. Representatives of the governments of all the Australian colonies and New Zealand attended the Conference. Parkes, whose efforts had prompted the gathering, opened the debates with a resolution and a long address. In this he covered a wide range of reasons setting out why the time was ripe for federation. Immigration control was not one of them. He asked: 'How much better shall we be for Federal Government?' His answer embraced subjects such as federal development of 'splendid sea-fisheries' and 'efficient lighting' of coasts. Although Parkes clearly searched desperately for answers to his own question, he made no mention of immigration. Later, on the sixth and last working day of the Conference after others had alluded to the topic, he seems to have realized that somehow he had overlooked the question. He then held that two of the most important objects of a central government related to 'the Asiatic races and to the islands of the Pacific'. He denied racial sentiment against the Chinese but opposed their entry so as to preserve Australia 'for a people modelled on the type of the British nation'.[7]

There was no sense of urgency in the remarks of the few other delegates on the subject. Indeed the first suggestion that immigration would be a proper federal power at all was put forward tentatively. Griffith listed some powers taken from the British North America Act, and said: 'To the latter, I think, may here be added the question of the regulation of the admission and exclusion of undesirable immigrants'. Thomas Playford, the next speaker, commented: 'well, I think a general Parliament of Australia would never have to deal with the question of immigration'. Deakin referred to the problems that a united Australia might be called upon to face: 'One has been in some measures already dealt with, but not yet finally solved—that of the influx of inferior races into the northern parts of the continent'. John Macrossan rebuked delegates for concentrating too much on the great advantage of intercolonial free trade to the neglect of others. These 'although not as important as that of a Customs Union' were 'indispensable to a complete Federation': he did not mention immigration.[8]

In sum there is little to suggest that the control of immigration was a vital issue with the delegates who made up the Australasian Federation Conference in 1890.

The National Australasian Convention was a direct result of the Melbourne Conference. Held in Sydney in 1891, it consisted of forty-five politicians appointed by the seven colonial parliaments. On this occasion Parkes, as president, opened with four principal resolutions. These foundation principles referred to a minimum surrender of powers to the central government, intercolonial free trade, federal control of customs and unified defence. The Convention waited until the sixth day to mention immigration. Kingston suggested that the 'necessity of protecting Australia against the influx of aliens, Asiatics, criminals, paupers, and other undesirable classes' was next to the protection from invasion. Later McMillan favoured a central government 'which will deal with the black question in North Queensland'. Griffith, in explanation of the sub-clause which like many others passed into the draft Constitution without debate, said: 'It may under some circumstances be a very useful provision'.[9] No other delegates appear to have stressed the issue.

The second draft Constitution was produced in the three sessions of the Australasian Federation Convention in 1897-8. Fifty delegates from five colonies assembled for the first session in Adelaide in 1897;

Queensland and New Zealand were not represented. After formalities had been completed Barton, as leader of the Convention, moved resolutions dealing with the basic conditions for federation. They embraced the same subjects as those of Parkes in 1891—the concern for the powers, privileges, and territories of the colonies; federal control over customs, excise, and military and naval defences; and 'absolutely free' trade between the colonies. Once again immigration was conspicuously absent. Although the session lasted seven weeks only two references seem to have been made to the topic. Higgins, in a debate on State rights, argued that true protection for small states would be obtained by limiting the power and functions of the central government. He instanced Queensland's Kanaka labour—'a question which affects that colony alone'—and implied that should Queensland federate some special provision would be needed. It would be necessary either to 'put that subject out of Federation, or put a qualification dealing with labor traffic in the Constitution Bill'. James Walker, formerly a Queensland resident for twenty-five years, alluded to Higgins' comment. If the Convention were to meet in Brisbane 'we would have an opportunity of seeing for ourselves that the employment of a certain proportion of colored labor is, in certain localities, necessary for the profitable carrying on of the sugar industry'.[10]

The short second session in Sydney produced the first use in the Conventions of the term 'White Australia'. Joseph Carruthers described the 'regulation of the inflow of population so as to secure a "white Australia"' as one of the greatest purposes of federation. Henry Dobson immediately challenged the view. This was a State right—'Queensland, for instance, could not possibly come in unless you had regard to her sugar plantations!'[11]

The only real airing of views took place in the third and final session in Melbourne in 1898. The discussion arose merely by chance because the exclusive power to make special laws for the people of any race, then under consideration, had been mistaken by a number of delegates for the concurrent power over immigration.[12] The debate, such as it was, was legalistic and remarkably confused and confusing even to the participants. However it is possible to make the following points which emerge from the short discussion.

First, there is no doubt that some delegates—Quick, Barton, Kingston, Reid, Cockburn (and later Deakin)—strongly favoured a White Australia. Nonetheless, few said anything on the issue and Wise could still assert 'We hope to see the Commonwealth embrace the whole continent, and it might be found desirable to establish practi-

cally a colony in which black labour might be employed.' This statement was used later to attack the Bill.

Secondly, a large majority of delegates, largely on the ground of
State rights, did not support uniform legislation to deal with resident
aliens. Deakin advocated a concurrent rather than an exclusive power
because he was not satisfied that colonial opinion was at an even
level. Besides, he added, 'It might conflict with what was absolutely
vital, for example, to Queensland, and we all hope that Queensland
will eventually become a part of the Federation.'

Thirdly, it was regarded as by no means clear in 1898 that federation itself could actually improve the situation and enable more
stringent measures to be taken. O'Connor said that there would be
very little difficulty in legislating against Chinese or Japanese already
in the Commonwealth, but

if you wish to make a law dealing with their introduction into the state,
you may be brought face to face with the obligations of treaties entered
into by Great Britain and other difficulties of that kind which cannot be
surmounted.[13]

Fourthly, delegates generally agreed that there would inevitably be
a long delay before the Commonwealth was able to legislate on these
subjects. Turner suggested up to five years could elapse as parliament
would be too busy with the tariff and other financial matters. Trenwith emphasized that the tariff would take up a great deal of time:
'Then there are the questions of finance, quarantine, ocean lights, and
a number of other things, each of them very difficult to settle . . . and
consequently it will take a long time to settle them.'[14]

Finally, Wise, O'Connor, McMillan, Walker, and Barton argued
that the one sure way to force the Commonwealth to legislate quickly
on a subject was to make that subject an exclusive power. As Barton
neatly put it: 'To make the power exclusive conduces at once to its
speedy exercise by the Commonwealth'. But the special race clause
was removed by a vote of 35 to 10 from the exclusive list. Immigration remained a *concurrent* power. Moreover, delegates recognized
that an exclusive federal power was stronger than a concurrent, that
where a question was vital it should be exclusive. Trenwith said,
'Give exclusive power where it is essential in respect to such matters
as may be deemed to be necessary to be dealt with by the central
authority'. But they ignored suggestions by Forrest and Quick to
make immigration control exclusive.

Thus it is evident that in the making of the Constitution at the

Federal Conventions in 1891 and 1897–8, the question of federal control of immigration was not dominant. The reports of the Conventions fill five volumes and more than six thousand pages. The urgent needs for federating, and the great benefits to be derived therefrom, were freely canvassed. At crucial stages when the Conventions looked like failing and delegates threatened to pack up and go home, passionate pleas were made on the great objects of federation. But very few words were devoted to the topic of immigration. Indeed the reports require careful reading in order even to find references to the subject. When they occur they are generally afterthoughts. The majority came about indirectly at the last Convention session because delegates such as Reid mistook the very clause which dealt with the question. Although it is clear that some delegates were staunch believers in a White Australia, several dissented and the large majority kept remarkably silent on the issue. At the second Convention, when Queensland was unrepresented, Higgins, Deakin, and others displayed a tender regard for that colony. Unlike two other traditional motives for federating—intercolonial free trade and defence —immigration was not included in the great principles put forward by Parkes in 1891 and by Barton in 1897. Unlike intercolonial free trade and defence, immigration was given no special status in the Constitution.

Independent of the official Federal Conventions unofficial conferences were held in Melbourne in 1890, Corowa in 1893, and Bathurst in 1896. These, termed the 'popular' phases of the movement, are generally credited with stimulating interest in federation, and then reviving it when legislative action on the Draft Bill of 1891 had broken down in colonial parliaments.

Australians from all the mainland colonies attended the Intercolonial Australian Natives Association Federation Conference in Melbourne. Delegates displayed 'Great enthusiasm and an intelligent interest in the cause of Australian union' and resolved that the time had 'now arrived for the Federation of the Australian colonies'. They further resolved that the central legislature be empowered to deal with some sixteen 'national matters': immigration was not one of them.[15]

The seventy-five members of the Corowa Federation Conference represented a wide range of organizations from Victoria and New South Wales. These included seventeen branches of the Australasian Federation League; six branches of the Australian Natives Association; the Chambers of Commerce and Manufactures; the Imperial

Federation League; the Protection, Liberal and Federation League; the Progressive Political League; the Commercial Travellers Association; and a number of progress associations and committees. 'The main principle', Quick said, 'was that the cause should be advocated by the citizens and not merely by politicians'. The main object was to advance federation 'by an organization of citizens owning no class distinction or party influence'. Delegates said much about 'cursed Border duties' but nothing about Asian immigration.[16]

Some 211 delegates drawn from all mainland colonies attended the People's Federal Convention at Bathurst. They represented an even broader social and geographical section of the community than the Corowa Conference. In addition to the array of leagues and associations many municipal, borough, shire and town councils were present. Invited members included academics, churchmen such as Cardinal Moran, and politicians such as Cockburn, Barton, Lyne and Reid. John West attended on behalf of the Trades Hall Council, A. C. Hammond for the Warringah Labor Electoral League, and Rosa for the Australian Order of Industry. Lyne observed, 'On the present occasion there were Conservatives, Liberals, ultra-Radicals, and even Republicans present'.

Delegates at the People's Convention made a variety of addresses and carried a number of motions. The mayor of Bathurst moved 'That the interests—financial, defensive, sanitary, and progressive— of the peoples of the several colonies of Australasia demanded an early union under a Federal authority'. The president, Dr Thomas Machattie, stressed the commercial and financial benefits in his inaugural address. He quoted Sir Mackenzie Bowell, Prime Minister of Canada, in Sydney in 1892: 'after Federation the Dominion advanced so rapidly that money was lent in the London market most readily at about half the interest paid previously by the Provinces'. Cardinal Moran delivered an impassioned speech on the advantages that must accrue from federation. Despite many stirring speeches not one single delegate touched the question of immigration.[17]

It would seem that the desire for uniform immigration control was not a pressing issue at the popular gatherings at Melbourne, Corowa, and Bathurst.

As a result of federal conferences and conventions, popular initiatives and parliamentary action, the issue of federation was eventually put to the popular test. The occasional appeal based on the topic can be found in the referenda campaigns of 1898. In New South Wales at the Hoopers' Hall, Crow's Nest, a J. F. Cullen said that federation should include all the colonies 'since nothing short of that would admit of the necessary means of defence against foreign aggression, or against the incursions of inferior races'. E. W. O'Sullivan, at Captains Flat, asserted: 'When Queensland joined the federation the Federal Parliament could abolish the black labour in that country'. An editorial and a special federation section in the *Sydney Morning Herald* stated that 'Federation is the only possible means of preserving Australia to the White races'. However, the latter serves to illustrate the insignificance of the question in the referendum. The special section 'The Coming Appeal' outlined the history of the federation movement. Articles and letters were printed from more than thirty leading politicians and public figures. Contributors numbered the New South Wales Convention delegates, the president and secretary of the Bathurst Convention, presidents of the Chambers of Commerce and Manufactures and the Women's Federal League, newspaper editors, Bruce Smith, Atlee Hunt, Bishop Doyle, Garran and Purves. There were in addition numerous unsigned articles and letters suggesting a large variety of reasons to vote for the Commonwealth Bill. In all the section took up twenty-five columns or more than three full pages of the *Herald*. But immigration and a White Australia was mentioned only once, and then by an anonymous contributor.[18]

Thus again it must be emphasized that references to the issue were the rare exceptions rather than the common rule. Apart from the near total absence of the subject, a few examples of glaring omissions may be given by way of further illustration. For instance, the *Herald* and *Daily Telegraph* published Barton's open letter 'To the electors of New South Wales'. The Bill afforded the 'freest play to individual and national energy in the field of commercial, industrial, and intellectual expansion'. It was an instrument 'by which the new several provinces may be shaped into a nation, great in material wealth, splendid in intelligence, and noble in humanity'. The letter did not allude to a White Australia. Again, the nationalistic and racist *Bulletin* listed twenty-three reasons to vote for the Bill; immigration control was not one of them. The *Bulletin*'s editorial on polling day elaborated twenty-seven points in its 'Case for the Bill' without touching the subject.[19]

A similar low priority was given to the question in the campaign in Victoria. The manifesto of the Australasian Federation League of Victoria mentioned the topic, as did an editorial of the *Age*. One speaker at the St Kilda Town Hall commended the Bill for including the power. Prominent federationists such as Turner, Isaacs, Trenwith, Peacock, Purves, and Deakin addressed an Australian Natives Association meeting at the Melbourne Town Hall; it was left to J. W. Kirton, MLA, to refer to immigration. The *Age* reported his remarks briefly but the *Argus*—a keen supporter—did not consider them worthy of inclusion in its coverage of the meeting.[20]

Otherwise there seems to have been silence on the issue. The *Argus* printed nine reasons for federation under the title 'A HALFPENNY PER WEEK'; immigration control was not mentioned. A federal manifesto signed by Turner, Quick, Deakin, Peacock, Isaacs, Trenwith, Berry, Fraser, and Zeal failed to include it. The manifesto said that acceptance of the Bill would 'inaugurate union, establish permanent friendship, strengthen democracy, hasten progress, and assure prosperity'. Its rejection would 'continue isolation and estrangement, retain barriers, encourage strife, prolong conservatism, and fetter industry'. The manifesto of the Bendigo Federation League apparently did not believe the question to be of sufficient importance. Harrison Moore at Melbourne University held that 'There were two great needs for federation—defence and the protection of our trade and commerce'.[21]

If the issue was scarcely touched, let alone blazoned forth, in the campaigns in the two larger colonies, it was even less important in the smaller. It appears to have been entirely neglected in Tasmania. It did not, for instance, rate in the top forty reasons given by the *Launceston Examiner* in its appeal for a 'Vote for Union'.[22]

In South Australia an extensive examination of the campaign as reported by thirty-four town, country and church newspapers revealed only a handful of appeals to federate to control immigration and thereby secure a White Australia.[23] The vast array of Convention delegates selling their product, leagues, politicians, businessmen, and newspapers who campaigned with great vigour apparently ignored the subject. Any attempt to give a complete list of omissions would be both difficult and tedious, but some may be given to make the point. It did not make the Convention delegates' manifesto, which accompanied copies of the Commonwealth Bill forwarded to all post offices for distribution to the electors. It was not included in the manifesto of the powerful Conservative Party organization, the Australasian National League. It was not one of the 'Benefits of Federation' in the appeal of the Commonwealth League, the body which co-ordinated the diverse elements supporting federation. Finally, it was not touched in the twenty-five editorials advocating the Bill in the *South*

1   *Billite and anti-Billite leaders, New South Wales*

2   *Anti-Bill cartoon*, Daily Telegraph

3 *Federal Convention delegates, Sydney, 1891*

Standing, left to right: Marmion, Baker, Webb (Secretary). Gillies, Wrixon, Fitzgerald, Loton, Gordon, Rutledge, Brown, Douglas, Deakin, Barton, (Clerk) Wright, Dibbs, Russell, J. Forrest, Playford, Moore, Hackett, (Clerk), Macdonald-Patterson, McIlwraith, Seated on chairs: Bray, Smith, Grey, Munro, Lee Steere, Atkinson, Parkes, Fysh, Thynne, Jennings, Griffith, Kingston, Cuthbert. Seated on ground: Suttor, (Serjeant-at-arms), A. Forrest, Donaldson, Cockburn, McMillan,

Australian Register between the end of the second Convention and polling day.[24]

Apart from the general absence of appeals on the issue in 1898 some indirect references throw doubt on its importance. One of the benefits of federation held out by the Billites was that the Commonwealth government would relieve South Australia of the burden of the Northern Territory. The prospect of this welcome windfall was disputed by the anti-Billites who argued that the federal government would not be prepared to accept the debt. In reply Holder—Convention delegate, Treasurer, and Minister controlling the Northern Territory—told of an offer to the colony on the Territory. The offer came from a syndicate

who would willingly pay all the debt on it, besides a good sum to the Government, if it were given permission to bring in colored labor. . . . However, if the Federal Parliament refused to take it over, they could easily bring them to their bearings by telling them that unless they did the offer of the syndicate would be accepted.[25]

King O'Malley echoed Holder. The Commonwealth's hand could be forced over the Territory by permitting 'Asiatics to come in, when for the sake of regulating such immigration, the Federal Parliament would insist on taking over the control of the vast district'.[26]

Now these extraordinary statements imply one of two things. Either Holder and O'Malley seriously believed that a federated South Australia would still be able to admit Asiatics and the like and that the Commonwealth would need to accept direct responsibility for the Territory in order to control immigration there—which suggests that federation was seen to have little to do with a White Australia. Or their arguments were sheer political expediency to counter the frequent anti-Billite charge that federation would cost too much— which suggests that immigration control was less important than the £70 000 per annum the colony hoped to save. In either event it says little for the mass appeal, the expectations of Commonwealth action, and the priority of the whole question in South Australia at the time of the referendum.

There are a number of illustrations which indicate that a White Australia and the Commonwealth Bill were not closely related in the campaigns of 1898.

The first comes from the Northern Territory itself; inappropriately, in view of its racial composition, this was termed a 'white' elephant by the Billites. The closest census returns show that the Territory had over 94 per cent of the Chinese resident in areas under South Australian jurisdiction and virtually all the Japanese. In April whites signed a petition to exclude all Asiatics from the Ferguson River goldfields. The *Northern Territory Times* expressed some concern about the naturalization of Chinese and Japanese and their competition in trade, industry, pearling, and mining: 'Naturalisation of Asiatics is a farce, pure and simple'. The local Literary Society debated the merits of a policy which would exclude 'the Asiatic aliens to the benefit of the White population'. Yet the *Territory Times*, though a staunch supporter of the Bill, made no appeal to federate to control immigration. Neither did V. L. Solomon, former proprietor and editor of the paper for many years. Solomon, Convention delegate and the Territory's senior member in the South Australian Parliament since 1890, had pronounced opinions on Asian immigration. In 1880 he toured the eastern colonies to address public meetings and interview Premiers to persuade them to press the South Australian government to close the Darwin door to Asiatics. Although Solomon campaigned in 1898 he did not propose federation as a means of keeping Australia white.[27]

Secondly, if in fact the Bill had been closely associated with immigration control, an excellent opportunity for Billites to exploit the issue occurred three weeks before the referendum. Newspapers reported the first case of leprosy detected in South Australia. The 'leper', a Chinese hawker, aroused anti-Asian sentiment. The *Weekly Herald*, for example, devoted one editorial to the 'detestable' Wah Lee: it attacked the British government for its attitude on immigration and regretted that 'the people of South Australia are for the present helpless'. But not one paper, delegate, league, or anyone else related the affair to the Commonwealth Bill. Moreover, Wah Lee was a resident of Hindley Street, the city's Chinatown in West Adelaide. The *Advertiser* wrote: 'The locality in question is quite a little nest on both sides of the street'. A joss-house existed there. Census returns show that West Adelaide had nearly one-half of the Chinese-born residents of the colony proper. That is, although a small electorate, it possessed almost as many Chinese as the other twenty-five electorates put together. Also, as it happens, West Adelaide was the constituency which Kingston—Premier, Convention president, and the colony's most popular politician and ablest statesman—had represented since his entry into politics in 1880. It was Kingston who had played a major part in the 1888 Intercolonial Conference on

Chinese Immigration and who touched the issue in the referendum campaign. But West Adelaide was one of only two electorates in the colony to reject the Bill. A bare 15.5 per cent of the qualified electors voted in its favour.[28]

A similar opportunity arose in Victoria. On 23 May, less than two weeks before polling day, a party of seventy-nine Indians arrived in Melbourne on the *Bucephalus*. A series of news items in the *Argus*— 'The Hindoo Host'—and in the *Age*—'The Shipment of Indians'— reported their arrival and subsequent attempts to get rid of them. The papers reported that the Indians, *en route* to sugar plantations in northern New South Wales and Queensland, had been refused permission to land at Sydney. The *Argus* expressed concern that the destitute 'brother Britons' threatened to become a burden to the colony. Customs officials pointed out that as British subjects the Indians had as much right to enter Victoria as 'the people of the United Kingdom and Ireland'. Judge Greaves asked the mayor of Melbourne to use his influence to have the whole party shipped to Sydney: 'These fellows will become a downright curse to the community, and unless the Indian Government is prevailed upon to advise them not to come here some repressive legislation is certain to take place.'[29]

Nevertheless, despite hostility to these unwelcome migrants, no Billite seems to have related the incident to the coming referendum. The *Age* gave its pre-referendum leader to the affair. But its purpose was not to exhort its readers to vote for federation but rather to suggest that the Victorian Parliament pass new legislation. The editorial said in part: 'There is no great difficulty in dealing with real colored aliens, that is, with colored races which are not subjects of the British Empire'. It would be useless for Victoria to legislate except in accord with Chamberlain's injunction although it was possible that 'if a Federal Parliament were to pass a more drastic measure Imperial Ministers might hesitate before declining to listen to the wishes of a combined Australia'.[30]

Thus there were no clarion calls to vote for federation so as to prevent such problems. In fact the contrary happened. In Adelaide the *Weekly Herald*, an opponent of the Bill, noted the arrival of the Indians, one of whom was ill. Its editorial on polling day warned: 'federation will be purchased at a costly price indeed if it means that we are to open our doors to colored immigrants and be flooded with disease-producing and dying Indians.'[31]

There seems no reason to believe that appeals on immigration were more evident in the 1899 campaigns for the second referendum in the four south-eastern colonies. On the other hand the anti-Billites developed a new criticism of the Constitution. The *Daily Telegraph* used Wise's comment at the Melbourne session—'it might be found desirable to establish practically a colony in which black labor might be employed'—to discredit the Bill. It also quoted a statement made in 1895 in the *Commonwealth and Empire* by J. Langdon Parsons, the late Government Resident of the Northern Territory: 'On the day of Federation, Australia will enter into her inheritance in the tropics. She can then introduce, use, and return to the place whence it came the labor necessary for tropical agriculture.'[32] The *Telegraph* conceded as possibly true that public sentiment would be on the whole against the introduction of coloured labour on the 'tremendous scale evidently contemplated' by some framers of the Bill. But under the Bill political power was entrusted to 'territorial divisions'. Queensland, Western Australia, and South Australia had predilections for coloured labour. Hence the deliberate provision for coloured labour can therefore 'be settled beyond controversy'.

Wise, in reply, denied that he had supported a proposal which would allow black labour to drift throughout the continent. What he had supported was an exclusive power over special race laws so that if the Commonwealth permitted black labour then it should have the power to 'prevent the labour coming below or outside certain tropical limits'. He also denied that the establishment of a black labour colony was amongst 'the openly cherished dreams of some of the most influential supporters of the bill'.[33]

Wise's first denial does not support the traditional view of the relationship between federation and White Australia. And the attacks continued. Several cartoons appeared on the theme of 'Federation, Black Labor, and Monopoly'; one depicted black ants swarming out of central Australia across the continent. A. B. Piddington, former academic and examiner in history, drew an analogy between the United States and the extension of slavery, and Australia and the Commonwealth Bill: because of equal State representation 'the colored labor States could, in the Senate, turn out any Ministry by rejecting its financial proposals'. Rosa, who also quoted Langdon Parsons, argued in like manner: one of the greatest dangers of equal representation was 'the probability that it will lead to the importation, upon a large scale, of colored labor, and, as a result, civil war'. The *Worker* joined the fray. It believed that Wise had attempted to make it possible—by leaving domestic control temporarily in the hands of the States—for any State to 'continue and extend its importation of colored labor until the Commonwealth's Parliament enacted some authoritative laws on the question'. The Constitution Bill provided special opportunities to block the passage of laws. Thus the importation of an inferior race might continue 'until legislation, as in the United States, was impotent to cope with the evil'. Under a South Australian Act of 1896 one hundred million acres of land in the Northern Territory had been pegged out in blocks from 1000 to 5000 square miles each by certain titled prospectors. This doubtless was to be 'the black labor State of which Mr. Wise spoke'. Who was to say how long it would be before Parliament legislated? Who was to say that it would not be conservative or corrupt enough 'to pass an Act which so far from prohibiting such immigration will sanction it? . . . The whole episode shows what unsafe ground we stand on in relation to the proposed Constitution'.[34]

As might be expected immigration was a more prominent issue during the campaign in Queensland in August 1899. Several Billites stressed the importance of the question on a number of occasions. At Bundaberg Thomas Glassey claimed 'united we can speak with a more powerful voice in the exclusion of aliens'. It was a 'momentous question, particularly with reference to the continued influx of Japanese'. Anderson Dawson referred to the 'alien curse in the North' and advocated the Bill 'so as to have the assistance of the larger army of democrats in the Southern colonies'. John Dickson believed the Commonwealth would be better able to keep out all orientals because a 'united voice' could be brought to bear upon the Mother Country. As for Kanaka labour 'let federated Australia determine whether the Kanaka or any other coloured man shall be allowed to remain'.[35]

But even in Queensland the question of how federal parliament would exercise its power was by no means certain. The Labor movement was split by federation and its relation to a White Australia. Eleven members of the parliamentary wing were reported to be in favour of federation and ten against.[36] Glassey, described as 'the pioneer' of the Labor Party, was opposed by the Workers' Political Organization and the Brisbane *Worker*, official organ of the trade unions. His local Labor paper the Bundaberg *Patriot*, a vociferous opponent of black labour, regarded him as a renegade. It asked: 'Is every other trade, profession, and everybody else to suffer because sugar is to be benefited, black slavery encouraged, and a few monopolists made into money kings?' As Glassey rose to speak at Bundaberg 'The flag of "White Australia" was unfurled by two or three Labour men who were opposed to the Commonwealth Bill'.[87] The *Worker* feared that certain powers had been put in the Constitution in order to hamper the progressive tendencies of the more forward States. Subjects such as 'black labour, immigration . . . which are really matters of domestic concern, have been removed from the control of the more advanced colonies'. Furthermore, the intentions of federal parliament with regard to 'the vital questions of the day are vague and undefined. . . . The intention of the Commonwealth as to the alien and black labour question should be distinctly stated'.[38] The paper addressed 'A Cingalese, Mahomed Abdul, and Yamashiro Maru' and assured them

There is nothing in the Commonwealth Bill to occasion you any alarm. The Federal Parliament 'shall have power' to legislate for your exclusion: but this, of course, doesn't mean that they 'will' or 'must' do so. Besides, the sugar-planters all say that Federation won't interfere with you.[39]

Views such as these cannot be dismissed simply as those of a prejudiced lunatic fringe. Clear statements of future policies in fact had not been made, and Queensland sugar interests believed on the whole that their black labour would not be affected. In February 1899 the *Sugar Journal and Tropical Cultivator*, Mackay, enthused about the 'tangible benefit' of federation—the exclusion of European beet sugar, Mauritius and China whites and the consequent relief from external competition. But it held that it was 'difficult at present to form any estimate' on the labour question as it was likely to be dealt with by the Commonwealth. It had, it said, frequently referred to the possibility of hostile action, but there was this consolation:

a Federal Government is hardly likely to interfere so long as there is no evidence that colored labor is a menace to the rest of Australia, and so long as Queensland herself, the colony most interested, does not attempt to force the Federal Government into taking action in the matter. Interference with labor must, we take it, come from this colony first . . .[40]

It counselled,

so long as the sugar producers remain true to their own interests in the colony, and refuse to sanction any political party opposed to the continuance of the employment of a few thousand Polynesians, so long may we expect that the Federal Government will not think itself called upon to interfere in the matter.[41]

In June the *Sugar Journal* was less optimistic about the benefits. What was good for the New South Wales industry was probably bad for the Queensland. As to the Kanakas, the advantages of transferring trust from the Legislative Council to another parliament were 'more than questionable'. Nonetheless it admitted that these were *minority* opinions. By August federation was actually seen as a means of preserving the *status quo* in the industry. 'Sugar growers and manufacturers', the *Journal* reported in its pre-referendum edition,

are largely being driven into Federation by fear of the results of a change in political parties in this colony, though they certainly do not recognize how much simpler it will be to effect a change when a dozen or so of our most enlightened statesmen have transferred their influence to the Federal Parliament.[42]

In summary there is little in the campaigns of 1898 and 1899 to support the view that a White Australia was the 'one issue' that brought about federation. Federal control over immigration in fact was rarely held out to the 'average citizen' in the south-eastern colonies as an inducement to federate. Not only did the Billites fail to exploit the incidents of West Adelaide's leper and Melbourne's 'Hindoo Host', but Holder and O'Malley made some strange statements on the subject. Indeed so little had been said of immigration control through federation in these colonies that anti-Billites felt able to campaign against the Bill because it included the power. Piddington, the *Weekly Herald*, *Daily Telegraph*, and *Sydney Worker* appealed for a vote of 'No' as the measure was likely to worsen the situation. So too in Queensland. Certainly some Labor men advocated federation as a means of ridding the colony of its Polynesians. But to others federation was a capitalist scheme destined to perpetuate black slavery. It would remove the topic from the local parliament and thereby forestall their imminent triumph on the issue. The Mackay *Sugar Journal* reported that growers actually saw federation as a possible way of retaining Kanaka labour. The paper itself believed that the Commonwealth would do nothing without a Queensland initiative.

Why then was a White Australia at best no more than a peripheral issue in the campaigns and in the federation movement of the 1890s taken as a whole? The answer is surely that the problem of Asian immigration which had bedevilled the colonies was commonly regarded as solved. The restrictive measures against the Chinese had proved effective. No colonial government wanted to relax or revoke them. None would have dared try even if it had. The later trickle of Japanese, Afghans, and Indians was a relatively minor nuisance compared with earlier Chinese invasions. Their arrival and subsequent activities were but irritations that were only becoming apparent after the federation movement was under way. Besides colonial Premiers were well aware that the problems, such as they were, could be dealt with readily by local parliaments. Chamberlain in 1897 had made it perfectly clear to them that even the sensitive question of excluding the Empire's British Indians could be met merely by an appropriate 'form of words'.[43] In brief Asian immigration was a dormant public issue simply because by and large it had been settled.

This view may be illustrated in a number of ways. For instance there were no great demonstrations, strikes, or public protests as there had been in earlier decades. Such affairs were things of the past. Early in 1888 the *Northern Territory Times* had campaigned energetically and bitterly against the entry of Chinese at Darwin. The Territory should be a prosperous British settlement 'and not the home for every class of Chinese convict and leper which the Imperial Kow may think fit to transport to us'. The whole of Australia was 'in a state of ferment on the Chinese question'. Ten years later in direct contrast the paper reported its current troubles with the Chinese and Japanese in the mildest terms. They were ignored altogether in its appeals for federation. The exclusion of Asiatic aliens was relegated to that of a debating topic for the Literary Society.

A similar low priority and lack of urgency was evident in Victoria when an Immigration Restriction Bill was introduced shortly after the first referendum. The Bill was a combination of the Natal and West Australian Acts of 1897. Its main purpose was to deal with problems caused by Afghan and Indian hawkers. Most members in the Assembly agreed that something needed to be done about the hawkers. But many could not see the necessity for this particular measure though they were prepared to pass it. One used the statistics on the number of Hindus provided by the minister to argue that there was 'no such urgency for passing this measure at the present time, as there was in Natal'. Duncan Gillies fancied that 'a great many honourable members imagine that this Bill is not an urgent measure'. The proper method was to deny licences to Indian hawkers. The legislation should be delayed in view of the horse export trade to India as 'persons are brought over whose business is to take charge of horses exported'. Gillies concluded: 'We are none of us in the slightest degree alarmed at the present situation'.[44]

Some members also took exception to the Bill because it was not uniform with those in other colonies. On this point a curious inversion of the traditional relationship between federation and immigration emerged. Uniform legislation should *precede* federation. The measure should be uniform with the New South Wales Bill so as to aid the federal cause. As Gillies put it during the third reading, 'In view of federation it was most desirable that, in dealing with this subject, the Australian colonies should adopt a uniform measure.'[45] The Legislative Council concurred. It appointed a Select Committee which examined ship owners, spokesmen for the Chinese and Indians, municipal sanitary inspectors, and the officer who issued hawkers' licences. Its report stated,

Your committee are of opinion that the legislation proposed in this Bill is not required at present for Victoria, evidence having been given that under the provisions of the Chinese Act 1890 the number of Chinese residents has steadily diminished, and that in respect of Indian immigrants the objections which have been urged to these as hawkers can be met by an amendment of the Hawkers and Pedlars Act 1890. . . . but, inasmuch as some Australian colonies have already passed Immigration Restriction Acts, and others are now dealing with Bills of the same tenor . . . your committee, with the desire to act in a federal spirit, have agreed to recommend that the provisions of the New South Wales Act, with some additions, be adopted instead of those embodied in the Bill referred to them.[46]

Perhaps the best example is provided by various working-class organizations. Throughout the second half of the century these had been in the vanguard of movements to make Australia white. For instance, H. A. Harwood, a prominent trade unionist, was president of the Victorian Anti-Chinese League. It was Harwood who proposed in 1885 that it be 'compulsory upon the Chinese to denationalise themselves by cutting off their pig-tails, and adopting European clothes and customs'. Chinese and coolie immigration was a vital topic at the first five Intercolonial Trade Union Congresses. Papers were delivered and resolutions passed on the subject from 1879 to 1888. At the latter delegates unanimously agreed 'that stringent and identical legislation be enforced by the various Australian Governments, with a view of preventing the influx of Chinese and coolie immigrants to these colonies'.[47] However, the next Congress took place in 1889 after the Chinese Conference in 1888. This one was the first to evoke no discussion whatever on immigration. Instead the last business resolution reflected general contentment. Harwood moved 'That this Congress records its satisfaction at the Acts of Parliament in the various colonies in restricting Chinese immigration, and, further, that, it is necessary restrictions should be placed upon all coolie immigration.'[48] At the Congress in Ballarat in 1891 only one of the five colonies represented included the topic on its list for consideration. The 26-point platform produced by the intercolonial committee did not incorporate immigration.[49]

Neither did that of the first Labor Party in 1891. Instead the New South Wales platform included 'Stamping of Chinese-made furniture'. A plank for the 'Exclusion of alien inferior races' was not inserted until 1895. With federation in the air the annual conference in 1896 drew up its federal programme. Arthur Rae's resolution, 'The incorporation in the proposed Federal Constitution of provision for the future exclusion from the rights of residence and citizenship in Federal territory of all undesirable alien races', was carried. John Christian Watson moved an amendment: 'That power be given in the Constitution of the Federal Parliament to exclude all undesirable alien races.' This was defeated. It is not clear from the reports what was meant by 'Federal territory'. Elsewhere the term was common usage for the capital territory, though it is possible it may also have embraced the Northern Territory in its use at the conference. Hence the implication of the acceptance of Rae's plank and the rejection of Watson's is that the current situation was under control. What needed to be safeguarded was not the existing colonies but rather the settled policy which the Commonwealth might possibly undermine in territory under its direct control. Be that as it may, Watson's version was certainly the stronger and it was lost. But even his used the word 'alien' and therefore did not cover Indians who were not aliens but British. A plank for the 'Total exclusion of colored and other undesirable races' did not become established in the platform until January 1900.[50] This of course was well after federation was assured.

The situation regarding contract Polynesian labour in the Queensland canefields was different to that of Asian immigration. In 1893 Griffith reversed his former stand and revoked legislation which was to end the traffic. Hence, unlike alien immigration, the Kanaka question was very much a lively issue in the 1890s, especially in Queensland. But how could the leaders of the federation movement make much of uniform control in the second Federal Convention and in the referenda when Queensland was boycotting the affair? How could they guarantee federation would secure a White Australia when it was by no means certain that the chief culprit would actually federate? Moreover to have done so would have been a serious tactical mistake. It would have jeopardized the chances of the Queensland Parliament passing the essential Enabling Bills to permit the necessary referendum in the colony. Even after Queensland's late entry it was noticeable that when Barton, Deakin, Kingston, Turner and others advocated the Commonwealth Bill in Queensland they carefully avoided the whole issue.

Nor is it really valid to argue that everyone understood what was to happen after federation. The *Sugar Journal*'s reports of grassroots opinion in the industry and the anti-Billite Labor views indicate this. Furthermore Griffith, the Bill's chief draftsman in 1891, weighed the probabilities. In 1896 he presented a paper to the Queensland government. Entitled *Notes on Australian Federation: Its Nature and Probable Effects* it said:

The question of the immigration of the coloured races is both a political and social question, and involves important issues in both aspects. It seems necessary that the ultimate power of dealing with the matter should be left to the Federal Legislature, for it may give rise to difficult political problems seriously affecting the external relations of Australia; and the question of the character of the future civilization of any part of the Federation concerns the whole of it. . . . But the probability is that the representatives of the Nation would rise to the occasion, and would decline to do any act that might inflict disaster on any part of the Continent merely in obedience to a popular cry.[51]

Griffith mentioned the lack of knowledge of the effect of climate on Europeans. This was 'so obvious to unprejudiced observers' that 'it may be anticipated, with some degree of confidence' that the Commonwealth would not 'until it is in possession of much fuller knowledge than is at present attainable' permit any action that would result in the 'definite condemnation' of any part of Australia 'to barrenness and desolation'. He expressed 'large confidence in the general intelligence of the Southern parts of the Continent'. He concluded: 'that the future State policy on this matter will exert the most material influence on the social condition of the people cannot be doubted. . . . Federation will not of itself make any great difference in this respect.'[52] In May 1899 Griffith delivered a paper to members of the Queensland Federation League before presenting it to parliament. He compared the new Draft Bill favourably with the old. The special race clause was now a concurrent power, not an exclusive one. (Griffith incidentally had suggested this in his first paper.) Hence,

The present Bill, therefore, gives a freer hand to the several colonies than that of 1891. It was admitted in both Conventions that the question of alien immigration must be left, in the last resort, to the Federal Parliament, but the Convention of 1897–8 has left the matter to be dealt with by the several states until the Federal Parliament thinks fit to interfere. The probability of the Federal Legislature interfering with the existing laws of Queensland with regard to Polynesians may be gauged by the fact that up to the present time the Legislature of New South Wales has never attempted to touch the subject, although it largely affects the Northern agricultural areas of that colony.[53]

Clearly Griffith, president of the Federation League, did not regard a White Australia as a fundamental part of the federation movement.

Moreover Queenslanders remained confident after federation took place. And even if it was possible to remove the Kanakas, 'their places would very soon be taken' by Indians. The British Empire contained a large proportion of coloured races and

The Federated Parliament will be more clearly a Parliament of the Empire, with more clearly defined Imperial duties. . . . The men who compose the coming Federal Parliament will in all probability be tried men of wide outlook, and the Parliament is not at all likely to attempt what is a proved impossibility—a white Australia.[54]

Barton's policy speech on 17 January 1901 at Maitland came as a shock. A resident of Proserpine regretted his vote for federation: 'It is surprising that a man of Mr Barton's ability should join in the stupid cry of a White Australia, and talk of the abolition of black labour for the whole of Australia'. One from Bundaberg feared that Indians 'will simply pour in' because 'a British subject has British laws at his back to enforce his just desires'. Thynne, a member of the first Federal Convention, held that though it was possible to keep out indentured Indian labour 'it will be found a difficult, if not impossible, thing to prevent the admission of British Indians who come of their own accord'.[55]

What then should be made of the idea that a White Australia was the compelling force for federation? It is evident that this is a gross exaggeration if not entirely incorrect. Apart from evidence and arguments already advanced the whole notion is riddled with anomalies. Parkes took his initiative at the very time that Asian immigration was least in need of attention. The Sydney Conference in 1888 had taken care of the Chinese and other Asians were not a problem. Even the Kanaka traffic was due to end in a few years. The 'Father of Federation' did not allude to the subject in his Tenterfield address. Again, the traditional guardians of a White Australia, the Labor organizations, were generally indifferent or hostile to federation. On the one hand, the Labor Parties in New South Wales, Victoria, and South Australia, and papers such as the *Worker* opposed the Commonwealth Bill. On the other hand, no major newspapers campaigned more whole-heartedly for it than the *South Australian Register* and the *Brisbane Courier*, traditional advocates of cheap coloured labour. The Victorian Legislative Council ardently supported federation yet believed an Immigration Restriction Act unnecessary for the colony. In South Australia Adelaide's Chinatown rejected the measure. In Queensland the tropical northern and central regions carried the day despite the hostility of the urbanized and southern Brisbane district.

What should be made of Deakin's famous statement? It should be recognized that Deakin was speaking to parliament and nation in support of a ministerial Bill. He was indulging in a piece of political poetic licence, carried away by his famous rhetoric. Historians, wise after the event, have taken his famous statement at face value. But those who wrote of the federation movement before the federal policy was announced ignored a White Australia in their accounts. For instance the best historical treatment of the federation movement is undoubtedly the introduction to the *Annotated Constitution of the Australian Commonwealth*, but Quick and Garran were utterly silent on the issue.[56] Perhaps most telling of all, though Deakin the Attorney-General made much of it, Deakin the historian did not. He began the *Federal Story* in March 1898 during the closing days of the Federal Convention and completed it in September 1900 just before the Commonwealth's inauguration. Yet in this, which Deakin himself called 'an inner history of the movement', he said not a word about immigration control or a White Australia.

In essence the standard interpretation of the relation between federation and a White Australia leaves much to be desired. As such it does not provide an adequate explanation for the origin of the Commonwealth's legislation.

The first statement of intent of Commonwealth action on a White Australia was given by Barton in his inaugural policy speech as Prime Minister on 17 January 1901 at West Maitland:

Legislation against any influx of Asiatic labor we shall regard simply as a matter of course. (Applause). Not so Polynesian or Kanaka labor. If we were at the beginning of it now, we should have quite as strong an objection to that, but we shall not be guilty of any oppression of those Kanakas already in Australia. But we shall take care to restrict the importation of more of them. (Loud cheers). We shall try to prevent any such importation as will increase the number of Kanakas in Australia under any circumstances, and we shall preach and ensure a gradual abolition of the importation. (Cheers). This legislation will be introduced without unnecessary delay.[57]

There are two related, but still distinct, questions that need to be answered in order to understand better the origin of Commonwealth legislation on a White Australia. In view of the neglect of the issues of Asian immigration and Polynesian labour by Barton and others in important stages of the federation movement, why did Barton include these in his ministerial policy? Secondly, why did the Pacific Island Labourers and Immigration Restriction Bills pass rapidly through the legislative process so as to become the first policy Acts of the Federal government? The distinction between the two questions is important because Barton's speech embraced a wide range of topics, some of which were not secured by federal legislation within the life-span of two or three federal parliaments, still less the first year of the opening session. Barton promised a Bill dealing with old-age pensions 'as soon as the financial situation is clear enough to enable us to provide the necessary funds': no ministry—the Barton, Deakin, Watson, or the Reid—introduced such a Bill until 1908. Barton said that Lyne would take charge of a Bill to establish the Inter-State Commission. Lyne did indeed introduce the Bill, but it received an unsympathetic reception, was withdrawn, and establishment of the Commission lagged until 1912. Other examples could be given, but the disparity between election campaign promises and their fulfilment is a common enough phenomenon.

Evidence suggests that leading members of the cabinet regarded White Australia merely as one of a number of policies calculated to gain widespread popular support, rather than as the triumphant expression of the federation movement. As the inauguration of the Commonwealth drew near, future ministers discussed their election tactics and policies. In September 1900 Kingston informed Deakin about the prospects of two good Labor candidates in South Australia and advised:

Free Trade and Protection are unlikely to be the issues here though one or two would like to see a fuss about them. . . . What about a White Australia, Old Age Pensions and Industrial Conciliation as further lines in a Liberal Policy. I have not sat down to think the matter out.[58]

In November Kingston outlined a platform for a projected local 'Liberal Association'.

1. Uniform Federal franchise and Adult Suffrage.
2. We must work in somehow local enfranchisement of Federal voters and state deadlock resolutions on basis of Federal Model. . . .
3. Tariff to meet present customs requirements and avoid sacrifice of industries.
4. Old Age Pensions.
5. White Australia.
6. Industrial Conciliation and Arbitration.
7. Federal Economy.[59]

By this time Deakin, perhaps influenced by Kingston's original letter, was thinking along similar lines. 'We must have a popular programme', he told Barton, 'and a government national in its character and composition and stable because of its breadth'. A Liberal Party platform could include 'equal citizenship for all adults except those of alien race whose numbers shall be limited and reduced as far and as fast as is consonant with justice to them and to many interests affected.'[60] A week later he referred to Kingston's programme 'which oddly enough was an exact replica of that I sent you'.

The Labour party in every colony are organising for the fray and unless we take care will anticipate us. We shall have to fight the Ultras—Tories and Labourites and socialists but with a progressive programme . . .[61]

In December Barton spoke of likely legislation on intercolonial free trade and the tariff, common defence, uniform postal services, and, he went on, 'it cannot be long before the immigration of persons and races not wanted in Australia will be regulated by one equable law'.[62]

Cabinet shaped Barton's Maitland policy speech at meetings in Sydney on 9 and 10 January 1901. These initial meetings were unique for a variety of reasons. Barton, not yet Prime Minister in his own right as elected head of a national party, presided over a caretaker cabinet composed of members representing no one but themselves. Ministers held no safe seats, commanded no parliamentary majority or political party. Indeed there was no Commonwealth Parliament.

There were no government or opposition records to defend or attack, no national party programmes. Cabinet also assembled in awareness that Reid—the acknowledged centre of the greatest public demonstrations at celebrations throughout the preceding week—was already campaigning in Tasmania. By a common consent confirmed by Reid, the great election issue would be the federal tariff.

In these peculiar circumstances the policy speech needed to be an appeal to both electors and candidates. But its major theme— moderate protection—would inevitably be divisive. At the same time, as Kingston pointed out, the conflict between free trade and protection would probably have less resonance in States other than New South Wales and Victoria. Hence what the ministry really required were popular, unifying policies to broaden their bases of support in the electorates and parliament. Given the liberal bias of the protectionist cabinet and the more conservative predilections of their free-trade opponents, cabinet sought a progressive platform.

A White Australia was one such policy that met the needs of the moment admirably. New South Wales, Western Australia, and Tasmania already had popular restrictive legislation modelled on the Natal Act in operation and no controversial principles were involved. Now that Queensland was actually a member of the union a continental White Australia became a physical possibility by ending the Kanaka traffic. Considerations—such as alienating vital support among Queensland parliamentarians, commercial, and sugar interests —which may once have restrained federal leaders were now gone. A new situation open to new tactics and expediencies existed. The policy's appeal cut across geographical, fiscal, and social divisions. Cockburn, now Agent-General for South Australia, explained to British readers that it was a mistake to regard it simply as a Labor question: 'A profound instinct against racial admixture pervades all classes'.[63] But it was doubly useful to attract Labor politicians because they were either divided on, or indifferent to, the great issue of the tariff. Moreover, although throughout most of the 1890s alien immigration had been a dormant public issue, the federation movement itself had aroused fears among some people of possible interference with settled colonial policies. They believed that a national parliament, with an anticipated conservative Senate, would be more likely to perpetuate or extend black labour than to banish it. Already, in January 1900, an intercolonial conference of Labor parties had placed 'total exclusion of coloured and other undesirable races' second to electoral reform in the federal platform.[64]

It seems unlikely, therefore, that Kingston and Deakin, who probably urged the policy at cabinet meetings, had to use their full powers
of persuasion on their colleagues. If cabinet needed a reminder that
the sections of colonial society which had done most to make
Australia white were now mindful of the subject, then they had just
been given one. On 7 January at a Trades Hall banquet attended by
unionists from three States and by Barton, Kingston, Lyne and
O'Connor from the ministry, E. W. O'Sullivan plainly told the
ministers what was expected.

The first great task that the new Government would have to take in hand
would be that of a white Australia. (Prolonged cheers). It was only a
question of time, perhaps only three years, when they expected the Federal
Parliament to carry a bill to abolish coloured labour, no matter whether it
was in Queensland or any other part of Australia.[65]

Besides, as experienced colonial politicians, they had learned the facts
of political life and knew well the desirability of gaining Labor support or acquiescence. In 1899 Barton had failed to get Labor backing,
Lyne succeeded, and as a result he, not Barton, took over from Reid
as the Premier of New South Wales. In South Australia the support
of the United Labor Party from 1893 had enabled Kingston to govern
the colony for an unprecedented six years. Solomon, his successor,
offended Labor and lasted exactly one week; Holder, his heir, found
it convenient to include the Labor leader, Batchelor, in his new
cabinet.

Similar considerations made a White Australia almost as good for
Reid, though free-trade papers like the *Australasian, Brisbane
Courier, South Australian Register,* and the Hobart *Mercury* opposed
aspects of the policy which they ridiculed as a 'false issue', an election
'catch cry', a 'catch penny phrase'. But Reid, unfortunately for him,
had not mentioned it at the start of his campaign early in January in
Tasmania, where he concentrated on the tariff. Objectively he could
be excused for the omission because Tasmanians were probably less
interested in the question than any other Australians. Asian immigration was no longer a great problem there (or anywhere else) and the
island was scarcely likely to be inundated with stray Kanakas. When
Kingston raised the issue in Hobart in February, a member of the
audience told him to stick to the tariff as a White Australia was 'a
far-off subject that was not now agitating the people'.[66] Tactically,
however, Reid made a bad mistake. Barton's Maitland speech pre-
empted his mainland campaign and thereafter Reid was reduced to

claiming that he had thought of the policy first, indeed that he himself had actually invented the phrase. But for a politician of Reid's reputed skill it was an unhappy start, a peculiarly inept performance.[67]

Nonetheless, despite the undoubted attractions of the policy as one item in a popular platform, the Maitland speech may still not have included it as a plank but for one further untoward circumstance. James Robert Dickson, Chief Secretary in the Philp ministry in Queensland and the State's representative in Barton's cabinet, was too ill to attend the Commonwealth celebrations and died on 10 January. Cabinet therefore drew up its programme in the absence of a Queensland representative. Now Dickson, like Philp, supported Kanaka labour and had advocated its retention in the federation referenda campaign in 1899. Had Dickson lived to attend the meetings, he may well have opposed references to this aspect of the issue. As Queensland's delegate in the negotiations on the Commonwealth Bill in London in 1900 he had proved himself capable of taking and maintaining an independent stand against the concerted pressure of Barton, Deakin, and Kingston. Thus, perhaps faced with a split it could surely ill afford at its first meetings, cabinet may have considered it wise to exercise discretion and exclude the item.

In these circumstances doubt must also be cast on the inclusion of Asian restriction in the Maitland speech. References to this aspect would have reopened the *whole* question and reawakened what was still essentially a dormant public issue. But with Queensland a member of the Commonwealth, a White Australia now meant to most people (if they had to think about it at all) the prohibition of Asians *and* the abolition of the Kanaka trade in the northern State. Moreover, a measure for uniform restriction would need to make special provision for exempting South Sea Islanders without complementary legislation dealing with the traffic.[68] Rather than take such a potentially dangerous and difficult course cabinet might have preferred to try to let sleeping dogs lie.

Possibilities like these must, of course, remain conjectural. But they serve to suggest that a White Australia, or at least its form and timing, was not an inevitable part of either the Maitland speech or early Commonwealth legislation. Further, it is worth noting that although Barton personally telegraphed Philp on 10 January to express his condolences, he did not take the opportunity to discuss the vacancy but waited until the 15th. The delay may have been due to a proper sense of respect for the dead and the solemnity of the occasion.

But it ensured that no Queenslander would see or directly influence the speech before its delivery.

Negotiations between Barton and Philp to find a Queensland replacement for Dickson proved difficult.[69] Others also involved included E. B. Forrest, a Queensland MLA; J. F. G. Foxton, Philp's Home Secretary; and Arthur Hobbs, Foxton's legal partner and Barton's nephew. Philp declined the portfolio of Postmaster-General and on 18 January (post Maitland) proposed Foxton, a supporter of Kanaka labour. Barton ignored the suggestion—and a second naming in order Foxton, Drake, Thynne, and Cowley—and offered the post to Forrest, an opponent of the traffic. He in turn rejected it. The tone of the negotiations became increasingly acrimonious. Barton threatened to look elsewhere. Philp insisted that Queensland needed representation particularly as her special interests were 'threatened with active interference', a charge which Barton blandly denied: 'I cannot see how expressions contained in my speech if report is accurate have been read as threatening interference in special interests [of] Queensland'. By this time Barton was beginning to find the delay politically damaging: 'The vacancy has now existed for fifteen days. . . . The pertinacity of the Press renders all delay very embarrassing to me.' He was about to capitulate and drafted a telegram to Foxton when a letter from his nephew apparently saved the day. Foxton, Hobbs told his 'dear Uncle', was afraid 'that he was being foisted on to you', Foxton's business interests were in Queensland, it would be inconvenient for him to reside outside Brisbane, 'and he told me that it would only be at the unanimous request of his colleagues here that he would feel at all disposed'. Barton scratched out Foxton's name and address and sent the telegram to Drake instead. The anonymous Sydney correspondent of the *Morning Post* (Deakin, who had tendered Barton advice from the sideline in Melbourne) told his British readers of the immediate challenge by the Queensland establishment to the White Australia plank in the Maitland speech. The Premier of Queensland and most prominent men there supported the continued use of coloured labour:

It may be [he coyly explained] that the explicitness of this Ministerial announcement is partly responsible for the delay which has occurred in selecting another representative of Queensland in the Cabinet in place of the late Sir James Dickson. . . . At all events there is some hesitation in the allotment of the vacant portfolio which may easily have arisen on this account.[70]

In the event the Maitland statement on White Australia stood. Whether or not the Barton ministry could implement it, or would want to try, depended on a number of factors: the priority and reception accorded the topic in the campaign; success in the election and the temper of parliament; and the ministry's assessment of the total political situation. The future of the policy was still by no means a foregone conclusion. As even the *Bulletin* realized (and warned) in its pre-election leader: 'To some extent the decision must hinge on the demand for a White Australia. It is questionable if the vast importance of this issue is fully realised even yet in the South.'[71]

Most editorial and other early comment on the speech ignored the subject and dealt mainly with the tariff or with the speech as a whole. The *Age* welcomed its 'strong note' on liberalism and its 'sound one' on protection. The *Sydney Morning Herald* thought Barton had declared 'the desire rather than the intentions of his colleagues', and termed its theme of moderate protection 'the merest skeleton of a fiscal policy'. Sydney commercial men were said to be disappointed that they 'merely got platitudes', and politicians described the speech as well constructed but 'dealing with much-worn topics not entirely in a new way'.[72]

But newspapers, sugar producers, and politicians in Queensland, and labourites everywhere, seized upon the references to a White Australia. The *Brisbane Courier*, up to this point confident, immediately denounced Barton's 'manifesto' as a blatant bid for the Labor vote. Thereafter it conducted a vitriolic defence of the Kanaka traffic and State rights. The *Bundaberg Mail* believed removal of the Kanaka impractical and unwise as a more undesirable race could not be kept out: 'we are apt to find that the Federal Premier's desire to achieve a "White Australia" has only succeeded in giving our cane-fields a magnet attraction for the Hindoo'.[73] Chambers of Commerce, cane-growers, and sugar manufacturers passed resolutions deploring the statement, prepared petitions, and organized deputations. Some suggested the appointment of a Royal Commission before the Commonwealth legislated; a Commission would recommend, asserted W. V. Brown, a Queensland delegate to the Intercolonial Australian Natives Association Federation Conference, 'graduated restriction of Kanaka labour' to 'degrees of latitude rather than periods of time'. Queensland Labor candidates such as Henry Turley thought Barton had 'clearly voiced the opinion of the large majority of the people of the Southern portion of Australia'; neither Barton, nor Reid, nor any other statesman would dare to 'stand up in New South Wales, in

Victoria, or in South Australia and speak in favour of coloured labour'. Hughes expressed a reaction typical of Labor in other States: 'Our chief plank is, of course, a White Australia. There's no compromise about *that*. The industrious coloured brother has to go—and remain away'. Philp invited Barton to visit the north and see for himself that his policy was impractical.[74]

Barton visited Queensland in late February and early March, and showed signs of softening the policy. Interviewed at Toowoomba by the *Courier*, he asserted that if legislation was not introduced in the first session there would be ample time for a Royal Commission, but he was 'not in a position at present to say whether it would, or would not, be dealt with in the first session'. At Brisbane he admitted, 'The question was not entirely to be solved by legislation, as the natural forces were much stronger than the forces of the members of Parliament'. He had been misunderstood in Queensland, perhaps through misreporting.[75]

Opponents in Queensland and other States, where the issue spilled over, observed these and other signs of wavering and supplied various explanations and interpretations. One spokesman at a special meeting of the Brisbane Chamber of Commerce suggested that Barton 'who perhaps only kindled it [the White Australia policy] for political purposes, found it very difficult to keep in hand, and now tried to qualify what he had said and alleged he was misreported.'[76] The *Australasian* believed Barton contemplated 'a lease of life' for the system for another ten years. He sought 'the support of the labour party on the ground that his Ministry is against black labour, and he equally claims the support of the sugar-growers on the plea that he will do nothing rashly.'[77] He seemed to be realizing at last that 'nature' was the true arbiter; in Queensland's climate cane-cutting was 'niggers' work'. Later, in 1901 after the government had introduced the Pacific Island Labourers Bill, Philp, alarmed for the first time, protested to Barton and referred to Barton's speech at Brisbane:

The statement of your policy on which Queensland most relied, and which was mainly efficacious in lulling any possible apprehensions of drastic treatment under Federal administration was that made in your speech addressed directly to the citizens of this State on 2nd of March this year. . . . such marked stress was laid upon the comparative futility of legislation when brought into conflict with natural forces as could not but produce the impression that the speaker clearly recognized the force of one of the strongest arguments in favour of the employment of black labour in tropical agriculture.[78]

He himself had understood, he told Barton, 'that you were entirely out of sympathy with those who hold extreme views upon the subject'.

Reid, who noted Philp's endorsement of the protectionist Prime Minister in March, commented: 'If Mr Barton could secure the support of the free-trade Premier of Queensland he would require watching on the black labour question'; Philp had 'squared' Barton. But Reid also hedged his bets in the North. At Toowoomba, where he outdrew his rival, he declared a White Australia a 'supreme necessity' but confessed he was 'staggered' to learn that £7 million was invested in the sugar industry and promised 'to go and study the problem for himself'. At Brisbane he said Queensland was dangerously close to 'hordes of aliens'. The Kanaka's presence gave him no pleasure but 'there was a wide difference between the position of the Kanakas and the position of the Asiatics'. The *Bulletin* dubbed the 'Yes-No' free-trader 'Black-and-White' Reid.[79]

The result of the general election sealed the success of the policy in its entirety. The ministry secured just enough support to retain office, and Labor held the balance in both Houses. In Queensland Labor won three of the six seats in the Senate (two candidates topping the poll), four of the nine in the Representatives, and the advocates of black labour were routed. The campaign strategy planned by Kingston and Deakin had succeeded and parliament was decidedly more radical than expected. Only in June 1900 J. V. Chataway, Queensland Minister of Agriculture, had assured sugar growers at Mackay that 'it would be foolish to imagine the Commonwealth Parliament acting on this matter [the necessity for Kanaka labour] with less consideration than the Queensland Parliament'. The central government would be 'less likely to be swayed by local or sectional prejudices'. The men who will compose it 'will be the flower of Australian Statesmanship and are not likely to take a course bound to land them in the most complicated of economic difficulties'. Besides, in view of the overwhelming vote they had given for federation in the referendum, the federal government

will not be so ungrateful as to forget the sacrifice and the exertions of the Queensland sugar-farmers in the cause of Australian unity. . . . Gentlemen, believe me, you will be safe in trusting the intelligence of the Federal Parliament.[80]

But a year later W. H. Groom wrote from Melbourne to Littleton Groom (who in September was to succeed his father as member for

Darling Downs) remarking on the quality and tone of the Commonwealth Parliament compared to the Queensland legislature:

Without question Victoria is profoundly democratic. It is astonishing to
find so many educated men embued with democratic principles, and
[regarding] Conservatism as opposed to the spirit and advancement of
the age. . . . I do not wonder at the progress of democratic legislation, and
the feeling felt towards Queensland in consequence of its intense conservatism.[81]

And the *Review of Reviews* commented on the 'startling triumph' of
the Labor Party in Chataway's own State:

It is a paradox—an example of the irony of events—that the party which
counts for so little in the State Legislature should thus have a commanding representation in the Commonwealth Parliament. . . . It is surely a
somewhat absurd result that the party which controls affairs in Queensland itself must depend on the representatives of the other States for the
safeguard of its own ideals in the Commonwealth Parliament.[82]

The influence of one particular item on the result of an election—
and Barton and his colleagues campaigned consistently on the full
Maitland programme outside Queensland—cannot really be assessed.
But Labor's unexpected victories, especially in the northern State,
were taken almost everywhere as a verdict on a White Australia. One
Queenslander, apprehensive as to the future of Polynesian labour,
wrote to Symon, who led the Senate poll in South Australia: 'Your
State has behaved splendidly. But when Q'land is mentioned I hide
my head and am silent.'[83] The *Courier* lamented: 'We have humiliated Queensland. We have sent our worst men when we might have
sent our best.' The *Bulletin* rejoiced: 'On his knife-handle Barton can
write "The Asiatic goes at once", and on his fork-handle, "The
Kanaka goes as quickly as possible".' Senator Keating, seconding the
address-in-reply, first voiced an opinion which was to be echoed many
times in both Houses: the vote in Queensland was 'a mandate' for
Commonwealth legislation.[84]

Indeed now, for the first time, it may safely be said that uniform
immigration restriction and steps to halt and finally eliminate the
Kanaka traffic were inevitable. The election result could scarcely have
been more conducive to the early introduction and rapid passage of
Bills dealing with the questions. Had either the Protectionists or the
Free-Traders gained an absolute majority the situation would have
been more flexible, more open to possible compromise, and the victor

could then have proceeded leisurely, set up a Royal Commission, or given priority to other measures. But with Labor holding the balance pressure was on Barton to give the policy top priority. On the eve of the first working day of parliament after the adjournment on the Governor-General's address, Labor caucus placed a White Australia at the head of its platform of five planks.[85] In a party that could agree on so little it had become the most important policy, both a means to, and a symbol of, its fragile unity.

The protests, resolutions, deputations, threats and entreaties from the Queensland government and the vested interests could be safely rejected or given their due weight. Barton could tell Philp that coloured labour was a 'burning question' in the election campaign in his State. The Pacific Island Labourers Bill expressed the 'overwhelming public opinion not only of the rest of Australia, but of Queensland . . . as demonstrated by the result of the Federal Elections'; surely, 'the people of Queensland [knew] their own business'.[86] If perhaps it had once seemed prudent to remain silent or equivocate, it now became a virtue, more a necessity, to speak out boldly. Deakin, Kingston, and the like who deplored the degradations of a labour system akin to slavery were not only free to act, but virtually compelled to do so. Besides, counter-pressures from sugar growers in northern New South Wales were mounting. Deputations and petitions urged Barton to proceed forthwith because cheap Kanaka labour gave Queensland growers unfair advantages.[87]

In these circumstances the debates on the Pacific Island Labourers and Immigration Restriction Bills became chiefly a matter of how best to achieve agreed ends. Putting a stop to the Kanaka trade was still controversial in the North, but 'Queensland had spoken her mind'.[88] The grosser abuses of the traffic, which had offended humanitarian statesmen and others in Britain and the colonies, may have ended, but the system remained a blot on a democratic society. The Immigration Restriction Bill involved no controversial aim. Even most of those who in the campaigns and parliament supported the retention of Pacific Islanders argued that of course they too stood for a White Australia, but that indentured labour, a system dependent on temporary residents, did not abrogate the principle.

Barton presented the Bill as a precautionary measure. The Natal representative at the inauguration had advised him to legislate early. C. H. Pearson in *National Life and Character* had warned of the swamping of Aryan races and the Christian faith. It was unwise to delay until the dangers were almost insuperable. Better to 'legislate against the thing, not because it is a pressing killing danger at the moment, but because, even if it is not, it may in a moment become so'. Later, after questions on the effectiveness of State measures and criticism by McMillan, acting Free Trade leader, he stressed the present perils and 'tendencies'. Information from Victoria and Queensland (which he claimed was all he had) showed that in the preceding five years the arrivals of Chinese in Victoria exceeded departures by 1297, and that in Queensland there had been an increase of 3998 in coloured races—including 1926 Polynesians and 847 Japanese. O'Connor, government leader in the Senate, spoke in a similar manner. Deakin suggested there were up to 80 000 coloured aliens in the country (in fact there were under 55 000) and the situation members had to face was an Australia which 'being only in part protected, is scarcely protected at all—excepting in regard to the Chinese'.[89]

Naturally ministers enlarged upon the perilous position and presented the state of affairs in its worst light, but the picture was not as black as they painted. Returns from New South Wales, Victoria, Queensland, South Australia and the Northern Territory, showed a total increase of only 1307 Chinese for the five-year period (departures of Chinese from New South Wales exceeded arrivals by 1968—a fact used by Deakin to demonstrate the success of legislation there). Barton somehow neglected to mention Tasmania, whose reply he had acknowledged two weeks earlier. Chinese immigration there was decreasing and in 1900 a mere fifteen had arrived (no departures given) : except for these, there had been 'no influx' of alien labour. As for other 'undesirable' races the New South Wales customs reported:

Practically there is no influx of Asiatic or coloured passengers from oversea. . . . only 51 men, 12 women, 3 children having been admitted from foreign places during the two years and eight months the Act has been in force.[90]

Barton somehow overlooked this return. Notes prepared for O'Connor showed that 10 aliens had invaded South Australia since 1899, 133 had swarmed into the Northern Territory from whence 151 had fled. A total of 191 non-Chinese had entered Western Australia since 1898 but 498 had left. Barton somehow omitted to point out that Queensland, where danger loomed largest, had regulated the entry of Japanese from 1898 under its treaty with Japan; apparently since then 304 had arrived, but 864 had left.[91]

But, of course, the effectiveness or otherwise of State legislation and the actual trends of the moment were really irrelevant. Indeed, the government introduced the Immigration Restriction Bill on 5 June 1901, well before it knew anything about actual 'tendencies'. Rather than being an urgent response to an existing crisis, or even a potential one, the Bill served other important purposes.

It gave statesmen and politicians an ideal opportunity to express patriotic, nationalistic sentiments, their fierce pride of race, in the new national forum. It enabled them to display a rare degree of unity on a popular principle amid the inevitable war of attrition on the tariff. Its popularity, of course, rested on that same complex blend of economic, social, and outright racist views which had erected the barriers in colonial days. Indeed, it would be difficult to decide who were the greater racists, the large majority who, fearing the corrupting influence of 'inferior' races, wanted an Australia 'pure and spotless' free from 'any racial defects';[92] or the small minority who for their own ends sought 'servile' races as hewers of wood and cutters of cane. An otherwise enlightened, democratic politician, Watson, respected in parliament and throughout the country as a thoroughly decent 'bloke', used the classic racist argument: 'The question is whether we would desire that our sisters or our brothers should be married into any of these races to which we object.'[93] (If the Labor leader was not a racist himself, then clearly he thought his fellow Australians were.) Finally, it had the supreme virtue of costing little to implement. In short it was the ideal policy for the occasion.

These then were the circumstances for the introduction and passing of the Commonwealth's legislation on a White Australia. But the reasons were not directly related to the drive towards federation as such. Deakin's contention (and the accounts derived from it by Willard, Hancock, *et al.*) that this was the 'motive power' for federation is difficult to sustain. The subject was apparently not prominent in Parkes' mind at the start of the Melbourne Conference in 1890, and delegates said little at all about problems of coloured immigration at the first Federal Convention in 1891. It was no more prominent at the second Federal Convention in 1897-8. Delegates seem to have waited until the second session in Sydney to use the actual phrase 'White Australia'. Several, including Higgins and Deakin, implied that Polynesian labour would still be needed in Queensland should the colony eventually join the federation. Some regarded the topic as a State right. The first real discussion of the question at the final session came about by accident. Speakers seemed to believe that there would be a long delay before the Commonwealth could possibly legislate as there would be more urgent things to do. At neither Convention did a White Australia find its way into the foundation principles stated by Parkes in 1891 and Barton in 1897. Suggestions by Quick and Forrest to make the immigration power exclusive were ignored. The passing of uniform immigration legislation was not made mandatory on the Commonwealth as was a uniform tariff and the introduction of intercolonial free trade within two years. The power finally appeared in the concurrent list of section 51 as sub-section (xxvii) behind such topics as weights and measures, marriage and divorce. Samuel Griffith, who might be expected to know something about drafting a Constitution, reassured Queenslanders that the Draft Bill of 1898 gave a 'freer hand' to the several colonies on race questions than its predecessor of 1891. Individual delegates were most certainly passionate devotees of a White Australia. But a few were opposed, most silent. There appears to have been no common recognition that the desire for uniform legislation was at the basis of the movement.

Nor was the subject especially prominent in the public phases. The Intercolonial Australian Natives Association Federation Conference in Melbourne in 1890 failed to include immigration in its list of powers for a federal legislature. No member of the 'popular' Conference at Corowa in 1893 or Bathurst in 1896—the new federation movement which resurrected the 'dead' one—even thought the topic worthy of mention. Some references to a White Australia can indeed be found in the referenda campaigns in the south-eastern colonies in 1898, but there is little to suggest that it was given a high priority. Newspapers, Convention delegates, politicians, pamphleteers and campaigners of all descriptions stressed other gains to be enjoyed, other losses to be endured should federation not come about. In New South Wales and Queensland in 1899 some anti-Billites opposed the Commonwealth Bill on the ground that federal parliament would likely perpetuate black labour, while Billite sugar farmers in the northern colony supported it for that very reason.

A new political environment existed after the inauguration of the Commonwealth. But the policy became a part of Barton's platform almost casually, simply as one item in a popular programme. Had Dickson lived it may not have been included. Had Reid not lost the premiership of New South Wales in 1899 then he, not Barton, would have been the first Prime Minister of Australia. Queensland may still have spoken. But would a 'Black-and-White' ministry, supported by prominent free-traders and black-labour sympathizers such as a

Symon, Walker, Sargood, and Bruce Smith, have listened? In the
event the result of the election ensured early legislation. The situation
was not without irony. The very people who had fought hardest
against the Commonwealth Bill, now, as a consequence of their
failure, were able to get what they most wanted. Others who had
campaigned for federation, now, because of their very success, were
getting what they least wanted. The Reverend J. B. Ronald, Labor
member for South Melbourne and an outspoken advocate of a 'snow-
white' Australia, pleaded unashamedly for the Immigration Restriction Bill because federal parliament had to deal with 'the great
purpose for which we were called into existence'. Deakin congratulated the reverend gentleman for echoing his own view. But in 1899
Ronald had signed manifestoes calling upon voters to reject the Commonwealth Bill, and as vice-president of an anti-Billite organization
had campaigned against Deakin, chairman of the Federation League
of Victoria.[94]

To conclude, it is therefore scarcely valid or necessary to invoke the
notion of the compelling desire for uniform immigration control to
explain the origin of Commonwealth legislation on a White Australia. Post-federation events had a dynamic of their own, and in
a sense the legislation was less the manifestation of a causal factor
than an effect of federation. This is not to deny the strength of the
belief in a racially homogeneous white society. On the contrary, this
was an article of faith held by all strata of Australian society and this
was why Barton included a White Australia in a political platform
calculated to win maximum support. But this emotional issue was
demonstrably not a prime cause of the federation movement if for no
other reason than in the colonies concerned the principle was no
longer in danger. Federal legislation did not, of course, found the
principle but rather reaffirmed it on a national scale made possible
because the union of *all* the colonies had taken place. In essence the
Immigration Restriction Act tied up the loose ends of colonial
measures which had themselves established the principles and largely
solved the problems. As Barton said in moving the second reading,
'We are not doing very much more than the States have done.'
Deakin in his own 'inner history of the movement' said nothing
about uniform immigration control or a White Australia. The
introductory sentence to his famous statement, 'At this early period
of our history we find ourselves confronted with difficulties which
have not been occasioned by union, but to deal with which this
union was established', must surely be treated with scepticism.[95]

3

TOWARDS A WHITER COMMONWEALTH

Some of the unforeseen dynamics of the growth and influence of the Commonwealth government can be seen in the working out of the White Australia policy in the first decade. The policy itself was essentially negative: directed to stopping the entry of coloured people, and to removing the South Sea Islanders. But the actual form of the two Acts embodying the policy, and their subsequent implementation, involved wide ramifications. The Pacific Island Labourers Act immediately raised the sensitive issue of State rights, and it brought in its wake a series of satellite Acts. The Immigration Restriction Act involved delicate negotiations with the British and Japanese governments, and it had certain repercussions which no one anticipated. The original measures, and the complementary legislation which stemmed from them, had to be administered in accord with public and parliamentary opinion. Pressures had to be resisted or accommodated. Machinery had to be created, precedents set, procedures adopted. As such the implementation of the White Australia policy also serves as an example of the functioning of the new federal machine. Ultimately, the legislation introduced the central government into areas where it was generally supposed to have little impact. What perhaps seemed the end of an issue in 1901 with the passing of the two Acts was in reality only the beginning for the Commonwealth.

The Commonwealth, having determined to banish the Kanakas, had now to discover how best to preserve the sugar industry. The problem of substituting 'white' for 'black' labour in the cane fields was unusual. Great changes had taken place since 1885 under the impact of Queensland's Central Mill System and the Sugar Works Guarantee Act of 1895.[1] Large estates—especially in southern districts—were breaking up, and sugar production had doubled while the number of South Sea Islanders remained almost constant. But elsewhere in the world, cane sugar relied almost entirely on the use of 'cheap' native workers. And cheapness apart, blacks, it was still commonly believed, were essential because whites were physiologically unsuited to perform sustained manual labour in tropical climates. In 1892 Griffith had found it prudent to repeal his earlier legislation, which had denied further importation of Kanaka labour, after a Royal Commission predicted the rapid extinction of the industry. Mechanization might provide an answer one day, but suitable machinery had not yet been invented. When it was, its introduction would be a slow process and the Commonwealth's hasty political decision could not await or depend upon problematical technical developments. An Australian tariff could, of course, protect local growers from the rival produce of cheap labour, but it could not supply alternative manpower. As Philp told Barton, and doubtless firmly believed: 'No matter what duties are imposed, the operation of the tariff will not affect the question of how and where the supply of field labour necessary for the production of sugar can be obtained.' White men were not willing to cut and trash cane and if they did they would 'gradually sink below the level of civilization'.[2]

Expert opinion confirmed such views. In June 1901 Barton commissioned Dr Maxwell, director of Sugar Experiment Stations, to investigate aspects of the industry. In August Maxwell reported that the white man attained

his highest value in the most temperate conditions of climate, and can become an economic impossibility in the conditions which are the natural environment of other races, and in which they reach their highest labour efficiency.[3]

The federal government approached its difficult new task in near total ignorance of the sugar industry. Indeed most federal parliamentarians probably knew less about the industry than Queensland growers and politicians knew about southern politics. Barton himself implied in November 1901 that he would have preferred to have waited until receiving Maxwell's report before legislating against the Kanakas. The government's solution was deceptively simple. The Customs Tariff Act 1902, put together by Kingston as Minister of Trade and Customs, placed the equivalent of a protective duty of £6 a ton on foreign cane sugar and £10 on beet. The complementary Excise Tariff Act placed an excise duty of £3 a ton on manufactured sugar to 1 January 1907, less a rebate of £2 to growers who used white labour only after 28 February 1902. If Australians wanted a uniquely white sugar industry, then they would have to be prepared to pay a price in the cause of White Australia. Federal parliament rightly judged they were.

The origin of this ingenious way through the complexities of the financial provisions of the Constitution is obscure. Maxwell was not asked for advice on this question, and he did not give any in his report, though he may have done so elsewhere. Others did offer suggestions. A Rockhampton resident recommended the tariff-excise-bonus mechanism to Barton in March 1901. T. Temperly, proprietor-editor of the *Richmond River Times* and president of the North Coast Anti-alien Society, claimed he had first promulgated an excise duty on black sugar in 1895. Whether in fact unsolicited advice of this nature reached or influenced Kingston and his advisers, or whether they devised the method independently, cannot be ascertained. Two points, however, are quite clear. First, there was no prior arrangement or understanding between Barton and Philp concerning a tariff, excise, or rebate of the sort to induce either Queensland to federate or Philp to lend Barton his support at the first federal election. Secondly, Barton himself considered the scheme unconstitutional. In May 1901 he turned aside a request for an excise duty on black sugar from a New South Wales deputation with the comment that the Commonwealth could not prefer one State to another. Earlier in the month Atlee Hunt rejected the idea of an excise duty on sugar with a rebate for that grown by whites only, because section 51 (ii) precluded discriminatory taxation. But the dubious validity of the method—as Kingston and Deakin (as Attorney-General) must have realized—was of less immediate importance than its acceptance and effectiveness.[4]

Unfortunately, the excise-rebate system quickly proved unacceptable because it operated inequitably. By virtue of section 93 of the Constitution, the States received excise on all Australian sugar *consumed* within their borders. But the rebate paid to eligible growers was charged *against* the excise payable to the States which produced the sugar. Therefore, in effect, Queensland and New South Wales, as sugar-growing States, bore the brunt of the financial burden of this facet of the White Australia policy. Their governments soon saw the flaw in the system. John See, Premier of New South Wales, protested in January 1903 that rather than being a direct charge against State revenue the cost should be met by the Commonwealth as a whole and distributed on a *per capita* basis. In February he added that while every State desired to give the White Australia policy a 'fair trial', the existing system imposed 'unequal sacrifices'.[5]

As a result of objections such as these from New South Wales and Queensland (and perhaps also because of the method's doubtful legality which could soon be challenged) the federal government introduced amending legislation. In July 1903 parliament passed the Sugar Rebate Abolition Act and its complement the Sugar Bounty Act. The new measure substituted a bounty, paid out of consolidated revenue, for the rebate. Henceforth all States contributed to the payment on a *per capita* basis.

Naturally not all State governments (or federal politicians) were as pleased with the impending change as those of the sugar-producing States. Symon, in the Senate's address-in-reply debate complained that the people of the southern States were being compelled to 'put their hands in their pockets and make up the loss to Queensland growers who raise sugar by white labour': this would give a 'very severe wrench' to the federal spirit in South Australia. Senator Gregor McGregor described seeing the South Australian Treasurer acting like 'a bear with a sore head'. But, the Labor leader in the Senate argued, if he and his fellow South Australians had to pay a little more for White Australia they had no reason to grumble.[6] In the event they had no choice as the new means to achieve old ends were approved comfortably.

But while the principle of some type of assistance to encourage white labour and save the industry went largely unchallenged, the Bounty Bill still provoked a great controversy. The dispute led to a test of strength between the House of Representatives and the Senate, and threatened the passage of the measure.

The Bill incorporated Kingston's promise to Queensland growers to grant bounties to producers who employed white workers exclusively after 28 February 1903 instead of 1902 as in the earlier Excise Act (i.e. a twelve-month extension on the use of black workers). Further demands grew to extend the bonus to growers who had employed whites only for a period of twelve months, even if they had used black again after the new deadline. Dugald Thomson (Free Trade, North Sydney), unsuccessfully moved an amendment to delete the new date and substitute the greater concession. When the Bill reached the Senate, Thomas Glassey (Protectionist, Queensland), moved an identical amendment. Greater concessions were needed because major planters such as Angus Gibson were anxious to subdivide their large estates for white settlement.[7]

4 *The first ministry of the Australian Commonwealth*
Middle: Barton. Clockwise from top right: Deakin, Kingston, Fysh,
Forrest, Turner, O'Connor, Drake, Lyne.

5 *Barton's cabinet at Parliament House, Melbourne, 1901*
From left to right as seated: Drake, O'Connor, Deakin, Barton, Lyne, Kingston, Forrest.
Turner was absent because of illness.

The technical question now arose as to the Senate's right to amend a clause of this nature because of the disabilities imposed by section 53 of the Constitution. Its President, Baker, delivered a passionate defence of the status and role of the States House. The Senate could not amend a Bill so as to increase the taxation burden on the people. But Glassey was trying to increase the number of people entitled to a rebate, and to enlarge the quantity of sugar on which it could be claimed. Thus the 'practical' result would be to *decrease* revenue and the burden of taxation. Senators Drake (Postmaster-General), O'Connor (Vice-President of the Executive Council) and Best (Chairman of Committees), believed that the Senate did not have the right. The Senate supported Baker, rejected a suggestion at least to put the alteration in the form of a request, and returned the Bill to the House. The House refused to entertain the amendment because, Speaker Holder declared, section 53 prohibited the Senate from 'originating a proposed law so as to increase any proposed charge or burden on the people'. O'Connor then moved that the Senate not insist on its amendment, and pointed out that if the Bill failed then New South Wales and Queensland would continue to suffer and no bonus could be paid. Baker contended that a request placed the Senate in an inferior position, and urged his colleagues to stand up and show that the 'Commonwealth is a Federation, and that the Senate is a Federal States House elected by all the people of the Commonwealth grouped in States to represent them as State units'.[8] This time the Senators backed O'Connor. They returned the Bill with a request enabling the bounty to be paid as the House wished, provided it could also be paid to growers who had used white workers for twelve months.

Barton observed with satisfaction that the Senate, which had exceeded its rights, had abandoned its original amendment. Turner, the Treasurer, informed the House that the ministry would not accept the clause in the form requested. Instead it would incorporate the request in its own new amendment which insisted that growers could not claim the bounty if they had used black workers for planting after the new date. The Bounty Act 1903 passed with the section as the ministry wanted.[9]

The actual effectiveness of the experimental legislation was also open to dispute. The bounty was to cease at the end of 1906 in order to coincide with the complete phasing out of Kanakas under the Pacific Island Labourers Act. But as the impact of the deportations came to be experienced during the transitional period, vested interests pressed for an extension of the bonus beyond 1906. In October 1904 Maxwell advised Arthur Morgan, Premier of Queensland, that the time allowed for the bounty in the Act was inadequate, especially for the northern districts. Earlier he had told Deakin in Brisbane that a three-year extension would be necessary. Now he believed that five years would be needed: 'Unless action is taken immediately, such action will come too late.' Morgan urged Reid, Prime Minister, to extend the bounty period. The current uncertainty was harming the industry. The vast majority of Australians wanted it to prosper and to be carried on by white workers: 'even in tropical Queensland the notion is gaining ground that both objects are attainable'.[10]

Conferences of sugar growers and millers, public meetings, shire councils, Chambers of Manufacture, Workers Political Organizations pressed the federal government directly and through the agency of the Premier and Andrew Fisher. Lyne, Minister of Customs, commissioned Maxwell to report. Maxwell was to provide answers to a series of questions concerning the 'further expediting and maturing of the Federal legislation relating to the placing of the sugar industry of Australia upon a basis of exclusive white labour'.[11]

In October 1905 Maxwell duly advised that the number of white growers was increasing—especially in the south and centre—but that less than one-third of Queensland sugar qualified for the bonus. The bounty of £2 was insufficient to induce the use of white workers on the large northern plantations, where Kanaka and other coloured alien labour had been driven. He recommended no alteration of the £6 a ton tariff, but suggested an increase of £1 in both the excise and bounty with an extension of seven years.

Lyne introduced the second Sugar Bounty Bill late in 1905. The measure embraced Maxwell's suggestions except that the bounty would be extended five years to the end of 1911 (the seven-year extension would have taken the bounty to 1914 by which time the Braddon clause could have long expired). The Bill encountered considerable opposition from Free-Traders as the deportation of Kanakas was assured by the Pacific Island Labourers Act and the proposed legislation savoured too much of protection. John McCay alleged that the bonus was designed 'to assist white as against coloured labour within the Commonwealth' rather than white labour in Australia against coloured labour outside: this was not what he understood by the White Australia policy. The House only narrowly defeated a move to limit the extension to three years followed by a reducing scale for the remaining two. The Senate approved four years followed by the sliding scale for two. Fisher, champion of maximum concessions, regretted the Senate's amendment but reluctantly conceded that the Bill had to pass quickly. Lyne, forced to deal with the mutilated measure on the spur of the moment, reluctantly concurred.[12]

Henceforth the Commonwealth conducted the final phase of its experiment in the decade under the terms of the Sugar Bounty Act 1905. But the nature of the tasks and problems facing the administration now began to change. In the great haste to deal with the Bill a novel provision passed into the measure almost unnoticed by members of the depleted Chambers. On 18 December Senator George Pearce (Labor, Western Australia), proposed an entirely new clause. Thus far the Commonwealth's legislation had benefited growers and manufacturers: the 'workers' ought now to share the benefits. The minister should therefore be empowered to withhold all or part of the bounty if he found that the rate of wages paid by the grower was below the standard ruling in the district. The minister was so empowered. The clause, a precursor of New Protection, became section 9 of the new Bounty Act with little debate and no division in the Senate or Representatives.[13]

The administration became involved with working conditions and the supply of European field labour as a consequence of section 9, and its control of immigration. The Department of Trade and Customs, because of the absence of actual agreements between employers and employees, found it difficult to discover the standard rate of wages in the various districts. The Bounty Act did not enable the minister to fix rates. But for the purpose of administering section 9, successive ministers determined minimum rates below which wages could not fall if the grower was still to receive the bounty. Government ordinances, after investigation by officials in the different localities, set out scales of wage rates and conditions of employment. These went into fine detail. In June 1907, for instance, regulations of the acting minister laid down a detailed scale of weekly wages, stipulated that contract rates must not be less than the equivalent of the weekly rate, and added 'No deductions for keep from weekly wages to be made on account of wet weather'. In May 1908 another dealt with rates for casual white labour in the off season. The minister directed that in future five conditions must apply: (1) period of employment to be not less than one day, (2) labour could be terminated without notice by either side, (3) wages to be forfeited if the worker went absent,

(4) except for absence, no deductions could be made from wages under any circumstances, (5) wages must be a minimum of five shillings a day, and keep, for eight working hours.[14]

The Department of External Affairs also became concerned with the operation of the sugar industry through its jurisdiction over the Contract Immigrants Act 1905. In February 1907 William Kidston, Premier of Queensland, informed Deakin of an agreement between his own government and cane farmers to bring out European migrants under contract. He asked for assurances that the Commonwealth would raise no objections to the scheme. The plan had to satisfy the Sugar Bounty Act and section 5 of the Contract Immigrants Act, and later the request led to lengthy correspondence between External Affairs, Trade and Customs, and the Queensland government. This was but the first of many such schemes. Four years later the Mackay Sugar Manufacturers Association sought permission to import 132 labourers under an agreement identical to the first. The request led to the usual enquiries by officers and later E. L. Batchelor, the minister, noted: 'Will approve if wages made 25/- minimum & found, 35/- not found'.[15] As it happened at this time, February 1911, the first murmurings of the great sugar strike were heard when Bundaberg workers demanded improved pay and conditions from the Sugar Producers' Association. The Commonwealth government, chiefly through the agency of W. M. Hughes as acting Prime Minister and Attorney-General, became deeply implicated in the conflict.

In sum the Commonwealth from 1901 to 1906 under the Pacific Island Labourers Act and satellite legislation, and from 1906 to 1912 under the new style Bounty Acts and immigration laws, came to exercise a considerable degree of influence on the operation of a State industry. In the process a striking change of attitude had taken place. During the strike the *Age* castigated Hughes for daring to hint that he might rescind the £6 tariff duty: 'The Commonwealth', it warned, 'whatever else it may do, cannot afford to destroy *its* sugar industry.'[16] A few years earlier the industry would surely have been thought of as Queensland's.

The *Age* also alluded to the industry as 'costly' and 'bungled', with its profits flowing to the Colonial Sugar Refining Company, that 'giant monopoly'. There may well have been substance in these charges but the fact remains that the original intentions of the Commonwealth Parliament had been accomplished. In 1910 Maxwell proudly reported the success of federal legislation in its 'expressed purpose' of removing the Kanakas and other coloured workers from the industry and placing production on a 'White Basis'. He addressed himself to two related questions: had the Kanakas gone, and was the industry now carried on by white labour? Returns from the Customs Department showed that on 31 December 1901 there had been 9841 Pacific Islanders in Australia: 4985 had been deported by Queensland, 4269 by the Commonwealth. The small balance still in the country consisted of persons specifically exempted from deportation by the Pacific Island Labourers Act 1906. Further statistics established that in 1902 Queensland and New South Wales had together produced 31 688 tons of sugar with white labour, 67 107 with black: in 1908 whites produced 146 429 tons, blacks 19 286. In 1902 whites represented 14.45 per cent of Queensland's labour, blacks 85.55 per cent. By 1908 the proportions had been reversed: 87.89 was white, 12.11 black.[17]

'In respect of the "Removal of the Kanaka",' Maxwell justly asserted, 'Federal legislation has achieved its purpose.' And 'Unquestionably', Maxwell rightly concluded, 'the Excise and Bounty legislation has achieved its purpose, in a most notable measure, in substituting white for coloured labour in sugar production in Australia'. Despite prognostications to the contrary, by the end of the decade the experiment had indeed succeeded.

Federal parliament took great care to state the intention of the Pacific Island Labourers Act and to define the precise means to accomplish clear ends. The situation was different with the Immigration Restriction Act. The intention of the measure was perfectly clear. But ministers took great pains to avoid any statement of intent within the Bill itself, and the mechanism of exclusion deliberately lacked precision.[18] The reasons for this are well known. At the Colonial Conference of 1897 Chamberlain had informed the Premiers that direct exclusion on the grounds of race or colour would be so 'offensive' and 'painful' to Her Majesty as to preclude sanction. He firmly recommended legislation on the model of the Natal Act with its 'education test'. In May 1901, just after the formal opening of the Commonwealth Parliament, the Crown refused assent to a Queensland Bill amending the Sugar Works Guarantee Act 1893-5, as one section disqualified aboriginal natives of Asia, Africa, and the Pacific Islands.

Barton therefore adopted the education test in the Immigration Restriction Bill (though he departed from precedent and used English and not a European language). In the circumstances, as Barton's private notes show, his reasons for advocating the test were surely sound. Experience in Natal and several Australian colonies had proved that it operated effectively. If the Bill passed in this form, the Governor-General could assent at once; if parliament insisted on direct prohibition, then he would certainly reserve it. The new Commonwealth needed to consider imperial relations and keep them harmonious. Why provoke trouble and delay uniform immigration control when satisfactory results could be secured by complying with the wishes of the imperial government?[19]

Nonetheless, the provision came under severe criticism from Labor and Free Trade members. It was 'crooked': the Bill should openly and honestly prohibit undesirable races and not resort to hypocritical subterfuge—Britain would not refuse assent. It would prove ineffective: educated and 'cunning' Asians might pass the test in English, desirable Europeans such as Scandinavians, Germans, and French might fail.[20] While the Labor Party was serious in its attempts to substitute a clause for direct exclusion, it was not prepared to defeat the Bill if the government refused to accept its amendment. In July, before the Bill's second reading, federal caucus decided to work for the total exclusion of all coloured races and firmly rejected a counter-move to approve the education test. But at the same time caucus roundly defeated a motion to oppose the second reading unless the government consented to an amendment in committee. After the defeat of the amendment, an extraordinary meeting of Labor Representatives determined to support the ministry's clause as it then stood (i.e. the education test with Barton's promise of a European language).[21] Therefore, probably much of Labor's renewed opposition in the Senate was shrewd propaganda—a token display of belligerent independence. Probably, also, some Free-Traders such as Reid supported the Labor amendment to curry favour for the forthcoming tariff battle. Others like Symon and McMillan may well have wanted to cause the Bill's defeat, as Barton himself suspected at the time. Barton noted after the unexpected savaging of the Bill by McMillan, acting Free Trade leader: 'We cannot impute an indirect motive, but if he had the distinct object of killing the Bill he could not have taken a course more fitting to that purpose.'[22]

Parliamentary pressure possibly contributed to Barton's decision to revert to a European language in the test: on 12 September he promised this course should the Labor amendment fail. But the decisive factor, as Yarwood suggested, was probably Chamberlain's attitude.[23] On 20 August Lord Hopetoun, Governor-General, had asked the Colonial Secretary about his powers of reservation: he referred specifically to the 'severe education test' in English in the Immigration Restriction Bill.[24] On 9 September Chamberlain telegraphed that he thought the Bill should be reserved if it went through parliament in its present form. European countries would continually object to the proposed test, which departed widely from existing policy: Hopetoun should therefore 'press for substitution of European for English language'.[25] The whole purpose of the exercise was to avoid assent being refused. Furthermore, as Barton probably sensed— or perhaps by now even knew—the Labor Party was prepared to accept the test in English rather than see the Bill defeated. He could ill afford to admit to British pressure or interference, especially as Labor was critical of his compliance to Chamberlain's dictum of 1897. It was simply good tactics to appear conciliatory when he must have been aware that he would have to abandon English anyway.

In the event, the Bill embraced the test in a European language, and received Hopetoun's assent: the official myth that the Commonwealth had no White Australia policy was born. Federal politicians openly stated the purpose of the legislation in the plainest racist language inside and outside parliament, but the measure itself used no such terms. Eitaki, Japanese Consul-General, protested about statements by Barton, Deakin, and Watson in the House. But Barton could innocently claim that 'the legislation of the Commonwealth does not enforce any discrimination against Japanese subjects'. The Prime Minister could also draw the fine distinction between Barton the statesman and Barton the politician. He did not feel himself called upon to remark on the utterances Eitaki had complained of: 'Members of the Commonwealth Parliament are not responsible for any statements they may make in Parliament to any authority except the people who elect them'.[26]

The need to maintain the myth imposed considerable strains on bewildered collectors of customs, tide surveyors, landing waiters, and other officers obliged to administer the Act. Their problems became evident at the outset. Barton informed collectors of customs in their initial 'strictly confidential' instructions that the law said immigrants 'may' be tested not 'must'. He advised officers to use tact and discretion, but urged them to 'join in the vigilant and effective administration of the Act'.[27] He warned collectors to disclose their instructions to no one but officers who were to administer the Act. In January 1902 Barton sent George Steward, his chief clerk, to Brisbane to convey verbally two passages considered too incriminating to include in the confidential instructions. Steward saw at once that the Act 'was by no means understood by Mr Irving, the Collector of Customs'. He therefore lectured Irving on the various sections, and gave illustrations of cases and explained how they should be handled. He then dictated the two passages, and pointed out the 'grave necessity' for these instructions to be kept 'secret'. Irving should send them to his officers 'on paper not bearing any official mark or character'. The officers should memorize them, and then destroy them so as to leave the collector's copy the only one in existence. Steward held Irving in contempt, but one can only sympathize with the collector's reaction, duly reported back to Barton by the ingratiating chief clerk:

it is all very well for you to explain these matters to me, but how do you think it is possible for me to explain them to my officers, some of whom are two thousand miles away? It is quite impossible . . . to post them up in the proper working of this Act, except by verbal explanation. All the points which have been dealt with are likely to crop up at any time . . .[28]

Within days poor Irving incurred Hunt's wrath for failing to comply with his confidential instructions. In self-defence he complained of meagre facilities of communication, postal delays, vast distances, and pleaded that he was 'overwhelmed' with the work of his own department. The hapless Irving was but the first of many officers to find the Act difficult to implement as it was intended.

The Labor Party, partly because it foresaw problems inherent in administering the deliberately vague sections of the Act, had sought to spell out the disqualifications on aboriginal natives of Asia, Africa, and the Pacific. Partly, too, Labor members distrusted the wide discretionary powers which, given the education test, had to be accorded the minister and his administrators. Labor members rightly suspected that not every federal politician—Symon, for instance—and therefore every potential minister was as fully committed to a White Australia as themselves. The term itself meant different things to different people, and there were different shades of whiteness. In 1904 the Labor Party did not know (but would not have been surprised if it had) that Symon soon tried to modify the policy. In June Symon, Free Trade leader in the Senate, implored Lady Lugard 'to bespeak an influential word' to the editor of *The Times* for a sympathetic leader or friendly comment in aid of a good cause. South Australia's 'crushing financial burden' of the Northern Territory could only be relieved by the 'admission of colored labor to develop her acknowledged natural riches'. A 'number of gentlemen' intended to ventilate the subject in *The Times* in order to gain 'world-wide' attention and influence English public opinion which might 're-act on the Commonwealth authorities'.[29]

For the Labor Party, then, the Immigration Restriction Act was too flexible, too amenable to modification or reinterpretation in the manner of Symon, to be left safely in the hands of unreliable ministers and maladroit officers. Therefore the close scrutiny and cross-examination of ministers about the administration of the Act became a feature of the work of members of the Commonwealth Parliament. These activities were not confined to Labor members, but Labor men were particularly well equipped to guard White Australia. Trades Halls, Labor Councils, Workers Political Organizations, and individual unions—especially the Seamen's whose members were well placed at ports of entry—kept their federal representatives well informed with alleged breaches or lax administration.[30] Information from these organizations, news reports, rumours, became subjects for innumerable questions in parliament or deputations to Prime Ministers.

So also did a related issue. The Labor Party, with the subject of immigration before parliament in 1901, seized the opportunity to protect Australian workers from cheap, white labour. In July, before the second reading of the Immigration Restriction Bill, federal caucus decided to try to prevent the importation of labour under contract. In October Watson duly moved a new sub-clause designed to bar entry to 'Any persons under a contract or agreement to perform manual labour within the Commonwealth'. Watson told the House that he had intended the clause to cover all classes of labour, but had agreed to representations to restrict the prohibited classes to artisans and labourers for the time being. Deakin moved an amendment enabling the minister to exempt workmen required in the Commonwealth for 'special skill'. The new provision met surprisingly little opposition. McMillan objected, but recognized there was a 'consensus of opinion' in favour of the clause, which became section 3(g) of the Immigration Restriction Act without a division.[31]

Probably no provision in the Act caused the administration more problems or greater embarrassment. Alleged evasions soon became the subject of numerous questions to ministers and investigations by officers. Generally these resulted from complaints by organizations directly affected by the competition of European migrants. As early as March 1902 the Kalgoorlie Trades and Labor Council complained that Barton had too readily accepted assurances that Italian workers had not arrived under contract. The Italians were aliens who did not assimilate. The federal government had been lax in its enquiries. Foreigners under contract were displacing 'boys of the bulldog breed'.[32] The charge of laxity may well have been justified and these and later migrants may indeed have landed under contract, but in fact the provision proved difficult to enforce because it lacked sufficient powers.

Problems of administration, unfavourable publicity in England, hostility in Australia (from what Deakin termed 'unpardonable misrepresentations of unpatriotic partisans') and growing demands for British immigration caused the repeal of the sub-section. In 1905 parliament tightened the Immigration Restriction Act and created the Contract Immigrants Act 1905, the direct progeny of the contract provision. The new measure established stringent procedures and safeguards for the admission of contract labour, and severe penalties for their non-compliance. Written contracts had now to be submitted to the Minister of External Affairs for his approval. The minister could approve the terms if in his opinion the contract satisfied strict conditions. The contract could not be made in contemplation of or with a view to affecting an industrial dispute. Employers must have experienced difficulty in securing workers of at least equal skill within the Commonwealth (British migrants exempted). Remuneration and other terms and conditions could not be below those of current workers in the same occupations. Officers were given powers of interrogation, contracts must be verified under oath if required, wilful evasion or misrepresentation incurred a penalty of £20.

The Contract Immigrants Act, therefore, remedied the weaknesses in the earlier legislation. But the fact that it, like its precursor, accorded a federal minister wide powers—most of them discretionary —was all the more reason for a vigilant parliament. Once again Labor members were especially well placed to scrutinize the administration. Throughout the decade the 'illegal' entry of Asians and contract labourers was brought before federal caucus more than any other issue. But the fact that an apparently insignificant sub-clause, inserted as a late amendment by a non-government member without a division, necessitated a powerful new Commonwealth Act is also evidence of the unexpected developments of central functions.

The operation of the Pacific Island Labourers and Immigration Restriction Acts and their by-products in the first decade of federation involved successive Commonwealth governments in complex political, economic, and social problems. These problems affected, and were influenced by, external factors but as thus far described their effects were chiefly internal. But the Immigration Restriction Act also raised the constitutional problem of the validity of an international treaty entered into by a colony before union. The main impact of this problem was in the field of external affairs, namely the relationship of the Commonwealth as a Commonwealth to the imperial government and foreign countries.

In 1894 the governments of Britain and Japan concluded a Treaty of Commerce and Navigation. Articles I and III conferred tariff preferences and reciprocal rights of residence and trade on contracting parties and their subjects. Article XIX provided that the colonies could adhere to the Treaty by means of a Protocol. An Intercolonial Conference of Ministers in Sydney in 1896 decided to forgo the opportunity.[33] Later, however, the Nelson ministry in Queensland accepted the offer with the proviso—agreed to by Japan—that the entry of Japanese labourers and artisans into the colony be forbidden. On 16 March 1897 Sir Ernest Satow, British minister in Tokyo, signed the Protocol for Queensland. The Protocol, which could be terminated after twelve months' notice, came into effect on 17 July 1899. The alleged entry of Japanese under false pretences (indentured labourers in the guise of businessmen) led to an Agreement in October 1900 negotiated by Dickson, Queensland Premier, and Iijima, Japanese Consul at Townsville.[34] Under this the number of Japanese in the colony would not be permitted to exceed the total of 3247 shown as resident in Queensland by the census of 1898. Hence, though a measure of the Commonwealth Parliament said by ministers to be directed mainly against the Japanese became law, there was in existence a Protocol and Agreement involving Britain, Japan, and Queensland permitting a limited entry of Japanese businessmen into the northern State.

The possibility of conflict between the Immigration Restriction Act and the Protocol to the Treaty was overlooked by all interested parties while the Bill passed through federal parliaments. In particular Eitaki and Philp failed to protest on this score. On the contrary, the then acting Consul-General for Japan in his very first communication to Barton in May 1901 had stated that his government recognized distinctly

the right of the Government of Australia to limit in any way it thinks for the number of those persons who may be allowed to land and settle in Australia, and also to draw distinction between persons who may or may not be admitted.[35]

Eitaki, on 21 December—two days before the Bill received the assent —belatedly drew Hopetoun's attention to a conflict between the Bill and the Agreement.[36] As it happened, Hopetoun had left Melbourne on 18 December for a tour of Western Australia. Captain Wallington, his private secretary, turned to Garran, Secretary of the Attorney-General's Department, for advice. What transpired between the two is not fully clear from the file, but Garran confidently denied all possibility of conflict in a private letter. He agreed that 'the date of assent is the date of His Excellency's telegram' but added 'It will perhaps be as well to keep back the messages & Bills'.[37] Apparently on 26 December Wallington acknowledged the protest, which, Eitaki assumed, Hopetoun had not received before assenting to the Bill. Eitaki informed Hopetoun that his government had instructed its Ambassador in London to take steps 'to disallow the Act, so far as Japan was concerned': Japan believed that the Agreement was unaffected by the Act.[38]

Hunt, Secretary of External Affairs, briefed Barton early in January, and suggested that the Attorney-General's opinion be sought as to the effects of the change in status of Queensland on the Treaty and of the Act on the Agreement. Barton immediately recognized the danger of the situation and minuted: 'If only Japanese labourers and artisans can be excluded under our Immigration Act while the Treaty stands, then other most undesirable people such as prostitutes must be let in.'[39] (Protection from 'unfair' competition was, of course, intended under the Act.) He referred the file to Deakin on 13 January 1902 and asked if notice of Queensland's withdrawal should be given.

Deakin's opinion—doubtless prepared by Garran—was prompt and unequivocal. The Immigration Restriction Act was not invalidated by any conflict with the Treaty, although if the Treaty still applied the use of the education test against Japanese who were not labourers or artisans would be a violation. But in fact the Treaty no longer

applied because the establishment of the Commonwealth had an-
nulled it. The control of immigration had passed from Queensland to
the Commonwealth and in this respect

> the boundaries between Queensland and the rest of the Commonwealth
> have been obliterated as completely as if the Commonwealth were a
> unified possession. The right of immigration into Queensland would prac-
> tically, and perhaps legally, amount to a right of entering from Queens-
> land into all States of the Commonwealth, though all the others had
> expressly refused to permit it. Under these circumstances the Common-
> wealth cannot be taken to be bound by the Treaty as accepted by the
> Colony of Queensland under a condition of affairs which [had] ceased to
> exist.[40]

The Agreement of October 1900 also did not bind the central government. It was 'clearly a temporary and provisional arrangement' made
on the eve of union after Queensland had decided to federate and the
Constitution Act had received the Royal assent. It was probably
desirable to convey the fact that neither the Treaty nor the Agreement
was still binding to Japan 'in the most diplomatic and considerate
manner possible through the Secretary of State for the Colonies'.

For some reason the Colonial Office was not informed of the affair
until 18 January, nearly four weeks after Eitaki's original letter. It
took an opposite view to Deakin's, which was possibly sounder in
practical nationalism than in international law. On 29 January
Chamberlain telegraphed Hopetoun that Crown Law Officers were
considering the question but his provisional advice was that both the
Treaty and the Agreement subsisted.[41] The Immigration Restriction
Act was inconsistent with the Agreement and Hopetoun should defer
assent. Hopetoun transmitted the message to Barton on 30 January
but omitted the belated advice to defer the Bill.

Meanwhile the administration was confronted with pressing practical problems. These were created by the activities of the Japanese
Consul in Townsville, Philp in Brisbane, and the arrival in Queens-
land of fifty Japanese with passports for entry approved under the
Agreement. The Consul informed Philp that Japan considered the
Treaty valid, and presumed that arrangements had already been
made for the new arrivals to disembark. Philp strongly recommended
Barton to admit the party (the *Brisbane Courier* erroneously reported
that Barton had already done so) and all other Japanese given
Queensland's permission before the passage of the Commonwealth's
Act. Shortly after Philp, in response to the Consul's complaint that

customs officers had denied entry, urged that any such refusal would place Queensland in a position of breaching faith and would reflect badly on the Commonwealth.[42]

Therefore Barton, fortunately for the Commonwealth, had occasion to communicate *directly* with Eitaki, and thereby unwittingly averted a possible crisis in imperial relations. He objected to the action of the Consul in Townsville forwarding the view of the Japanese government to Philp, and suggested on 17 January that matters of such importance 'should be made by the principal representative of Japan in Australia to the head of the Federal Government'.[43] He took the opportunity to convey Deakin's opinion that the Agreement had terminated.

The Japanese response was uncompromising. Eitaki contended that it was difficult to see how the Constitution affected the issue as the Agreement had been made after the passing of the Constitution Act. The Japanese government had proceeded 'in the full belief that the Queensland Government had both the right and the power to keep faith with it': his country considered the Agreement operative.[44] But on 30 January, the day Barton received Chamberlain's unfavourable opinion, Eitaki was more conciliatory and unknowingly conceded a strong position. Japan considered the Agreement valid, but would defer to the wishes of the Commonwealth Parliament and now consider it terminated provided Japanese already issued with passports be allowed in: 'That the Queensland Government, or any other State Government cannot continue operations under any Agreement, the terms of which are in conflict with a subsequent Act of the Commonwealth Parliament is beyond question.'[45]

Barton agreed at once to this 'courteous and reasonable request', as well he might. He immediately informed Hopetoun that the proposal had been given 'careful consideration' and asked him to advise Chamberlain.[46] The alacrity of the normally dilatory Prime Minister in replying (especially when dealing with Eitaki), and the fact that he did not yet know how many Japanese were involved, strongly suggest that he was already aware of Chamberlain's view. Philp registered no objection, and later supplied a list of the 208 outstanding cases. Barton announced the outcome in parliament on 13 February, believing that the subject was closed. But in an interview with an *Argus* reporter on the Anglo-Japanese Treaty (which had been announced in London that day), Barton made further comments on the issue.[47] From these Eitaki learned for the first time Deakin's opinion that the establishment of the Commonwealth had nullified the Treaty as well as the Agreement. Eitaki complained that Barton had created the false impression that Japan had conceded both the Agreement *and* the Treaty. Barton denied the charge, but admitted the Treaty had not been mentioned in their negotiations. However, while Japan held it existed, the Commonwealth did not.[48]

The dispute ended in deadlock. Eitaki retorted that Japan remained 'firm in the conviction' that the Treaty stood, and would continue to apply the Convention tariff to imports from Queensland. Nonetheless, Barton must indeed have felt elated to have emerged from such a potentially dangerous situation at so light a cost. Under section 59 of the Constitution the monarch could still disallow the Act within one year of the Governor-General's assent. In June an anxious Deakin informed Barton in London that the Commonwealth had not yet heard that the King 'will *not* be advised to disallow the Immigration Act' and urged him to secure this intimation before he left England.[49] But the Crown, presented with a *fait accompli*—the immediate cause of dissension resolved and the Agreement abandoned—did not feel disposed to use its prerogative. This early exercise in diplomacy, largely as a result of a badly informed Colonial Office, an unnecessarily compliant Japan, and sheer good fortune—adroitly exploited by Barton—concluded on a highly satisfactory note for the Commonwealth.

Still, the question of the Treaty remained unresolved, and therein lay the seeds of further pressures. On the one hand, the fact that the exports of Queensland and other signatories received preferential treatment led to demands to secure the benefits for all Australian States. On the other hand, the very existence of a Treaty, and the disputed existence of Queensland's Protocol to it, left open a way for possible concessions to a more assertive Japan. It thereby disturbed a Labor Party ever alert to signs or chances of a weakening of White Australia.

In June 1901 McMillan asked Barton to consider securing the trading privileges of the Treaty for the Commonwealth while preserving 'all rights for the control of the influx of Japanese labour'.[50] Nothing came of the suggestion. But in 1904 Joseph Carruthers, Premier of New South Wales, began a sustained campaign to achieve Australian adherence to the Treaty even at the expense of renewed Japanese immigration. Ironically Carruthers had been the first delegate at the Federal Conventions to use the term 'White Australia'.

In November Carruthers informed Reid, then briefly Prime Minister, that his attention had been drawn to the severe handicap imposed on locally produced leather goods by Japanese import duties. The State's Commercial Agent in Japan had been surprised that New South Wales was unable to compete with American leather; obviously the differential tariff was responsible. In December Carruthers urged Reid to make representations to secure the Commonwealth the special treatment accorded Queensland, and forwarded a report from his agent. Japanese imports were rising despite the war with Russia. Prospects for increased trade, especially in wheat ('coolies' were rapidly taking to bread) were very good. Sir Claude MacDonald, British Ambassador in Tokyo, felt the time opportune for other States to adhere on the same footing as Queensland. The Ambassador and the Colonial Secretary, he had been assured, would do their utmost to assist, though he himself favoured a direct approach by the Prime Minister. The situation was hopeful, 'but not without compensating concessions on behalf of the Commonwealth'.[51]

The Comptroller-General of Customs advised Reid that nothing could be done in the absence of a Convention or Treaty tariff. Reid rejected Carruthers' proposition in January 1905. No action would be taken because the colonies had rejected the Treaty in 1895 and 1897, and because of legislation affecting the right of Japanese to enter Australia.[52] In May he interviewed the acting Consul-General and decided not to pursue the issue.

Carruthers tried Deakin in October 1905. Canada was about to join the Treaty and he believed that the new passport regulations had partially allayed Japanese irritation over Commonwealth legislation. If Deakin would 'further modify' the Immigration Restriction Act, then Japan would certainly admit Australia to the trade benefits reserved for Treaty members. If Australia did this without pressure from Britain or Japan, 'it would be deemed a grateful recognition of the alliance recently renewed'. He had no apprehension of a great influx of Japanese, except for trading purposes. In March 1906 he sent a reminder and added that the newly amended Immigration Restriction Act made the time even more favourable.[53] Deakin, like Reid, opposed the idea. Circumstances had not varied sufficiently to justify reversing his predecessor's decision.[54]

Carruthers, who throughout his premiership persistently feuded with the Commonwealth, placed the question on the agenda of the Conference of Commonwealth and State Premiers in April, and submitted a paper on the subject. The paper traversed earlier arguments, and then claimed that the whole range of circumstances had changed since 1894. Japan had advanced in science and trade. Japan, because of her victory over Russia, had entered so fully into the 'comity of Nations' that she now stood as a bulwark of peace and 'defender of Australia through her alliance with Great Britain'. As to immigration, the Commonwealth had already felt the necessity to deal more leniently with the Japanese. A change of policy regarding a Treaty with Britain's ally was warranted in the interests of trade and good will. Deakin pointed out that a free access of migrants would conflict with the way existing legislation was applied, but promised to examine the Treaty to see if some way round this 'serious obstacle' could be found.[55]

In the meantime Morgan, Premier of Queensland, had asked Deakin if the Commonwealth believed that the Treaty still held: the Japanese tariff was 'most indulgent' and his own Attorney-General had advised that the question was 'really one for the Japanese Government to decide'. Isaacs, Commonwealth Attorney-General, gave his opinion in April 1906, two days after Deakin's statement at the Premiers' Conference. He agreed with his Queensland counterpart that there was nothing to stop local merchants from enjoying their advantages, but suggested that Deakin request Britain to make representations to Japan in order to remove the anomaly and secure equality of treatment.[56]

On 1 May 1906 Deakin made a formal request for Australia to become a party to the Treaty without conceding the right to control 'undesirable' immigration. Trade with Japan was increasing, and, he ingenuously informed the Colonial Secretary, merchants from New South Wales, Victoria, and South Australia were 'at a loss to understand why discrimination should be made between shipments of goods from different parts of the Commonwealth'. Japan had made no sustained attempt to keep up the number of Japanese in Queensland. The informal passport arrangement of 1904 could be embodied in a formal Convention.[57]

Japan, victor over Russia and ally of Britain, proved a tougher proposition than in 1901–2. In October 1906 Lord Elgin cabled that the Japanese government was willing to extend the commercial benefits but expected to be met half-way and would 'certainly require arrangements similar to those made by Queensland in 1897'. Viscount Hayashi, Minister of Foreign Affairs, had informed MacDonald that Deakin's passport provisions of 1904 were 'altogether too stringent'; Canada had adhered unconditionally to the Treaty. On 16 January 1907 Deakin received a copy of the letter from Hayashi to

MacDonald: Japan would be glad to negotiate provided the Australian government had 'no objection to the putting of proper restrictions upon the unrestricted right of legislation possessed by the Australian Parliament in regard to Japanese immigrants'.[58]

Before Deakin received Elgin's cable, he, like Carruthers, came under direct pressure from business interests. In July 1906 the New South Wales Chamber of Manufactures forwarded a resolution urging reciprocal relations with Japan to secure the advantages of the Convention tariff. A week after getting the cable, the Commonwealth received details (supplied by Queensland's Commercial Agent for the East) of the revised tariff which came into effect on 1 October. The Customs Department was asked to report. Deakin apparently awaited its reply before making a decision on the whole question, though by this time he must have known the contents of the cable for several months. The Comptroller-General's memorandum, approved by Lyne on 15 December, stated that it was not worthwhile to arrange reciprocal terms, as prospects of trade with Japan were not great. On 23 January 1907 Hunt minuted that the Prime Minister, 'having seen' the memorandum, directed no action.[59]

Up to this point negotiations had been prudently conducted with a minimum of publicity. In October 1905 the Senate had debated a vague motion by Senator Pulsford (Free Trade, New South Wales) affirming the desirability of conducting a treaty between Australia and Japan under which 'all questions relating to emigration and immigration may be arranged'. On the same day Senator Higgs (Labor, Queensland) pointedly caused a copy of the 1894 Treaty to be printed as a Commonwealth paper. In June 1906 the *Argus* had briefly referred to Carruthers' letter to Deakin earlier in the month and to the Premiers' Conference: but the paper he submitted was not published with the official report of the Conference.[60]

In November 1907 the issue came into the open when Pearce first suggested termination of the Treaty. Pearce, one of the most fervent opponents of Japan in federal parliament, asked a series of questions on the Treaty, Protocol, and Agreement. Senator Best, for the government, admitted that representations had been made for the Commonwealth to join, but stated that no further action was being taken and promised to consult parliament in future: no intervention to terminate the Treaty was considered necessary. In the debate on supply later the same day, Pearce denounced the government's policy. Japan, he ventured to suggest, had insisted that Australia must open her ports to immigration. Riots had followed the influx of Japanese into

British Columbia after Canada had adhered to the Treaty. The Commonwealth should induce Queensland to give the required twelve months' notice in order to close this 'loophole' in the White Australia policy. Failing this the federal government should take steps of its own.[61]

Earlier in the year Deakin had attended the Colonial Conference of 1907, before which he had placed the resolution: 'That the Imperial Government be requested to prepare for the information of Colonial Governments, statements showing the privileges conferred, and the obligations imposed, on the Colonies by existing commercial treaties'.[62] In preparation, he asked Littleton Groom, Attorney-General, for an opinion on how far the Commonwealth was bound by the commercial treaties of the Empire, especially ones 'to which some only of the Colonies which now form the Commonwealth gave their adhesion'. Groom, doubtless briefed by Garran, took a position similar to Deakin in 1902:

Under federation the position has been changed; a new political entity has been created; the six States have in certain matters become subordinate. . . . In the case of the States of the Commonwealth, owing to the action of the Australian people in depriving the States of the power to deal with matters under section 51 and by the exercise of the transferred powers by the Commonwealth, treaties made with respect to these matters may become impossible of performance. . . . As far as the Commonwealth is concerned, it is not bound by any treaty made with the States and to which it has not adhered.[63]

The minutes of the Conference do not reveal what took place when Deakin's resolution came under consideration because delegates retired for 'discussion in private'. But from subsequent correspondence it is apparent that Deakin referred to his opinion of January 1902 and to Groom's of March 1907, and cast doubts on the binding force on the Commonwealth of treaties binding on the States before federation. Also, as it happened, later in the year the Japanese Ambassador enquired at the Foreign Office on the present position of Queensland under the 1894 Treaty.

In January 1908, therefore, Lord Elgin, as a result of these events, forwarded a lengthy despatch on the question after consulting Crown Law Officers and the Foreign Secretary. The despatch alluded to the opinion of the Law Officers in 1902, the sense of which Chamberlain had given Barton in July of that year when Barton was in London. Until recently the imperial government was under the impression that the Commonwealth government had acquiesced to this opinion. In May 1906 when the Commonwealth had attempted to join, Deakin had mentioned Chamberlain's view without suggesting that he considered the matter still open. In correspondence on the 'Vondel' case all sides had assumed that the Anglo-Dutch Convention of 1856 retained its original binding force in Australia. All the precedents cited by Deakin and Groom related to independent sovereign states. But the Australian colonies were not independent states. Nor was the federation in which they had merged. A treaty binding on a colony before federation was not between the particular colony and the foreign power, but between the Crown and that power. Federation may have made it impossible for the Australian States to give effect to certain obligations, 'but the question is not whether it is possible for the States to carry out those obligations, but whether it is possible for the Crown to do so'. Therefore the British government proposed to inform the Japanese government that the Treaty of 1894 bound the Commonwealth in respect of Queensland. Principle apart, Elgin concluded, it would be difficult to answer otherwise in view of the fact that Queensland's exports to Japan since federation had continued to be admitted to the commercial benefits of the Treaty.[64]

Within two days of receiving Elgin's forthright despatch Deakin decided to terminate the Treaty.[65] On 16 March he informed the Colonial Secretary that this was necessary because the continued acquiescence of the federal government in an arrangement repugnant to the Constitution involved differentiation between States.[66] By this time Deakin seems to have been somewhat confused. He added that he presumed Japan would continue to refrain from attempting to secure the admission of Japanese labourers to Queensland in accord with the terms of the Agreement of 1900. In fact, as Lord Crewe, the new Colonial Secretary, quickly pointed out, Japan had abandoned the Agreement in 1902: the British government assumed, Crewe added, that Queensland had been consulted.[67]

Queensland had not, but William Kidston, the Premier, happened to be passing through Melbourne *en route* to England. Kidston, for reasons best known to himself, apparently readily agreed to a 'proposed' step seemingly opposed to the interests of his State. In a hurried note from Fremantle he told Deakin that it was in his hands but he saw no objection; Deakin had better write formally to his deputy to make sure no interests were involved. On 19 May Deakin duly misinformed the acting Premier of the action that the Commonwealth 'proposed to take', mentioned Kidston's concurrence, and hoped there were no objections.[68] There were none, and on 31 July the British Ambassador in Tokyo gave the Japanese government twelve months' notice of termination.

Deakin gave Queensland three reasons for withdrawing from the Treaty. These were his unwillingness to provide Japan with any ground to claim special privileges for her citizens, equality under the Constitution, and the imperative necessity to be able to legislate on the Navigation Bill which was then before the Senate. Probably these factors do largely explain Deakin's action, but at least elements of all three had existed for some time. The first, if valid, had been the position from the very outset (though now Britain was to inform Japan that she considered the Treaty binding on the Commonwealth); besides, when Deakin actually gave notice in March 1908 he seems to have believed that Japan had refrained from insisting on the terms of the Agreement since 1901 merely out of friendliness. Similarly, inequality under the Constitution had applied all along; demands from Carruthers for an attempt to level them upwards had initially been rejected, and when acceded to had long since failed. Thirdly, Deakin tried to join the Treaty barely five months before he promised to revive the lapsed Navigation Bill in his policy speech in October 1906; besides, the Bill was introduced into parliament on 12 September 1907, but in November the government rejected Pearce's suggestion to terminate the Treaty as 'unnecessary'.

Clearly then these reasons do not completely account for the change in policy. In part the reversal probably reflected the growing public uneasiness about Japan, which was coming to be seen less as the present ally of Britain and more as the future enemy of Australia. The earlier acclaim which greeted Japan's military and naval successes had given way to a reappraisal of Australia's increasing vulnerability. Fear of Japanese intentions was being skilfully aroused and exploited by organizations such as the Australian National Defence League, in which Labor men were particularly prominent. The Labor Party itself, influenced chiefly by the threat of an *armed* yellow peril, was moving inexorably towards compulsory military training. Already in December 1907 Deakin had announced his own compulsory scheme. Therefore, now that the subject was in the open *and* Britain was about to inform Japan, it no longer made political sense or seemed consistent with its own defence plans for Deakin to appear to fail to shut all possible doors to a potential fifth column.

The reversal of policy also probably stemmed from the very tone of

Elgin's despatch. The despatch flatly denied Deakin's practical-nationalist opinion, and firmly put the Commonwealth in its insignificant international place. Deakin, ever the sensitive Australian nationalist when dealing with the Colonial Office, must surely have been offended by the insensitive response of men who were never in sympathy with the White Australia policy. The denunciation of the Treaty—the first of many from which the Commonwealth was later to withdraw—was a small sign of independence, a slight rebuff to the imperial government and her ally.

Whatever the motives, the passing of the Immigration Restriction Act in 1901 and its inadvertent clash with Queensland's Protocol to the 1894 Treaty had unexpected repercussions. The Constitution gave the Commonwealth no specific treaty power. In May 1901 Deakin himself had asserted:

The Empire as a sovereign independent state possesses full contracting powers which are exercised by the Imperial Government alone. The Commonwealth has no Treaty powers of any kind under its Constitution and being a dependency can acquire none save those with which it may be specially endowed from time to time.[69]

But the conflict soon raised the questions of treaty powers and the international status of the Commonwealth. No doubt it was inevitable that these questions would arise one day, but the fact is that they arose immediately in an unforeseen manner. In April 1910 when Deakin left office for the last time the constitutional position remained unchanged. But following the Imperial Conference of 1911, where the subject was aired again, the imperial government opened negotiations with a number of countries to enable the release of the Dominions from obligations under those treaties: henceforth commercial treaties contained, when possible, clauses whereby Dominions could accede or claim most-favoured-nation treatment.[70] The original conflict, the negotiations, the denunciation were small, tentative steps in the continual climb from penal colony to nation-state.

4

FEDERATION AND DEFENCE

On 1 March 1901 the Commonwealth assumed control of the naval and military forces of the States by proclamation under section 69 of the Constitution: from that date the defence of Australia became the sole responsibility of the federal government. The major achievements of the eight ministries and three parliaments in the first decade are well known and it is sufficient to outline them here.[1]

In naval affairs the Commonwealth inherited a motley collection of obsolescent coastal defence vessels and the Naval Agreement determined at the Colonial Conference of 1887. Barton and Forrest negotiated a modified Agreement at the Colonial Conference of 1902 that provided a larger and more modern squadron for the next ten years. In 1909 Andrew Fisher's Labor government ordered the construction of three destroyers, the first of which was launched in 1910 at the yard of the Fairfield Shipbuilding Company, Govan. Finally, the Fusion ministry, directed by Deakin, decided to build a modern fleet unit. In 1910 the keel of the *Australia*, the nation's own Dreadnought, was laid at John Brown & Co.'s. When the pride of the fleet steamed through the Sydney Heads with the new squadron on 4 October 1913 the Royal Australian Navy was seen to be well and truly under way. The Minister of Defence, Senator Edward Millen, proudly greeted the fleet: 'Since Captain Cook's arrival, no more memorable event has happened than the advent of the Australian Fleet. As the former marked the birth of Australia, so the latter announces its coming of age'.[2] From the few old and unseaworthy ships, gun and torpedo boats in 1901, Australia now had a powerful battle cruiser, three light cruisers, and three destroyers in commission.

Developments in the military field were no less spectacular. The appointment of General Sir Edward Hutton as General-Officer-

Commanding brought the array of permanent soldiers, militia, volunteers, and rifle clubs constituting the military forces of the colonies under one command: between 1901 and 1904 Hutton attempted to reorganize the forces and implement his reforms. Sections 46 and 49 of the Defence Act of 1903 provided for the calling up of citizen forces for war service within the limits of the Commonwealth and its territories. An amendment in 1909 defined those eligible as 'All male inhabitants of Australia ... who have resided therein for six months and are British subjects and are between the ages of eighteen and sixty years'. The Fusion ministry's Act of 1909 introduced universal peace-time service with compulsory military training for cadets from 14 to 17 years of age and for adults from 18 to 20. Before these provisions could come into effect the second Fisher government embodied Lord Kitchener's recommendations into its Defence Act 1910. This extended service to boys of 12 in the cadets and to men of 26 in the citizen forces. Australian legislation to establish universal service attracted world attention. The military correspondent of *The Times* wrote of the first attempt in 1908: 'Deakinize the Haldane plan and what more is needed?' The Seattle *Saturday Evening Tribune* described the scheme as 'the most perfect on earth. ... This is militarism with its vicious features eliminated'.[3]

Thus while it remained true that the ultimate defence of Australia still depended upon the Royal Navy, within ten years of federating rapid and important changes had taken place. Not only was the fleet unit under construction and compulsory training approved, but the essential infrastructure was also being created. Senator Pearce's first memorandum on the progress of the Navy Department reported the setting up of the Naval Board under Rear-Admiral Sir William Creswell precisely ten years after the Commonwealth had assumed the defence power. A site for a Naval College was under consideration, the boys' training ship *Sobraon* purchased, and some 3200 cadets selected for training. Steps had been taken to found a gunnery and torpedo school and State governments asked to reserve land for further naval works. Factories had been established for the manufacture of cordite, rifles, small arms, harness, saddlery, leather equipment, and uniforms.

Historians have nominated defence as one of the great reasons for federating. Like the strong desire for a White Australia (with which it is sometimes directly related) the great demand for increased security by means of an Australia-wide system of defence is said to have also prompted, sustained, and ultimately led to the success of the federation movement. Viewed in this light the preoccupation of Commonwealth governments and politicians with the subject could be seen as but the inevitable outcome of union.

The purpose of these two chapters on defence is to examine the place of the defence question in the federation movement, and to show that the dramatic events which took place within the decade owed less to what happened before federation than to quite unrelated developments after. The priority given to building up the armed forces should be regarded as the result of factors which stimulated innovation over those that opposed change, rather than as the deliberate result of federation. The specific topics which will be considered are aspects of early administration and the Hutton reforms, the Naval Agreements of 1903, compulsory universal military training, and the birth of the navy.

The notion that the question of defence was of prime importance to the federation movement is based largely on the use made by Parkes in 1889 of the memorandum by Major-General J. Bevan Edwards. In part too it is founded on the belief that colonial statesmen, and perhaps behind them their supporters and electors, were seriously concerned about Australian security and genuinely interested in defence in the period that federation was accomplished.

The Edwards report consisted of six separate reports to the colonial governments on the condition of their individual forces and an accompanying memorandum entitled the *Proposed Organisation of the Military Forces of the Australian Colonies*.[4] In the memorandum Edwards noted the differing organizations and the practical and legal impediments to the employment of colonial troops beyond their own borders. But co-operation was essential because 'If the Australian Colonies had to rely at any time solely on their own resources . . . [their] position would be one of great danger'. The state of affairs in Europe, the role of the unforeseen in war, demanded a 'common system of defence' which was impossible without a 'federation of the forces'.

Parkes in his telegrams to Duncan Gillies and other Premiers on 15 October and in his Tenterfield address later in the month referred to the Edwards memorandum.[5] This reference became in his autobiography: 'The first movement worthy of the noble object of bringing all Australia under one National Government [arising] from my initiation in October 1889.'[6] Now probably only Parkes could have successfully launched the federation movement and he merits his title 'Father of Federation'. But as Professor La Nauze has pointed out Parkes in fact proposed the immediate consideration of a scheme for federation to Gillies in a private letter on 15 June, the text of which was not available until first published by Geoffrey Serle.[7] Edwards left Hong Kong on 16 June, reached Darwin on 28 June,[8] and dated his memorandum 9 October. In other words, Parkes suggested federation in 1889 *before the memorandum was written and indeed before the general had even left Hong Kong, let alone set foot in Australia.* Parkes made no reference to questions of defence in his letter. He wrote privately again on 25 June in response to Gillies' reply of 21 June (which apparently has not survived). It is clear from this second letter that Parkes regarded the time ripe for federation not because of any problem of defence, but because the political situation in New South Wales was favourable. He explained that he saw grounds

for apprehending that difficulties in the way of any comprehensive scheme of federation will be increased by further delay especially in this colony. It was indeed this apprehension which induced me to open communication with you on the subject.[9]

His anxiety to open the question of federation before the defence issue was aired may be gauged from the offer to share with Victoria the site of the federal capital. This very subject was later to prove an acute problem but Parkes suggested the capital could be 'in Victoria and New South Wales (as the two largest colonies) at some point on the Murray the Executive Offices on one side and the Legislative Chambers on the other'.

Furthermore the relationship between Edwards and Parkes became close, and it appears very likely that the ambitious general, inspired by the astute Premier, added the opportune memorandum to the reports in order to provide Parkes with a concrete reason for renewing his call for federation. The possibility of actual collusion between the pair is strongly suggested in a speech by Edwards at the Royal Colonial Institute in 1891. He told how he was charged in one colonial parliament with trying to further imperial federation and in another of being a 'political tout' and commented, 'an Opposition is nothing if not critical'. He then went on to say that when in Australia he had had the privilege of meeting leading people,

amongst others, that eminent statesman, Sir Henry Parkes, the Premier of New South Wales. I gathered that there was a consensus of opinion favourable to Federation, but that the realization of some common need was required to bring it about. Sir Henry Parkes, who as a responsible Minister had to consider my recommendations, saw at once that combined action for purposes of defence was impossible without a Federal Government to direct and control it. He therefore became the champion of the great question of Colonial Federation.[10]

Edwards named only Parkes. As Edwards was leaving Darwin for Hong Kong, Parkes telegraphed 'All going well.'[11]

In return for supplying 'some common need' Edwards hoped to become Inspector-General of the forces to prepare them for federation. It is evident from letters to 'My dear Sir Henry Parkes' from Edwards on his return to Hong Kong that this idea had been discussed in Sydney. On 24 January 1890 he asked: 'Will you be able to discuss the defence question at your meeting [the Melbourne Conference]? I am anxious that you should at all events agree to get the Inspecting General as soon as possible'. Getting seven parliaments to agree would be difficult 'but *you* might be able to manage it. . . . The fact is that I have lost my heart to Australia and its charming people'. Parkes asked Gillies to agree to the permanent appointment of an inspecting officer, but Gillies rejected this as 'premature'. Edwards then hoped to fill a rumoured vacancy in the governorship of Tasmania and thereby to perform the dual roles of governor and Inspector-General.[12]

Edwards' attempt to aid Parkes and the good cause did not end there. He sent Parkes an article on the foreign policy of China from a Hong Kong paper and as he wrote,

A portion of the Chinese Imperial Squadron is now at anchor under my windows consisting of 2 magnificent iron clads of the newest type and 4 very fine and heavily armed Cruisers.
Admiral Ting who commands is an old comrade of mine. . . . I have been urging him strongly to take his fleet & show his flag in foreign parts especially in Australia but he cannot go this year further than Singapore. Would not that help your federation?[13]

Whether or not there was an explicit arrangement or a tacit understanding between the two it is evident that Edwards was not the very model of a modern major-general. He exceeded his instructions and his alarmist views utterly contradicted official British assessments of danger and incurred the severe displeasure of the Colonial Defence Committee. But whatever the motives of Edwards and the role of Parkes in the affair, the memorandum provided a convenient opportunity. Indeed it was particularly opportune for a number of reasons.

It gave Parkes both a 'common need' and the excuse he needed to by-pass the existing Federal Council. Gillies advocated use of this body in response to his overtures. But Parkes' counter that the Council did not possess the power 'to constitute, direct, and control an united Australian army'[14] had merit and could not be dismissed lightly. Also the memorandum enabled Parkes to outmanoeuvre Gillies and at the same time to appear conciliatory as in 1888 he had declined to join the Victorian Premier in a formal request to Britain for the inspection: 'In the necessary preparation and organization for our defence, we must act for ourselves, and rely upon our own resources, as in other scarcely less important provinces of self-government.'[15] Having seized, perhaps created, the opportunity Parkes made much of the subject. Thus defence, unlike immigration, featured in the Tenterfield address and in the principal resolutions at the Convention of 1891 as an exclusive power. In the circumstances he could scarcely have done otherwise. But in essence the memorandum was the occasion rather than the cause of Parkes' public sponsorship of federation in 1889.

Apart from the chronology of the initiatives of Parkes and the origin of the Edwards memorandum other factors suggest that in the late eighties and throughout the nineties as the federation movement reached its climax the security of the colonies was not a pressing problem. Rather there was indifference towards questions of defence. Moreover, while there can be no doubt that if federation was to come then a united system of defence would be a natural corollary, these factors show what federal leaders and others actually expected of federation in respect to defence.

For instance the inspection of colonial forces by Edwards took place only because the British government persisted and paid for the tour. At the Colonial Conference of 1887 Stanhope, Secretary of State for War, agreed to Griffith's suggestion for a periodical inspection by a General Officer. But afterwards the colonies could not agree on the apportionment between themselves of the cost of the visit and the proposal lapsed. The War Office revived the idea in April 1889 and suggested that as some action was very desirable 'the question of expense should be waived for the present'. The Colonial Office agreed and informed colonial governments that in order to carry out the inspection, 'The expenses of this visit are to form a charge upon Imperial funds.'[16] On the arrival of Edwards in Sydney in July the *Sydney Morning Herald* alluded to the Conference proposal and wrote: 'This was not carried out through some question of the expense likely to be incurred . . . and the idea that such a visit was premature'.[17]

Again, the proceedings of the Colonial Conference itself reveal in a wider context the complacency of colonial delegates. Lord Salisbury, Prime Minister, pleaded in his opening address for the colonies to take a 'fair and legitimate' part in their own defence so as to lighten the British burden. He had, he said,

observed a tendency to the impression that the defence of the Colonies ought to be entirely a matter for the Imperial Government, because any danger that the Colonists might run was exclusively the result of Imperial action and policy.[18]

The Conference considered the Admiralty scheme which had first been discussed with Rear-Admiral Tryon by Sir Patrick Jennings, Griffith, and Gillies in 1886. The proposal was to build an auxiliary squadron for use in Australian waters. The colonies were to pay the original cost and annual maintenance. After ten years the ships would become the property of the colonies. None accepted the scheme. Downer for South Australia and Forrest for Western Australia supported the suggestion of the Victorian government to bear the maintenance charge only.

The statements of the Victorians hardly indicate that they were worried about their security. Deakin stressed that their shipping interests were small compared with other colonies. The floating trade was therefore not so important to Victoria. Most of the tonnage cleared there was British-owned. Australia had 'already contributed very largely to her own defence'. The maintenance charge would be 'a large sum to pay for the security of Australian shipping, and for the security of Australian product'. As to the Victorian offer,

We feel that when we in the Colony of Victoria go down to vote at one stroke to add £26,000 a year by special appropriation to our expenditure in time of peace and £45,000 in time of war, we are making a demand which is very rarely made by any treasurer. Besides which there is a proportion of the population in every community which looks upon every expenditure for war as a very unprofitable expenditure.[19]

Sir James Lorimer, Minister of Defence, added that Victoria had 'a very efficient navy'. Cargoes were 'an insurable interest'.

It could be argued, perhaps, that the unfederal and complacent remarks of Deakin and Lorimer, and the attitude of others, were merely attempts to strike a good bargain with the British. But a close reading of the reports shows that, with the possible exception of Griffith, delegates were not greatly perturbed about the state of their defences.[20] Only one delegate bothered to turn up at the Admiralty for a meeting arranged by the First Lord to discuss the actual type of vessels for the squadron.[21]

Colonial ministers, then, begrudged every penny when the colonies were at a peak of prosperity in the late eighties. It is hardly surprising, therefore, that after the financial crises and depressions of the nineties they should appear more concerned with the security of their stocks than of their coasts. In the decade in which the new federation movement triumphed the colonies cut their defence expenditure, generally drastically. Victoria, for instance, expended £350 821 on her forces in 1889–90; by 1897–8 the Turner government had slashed this to £184 316. South Australia spent £52 169 in 1890; by 1898 Kingston had reduced expenditure to £21 786.[22] In 1895 Kingston contemplated pruning the estimates to £8500.[23] The South Australian example is of particular interest. Kingston was one of the great figures in the federation movement. He was also one of the more nationalistic Premiers who believed Australians should rely less on the British. At the Colonial Conference of 1897 he alone opposed the continuance of the Naval Agreement.[24]

Similar attitudes to defence expenditure existed at the Federal Conventions. The propriety of ceding the defence power to the Commonwealth went almost unchallenged: one reason for granting full taxation rights was to provide finance to cope with a national emergency. Nevertheless, delegates considered an emergency more of a theoretical possibility than a practical probability. Many observed that whereas others like the United States and Canada federated because they feared external enemies Australia had no such pressure. Hackett, from the remote and sparsely populated Western Australia, where it might be expected that the dangers of attack would be most keenly felt, said in Sydney in 1891: 'we meet here under no menace from foreign aggression' but 'with tranquillity at home and abroad'. Others spoke out against unnecessary expense, and the threat to democracy, of a standing army.[25]

Furthermore, behind the great debates on the strength of the Senate and the finance of the States lay fears of the use and misuse of the defence power. At the first Convention Cockburn argued for a strong Senate. He made a prophetic statement:

We all know that the tendency of all governments, and rightly so, is to augment their own importance and to act up to the full extent of their authority. . . . Under the heading of military and naval defence of the commonwealth, they can do almost everything. They can make roads; they can build railways; they can lay submarine cables; they can erect enormous public works. You give them the power under that one heading of spending nearly the whole of the money.[26]

Six years later in Adelaide Holder advocated the return of a fixed proportion of customs revenue to the States. The Commonwealth

might launch out into heavy naval and military expenditure. We all know how easily money can be squandered in that way. Millions are nothing. Unless there were some safeguard . . . we might find some fine day that, though we had arranged for an absolutely equitable distribution of the surplus, there was no surplus to distribute.[27]

If, as seems likely, the proceedings of the unofficial conferences and the referenda campaigns are guides to public opinion, then statesmen and politicians acted in accord with colonial sentiment. The popular phases of the movement gave no special place to defence. At Corowa in 1893 only E. W. O'Sullivan referred to the question: 'The growing power of the Chinese nation was a menace to Australia, and it could only be met by a federated power.' At Bathurst in 1896 the mayor of Bathurst and Cardinal Moran mentioned briefly the advantages of federal defence. On the other hand the Convention president observed that members could be 'calm and collected' in their discussions because they were 'sitting with no present fear of the warlike intention of any great Power'. Reid made the curious statement that 'One great reason [defence] for Federation has been wisely placed in the background'.[28]

It would be tedious to dwell again on the referenda campaigns. Certainly the Billites referred to federalized defence more frequently than to uniform immigration control. But these appeals were neither common nor prominent. For example, the manifesto of the Australian Federation League of Victoria occupied over 350 lines in the *Age*. Yet all that was said on defence was 'the powers of the Federal Parliament embrace, in addition to the control of Customs, Post Office and Defence departments, the right to give bounties and bonuses for the development of new industries'.[29] By comparison the financial features received 37 lines, the federal tariff 21, the Inter-State Commission 16, constitutional amendments 16, and the removal of the stock-tax 27. The nine Victorian conventionists ignored the issue altogether in their own federal manifesto. So also did Barton in his personal appeal to the electors of New South Wales. And in South Australia the Commonwealth League failed to include federal control of defence in its list of the 'Benefits of Federation'.[30]

This omission by the League was probably deliberate. Anti-Billites strongly attacked the Bill *because of* its defence provisions. Hence, while any talk of invasion was 'utter-nonsense' federation could lead to a standing army which would give the 'Fatmen' the power 'to shoot us down in case of domestic strife. "Fire low and lay them out"'. Undoubtedly charges against the financial aspects were the most effective. There would be 'no limit' to defence expenditure. South Australia would be 'compelled to take over the debt of thousands spent on the now obsolete defences of Victoria'.[31] Delegates, complained an Anti-Bill League circular, were 'ominously silent' about this and the cost of the proposed standing army.[32] Even one of the Bill's supporters, the *Mount Barker Courier,* observed: 'Extravagance by the Federal Parliament in the matter of defence or by some other big undertaking seems to be the only danger which now presents itself'.[33]

Billites seemed so concerned about these criticisms that they tended to play down the necessity of federating for this purpose. Glynn, who on 1 April argued in the *Southern Cross* 'by speedy federation, we should be better prepared as a united nation to deal with the momentous question of national defence', failed to mention defence in his final appeal in the same paper on 3 June. Holder, the most travelled campaigner of all, held that 'In times of difficulty countries had combined. But it was not owing to any threatened danger that they were called to federate in the colonies.'[34] Moreover, on the eve of the referendum Holder referred to the damaging findings of the Sydney committee of enquiry which reported that the cost of federation had been considerably underestimated. He countered,

The £75,000 for defences is on the ground that our present defences are inadequate for these troublous times, and must be made more effective. This is very much open to argument, but it is clear that if more defence is required than we have now it is not the result of Federation . . .[35]

Had the prospects of federating for purposes of defence been such a popular and powerful issue, it is unlikely that the leagues and delegates—shrewd politicians—would have avoided the issue. Nor would their opponents have challenged the early appeals as confidently as they did. With intercolonial free trade, for instance, anti-Billites

6   Members of the first Commonwealth Parliament

Holder is the Speaker. Barton is seated at the government side of the table, Kingston is standing. Reid leads Free Trade members on the opposition side.

7 *John Christian Watson, first Labor Prime Minister, 1904*

8 *Reid–McLean ministry, 1904–5*
Standing, left to right: Smith, Thomson, McCay, Drake. Seated: Turner,
Reid, Lord Northcote (Governor-General), McLean, Symon.

equivocated. Free trade was good in principle, or proper in a few years, or the Bill should be rejected as its unsatisfactory provisions did not ensure true free trade. But in any event the war drums which started to beat as the delegates returned from Melbourne were muffled, if not entirely silenced, by the campaign's end.

Perhaps then the various strands of the argument may now be drawn together and the relationship of the defence question to federation summed up.

It is perfectly clear that federalists sought federal control of the forces and that if the colonies were to federate then central direction of defence was obviously desirable. As Parkes put it at Leichhardt,

> There might be persons who were opposed to raising armed men at all—(hear, hear)—there might be wide differences of opinion on that subject; but if it were done, clearly it were better that those forces should be in a position to operate upon any part of Australia . . .[36]

But this does not mean that the issue was necessarily a compelling motive for federation and, as the chronology of events shows, it was less the cause than the occasion of Parkes' initiative in 1889. Defence does not appear to have been a deep concern of politicians and others who prompted federation. On one occasion even Parkes admitted, 'This military question, however, was by no means the greatest question.' On another he coupled a call for defence union with holy matrimony: 'We ought to have one marriage law for the whole of the colonies, and this was also matter for the Federal Government, and we could not shut our eyes to the question of defending ourselves.'[37] Indeed the words of politicians abroad at Colonial Conferences and their deeds at home in local parliaments suggest rather that the subject had a very low priority. This is not surprising. The fact is that the years between 1889 and 1899 when the battle for federation was fought and won were remarkably free from external threats. The Colonial Defence Committee in a memorandum to the colonial governments in May 1890 expressly repudiated the alarmist nature of the Edwards memorandum. The Committee disowned what it termed the point of view from which the major-general appeared 'to regard the military requirements of this portion of the Empire'. No country could provide against every 'remote contingency' and moreover, 'On account of their geographical position, and of the now considerable population in all . . . except Western Australia, there is no British territory so little liable to aggression as that of Australasia'. A small-scale attack would 'court disaster', a large could not hope to reach its destination until the British navy had been definitely worsted. Even then the difficulties and the risks would be so considerable, that . . . it is almost inconceivable that the attempt would be made. History affords no parallel of such difficulties successfully over-come.[38]

The Committee disagreed with Edwards that it was necessary to contemplate the concentration of a force of '30,000 or 40,000 men' to repel invasion, and purposely refrained from marking his memorandum 'Confidential'.

Parkes, and later O'Sullivan, did raise the bogey of Chinese troops stealthily 'effecting a lodgement in some thinly-peopled portion of the country, where it would take immense loss of life and immense loss of wealth to dislodge the invader'.[39] But China was soon exposed as a paper-tiger by her defeat by Japan in 1895. Besides, it is very doubtful if their bogey-mongering ever had much impact. G. C. Craig, author in 1897 of a polemic, *The Federal Defence of Australasia*, complained of Australian reaction to the Edwards naval propaganda, part of which Parkes made public.

When Sir J. B. Edwards saw a powerful Chinese fleet floating before his windows at Hong Kong one day, he thought that the Australasian Colonies should accept that Chinese naval demonstration as an object lesson in Federal defence. The Press, people, and Parliament laughed at the idea . . .[40]

Nor, he continued, should the power of Japan be dismissed lightly:

Commandants have pointed such dangers out in reports and speeches, but their words of warning fell 'as the idle wind, which none regardeth'. Nothing will convince some legislators of the dangers of raiding and invasion until a shell strikes the Post Office tower in Sydney, or one explodes in King William Street, Adelaide.[41]

In 1898 Rosa held that China's defeat demonstrated Australia had nothing to fear from the 'heathen Chinee' nor for that matter from any other foreign devil.[42] At the Colonial Conference of 1897, Chamberlain, exasperated at his futile attempts to encourage co-operation between the colonies before they federated, lost patience with the Australians and exclaimed: 'Well, you are all acting as though war was impossible'.[43]

But though political leaders, secure in their isolation, displayed little interest in defence, they were deeply disturbed by the condition of the colonial economies. Hence retrenchment was the order of the decade. Victoria's 'very efficient navy', for instance, attracted Turner's attention. Whereas the Treasurer's actions were generally credited with limiting the ill-effects of the slump, Craig, a voice in the wilderness, lamented: 'The virtual abolition of the Victorian Navy, and its splendid body of naval defenders, was a double crime against patriotism. It will always be a blot upon the Ministry of Mr Turner.'[44] Turner was Premier and Treasurer from 1894 to December 1899, and again in November 1900 until he became Treasurer in Barton's first federal administration.

The point is surely this. The inclusion of defence as an exclusive federal power was largely a matter of precedent as existing federations possessed the power. Whatever existed in 1889 in the nature of a genuine interest in the security of Australia through federation largely evaporated between 1893 and 1899. Apart from the removal of legal restrictions on the use of colonial forces beyond their own boundaries, what was wanted of federation was not bigger and better forces but the efficiency and economy of a central command. Barton said at the Adelaide session that defence should cost less under the federal parliament. Turner agreed.[45] The *Bulletin* supported the Commonwealth Bill because the amalgamation of the separate forces would be 'cheaper as well as more efficient'.[46] What was not expected of federation was innovation. No one of consequence in the new federation movement seems to have linked federation with a demand for an Australian navy. Three weeks before the inauguration of the Commonwealth Barton wrote: 'Our fleet, *if we ever have one*'.[47] Kingston and Deakin were not even aware of each other's thoughts in private on conscription. The two federal leaders attended both Conventions and were closely associated for three months in the last act in London early in 1900. Yet in September 1900 Kingston wrote to Deakin: 'I don't know how you are on conscription for defence purposes but I always think it is our duty in time of peace to get ready to defend ourselves in time of need.'[48] Perhaps, as a Methodist minister explained to his flock, 'The soldier had not helped much in this discussion because we have not been driven to take counsel of him. Herein we differ from most federated states'.[49]

The construction of the first federal ministry under Barton reflected the low priority accorded defence at the outset of the Commonwealth. Barton himself took charge of External Affairs, Kingston Trade and Customs, Lyne Home Affairs, Turner the Treasury, while Deakin and Forrest became Attorney-General and Postmaster-General respectively. Dickson, the man of least stature in the whole cabinet, received the defence portfolio. A member of the cabinet because Philp declined Barton's offer, Dickson was the only one not to have attended either Federal Convention. Although he campaigned for federation in Queensland in 1899, he was best known for his role as his colony's representative in London in 1900. There he sided with Chamberlain against Barton, Deakin, and Kingston on the issue of appeals to the Privy Council.[50] After Dickson's death on 10 January 1901, Forrest became Minister of Defence. Forrest of course was a man of stature in Western Australia and the federation movement, but this was probably no late recognition of the importance of the post. Newspapers reported that he gratefully relinquished his first position. The difficulty of amalgamating six separate postal departments with six different sets of regulations and systems of control was not to his liking. Already he and the Victorian Postmaster-General had clashed. Certainly Barton believed defence was the simpler task. On the day Forrest exchanged portfolios he declared: 'The interests concerned in the Post and Telegraph Departments are much fuller of complexity and variety than those concerned in the Department of Defence.'[51]

Nor was the ministry eager to proclaim a defence policy. Apart from Kingston's question to Deakin no thought seems to have been given one. Indeed, Kingston in his subsequent letter and telegram did not include a plank on defence in his proposed platform. Deakin suggested merely 'adequate Defence Forces' to Barton.[52] While few could quarrel with such a laudable aim, the meaning of 'adequate' or what precisely needed defending, and how, was not considered. Cabinet meetings, which determined the election platform announced at Maitland, were held in the absence of Dickson. Hence no member was specifically responsible for the department. The platform contained a passing reference to defence and a few platitudes. The department was 'second to none in importance'. Time must be allowed to make the transfer 'judicious and effective'. A 'united administration will produce even greater results than those of which we have been so proud when Australia really did meet as one in South Africa'.[53]

Amidst the great events of the early months of the Commonwealth, the actual transfer on 1 March attracted little comment. This was not yet another coming of age. The inevitable confusion as departments were taken over or created affected defence, which got off to a particularly bad start. Though the difficulties were relatively unimportant in themselves, they serve to illustrate the lack of consideration given to the transfer and the small attention it attracted.

The trouble began with Forrest's first commands. On 27 February he forwarded instructions to the New South Wales military and naval commandants by way of the local Minister of Defence. Forrest asked the minister to act on his behalf, pending federal legislation, on urgent matters referred to him by commandants. Forrest informed commandants that their forces would remain subject to local law and as far as possible he intended 'to allow matters to continue as at present'. If actions required ministerial authority they were to confer with the minister who controlled defence in their State before 1 March. Barton, unofficially shown these letters by the New South Wales government, rebuked Forrest in a private note: the gentleman who was lately New South Wales Minister of Defence could not legally perform ministerial or executive functions for the Commonwealth Minister of Defence. Orders issued by the State's Executive Council would be *ultra vires*. It would be 'a very wise step', he advised Forrest, 'if you were to consult Deakin privately on the subject.'[54]

Seven weeks after the transfer Sir Frederick Darley, Lieutenant-Governor of New South Wales, pointed out to Barton that, as the Commonwealth had assumed control, all defence powers vested in him no longer existed. He confessed that he had continued to sign documents and protested that

formal notice ought to have been sent to me as Lieutenant-Governor that such day was fixed. In point of fact I was quite unaware that any change had been made till recently when my attention was drawn to the matter, but not officially.[55]

The British government continued sending despatches on defence to Darley during this period. But whereas Forrest was bemused as far as finer details of administration were concerned, he understood one fundamental point: costs must be contained. Promotions and new appointments, he cautioned commandants, could not be made because 'every effort' must be taken to limit expenditure. Every care must be taken to base expenditure upon appropriations made by the government of New South Wales.[56]

Any compulsion upon the cabinet to introduce ambitious schemes, if it had any, disappeared with the results of the general election. Barton and his supporters had failed to get an absolute majority over

Free Trade and Labor. In the House of Representatives the Protectionists outnumbered their arch-rivals but in the Senate the Free-
Traders were the largest of the three parties. Hence the political
situation militated against Commonwealth extravagance, especially
in defence. On the one hand, Free-Traders had good cause to limit
expenditure in this field or in any other; the greater the expenditure,
the higher or the more extensive the tariff. On the other hand
Labor, though divided on the tariff, looked upon defence expenditure
as an undesirable diversion of funds away from vital social improvements. Alternative sources of revenue were out of the question and
it was generally accepted that for at least the ten years' duration of
the Braddon clause the Commonwealth would rely solely on customs
duties. Neither Free Trade nor Protectionist favoured direct taxation.
Loans were anathema to Labor.

The Governor-General soon confirmed at the opening of parliament that the government had no great plan. The speech promised
'Extravagant expenditure will be avoided, and reliance will be placed,
to the fullest reasonable extent, in our citizen soldiery'. As might be
expected this was not a controversial part of the programme. As
Senator Fraser said, in moving the address-in-reply, a citizen-soldiery
was 'ample' because Australia had no military frontier: besides, 'the
people of this country cannot afford a very extravagant military
system'. But Reid could not resist a gibe at the ministry's 'perfectly
reckless courage. . . . Just think of the number of members in these
two Houses who are clamouring for a big standing army!'[57]

The Defence Bill introduced by Forrest in mid 1901 was a hotch-
potch of State Acts designed chiefly to amalgamate the existing
systems. Forrest feared the worst and, in an uncharacteristically apologetic manner, stressed his lack of expertise in military affairs. His
premonition proved well founded. The Bill evoked no enthusiasm
and was soundly criticized on technical grounds and on principle.
Hughes, in a typical reaction termed it: 'an *olla podrida*, a jumble of
clauses and provisions extracted from the various Defence Acts'.
Moreover, it aroused widespread hostility to 'militarism'. Radical-
Protectionists such as Higgins and Quick, and Laborites such as
Watson and Pearce, denounced the clauses which enabled permanent
forces to be sent overseas and provided for the calling up of citizens in
'times of emergency'. Free-Traders such as Reid ridiculed the 'gold
lace' provisions. In all fifty-two amendments were proposed.[58]
Though Barton stoutly defended the measure, cabinet recognized its
unpopularity and made substantial concessions. In particular the

discretionary powers of the Executive and the professional commanding officers were curtailed and the service of permanent and citizen-soldiers confined to Australian territory. Ultimately, however, the Bill, which barely reached the committee stage, was abandoned.

It was against this background of complacency as to security, distrust of militarism, and above all the overwhelming desire to restrict expenditure, that Major-General Hutton assumed command of the Commonwealth forces in January 1902. To be sure the Boer War had stimulated a public interest in defence in general, and military affairs in particular, not evident earlier in the nineties. Undoubtedly the war was well supported, if unexpectedly in some quarters. The *Bulletin*, the Bushmen's Bible, confidently predicted that bushmen 'would know themselves disgraced if they permitted themselves to be exported to shoot Boers or any other race fighting for their own country'.[59] But the 16 000 volunteers who eagerly competed in skills with rifle and horse to win coveted places in the contingents confounded the *Bulletin* and isolated other critics such as Higgins and Cardinal Moran. Deakin, the Australian nationalist, told his readers in the *Morning Post*: 'The Mother Country stood alone. In an instant the cry was "Australia for the Empire"'.[60] But the disasters inflicted on British regulars by Boer guerrillas and the exaggerated success of Australian amateurs reinforced suspicions of the so-called military expert in the field. Detailed schemes, elaborate military training and preparation, were as unnecessary as they were wasteful. What Boer irregulars had done, so too could Australians in defence of their homeland should the need ever arise. As O'Malley colourfully put it: 'A small skeleton of an army in the Federal capital, with a native Australian De Wet as Commandant, whether he knows anything about "European military tactics" or not'[61] was all that was required.

Therefore, although Reid welcomed Hutton's appointment, parliament was not likely to be sympathetic to the natural aims of the dedicated professional. During his three years as General-Officer-Commanding the Commonwealth Military Forces the emphasis remained more on economy than on solving the problems of effective reorganization and basic strategy.

Hutton in his *Minute upon the Defence of Australia*, April 1902, accepted the orthodox views propounded by Colonial Defence Committee memoranda as to the degree of risk and nature of possible attack on an Australia shielded by the Royal Navy.[62] The geographical position of the continent certainly 'renders it less liable to aggression from any foreign power than most parts of the Empire'. No expedition could hope to reach its destination 'until the British Navy had been definitely worsted'. Attacks 'will in all probability therefore be reduced to raids by an enemy's cruisers based on his defended ports'. As the future development of the country depended upon immunity from attack the Sydney naval base and 'great trade centres' should be protected. Access should be denied to all cities, towns, harbours of commercial importance, and the establishment of a hostile expedition on Australian soil made impossible. To this end garrison troops should man the fixed defences and a mobile field force should be created to concentrate at any threatened point.

But Hutton regarded the simple protection of Australian territory as an inadequate policy based on defective strategy: the nation's 'interests' also needed defending. Sound principles of defence, he went on, were not 'limited to those of a purely passive kind. History has shown that the surest and best defence is by a vigorous offence.' Markets for Australian produce were outside territorial waters. It followed therefore that 'Australian interests cannot be assured by the defence alone of Australian soil'. Nor was it consistent for a 'young and vigorous nation to neglect her responsibility' and leave the protection of her interests in the hands of the imperial government and imperial forces. Developments in the Far East pointed to the Indian Ocean, the northern Pacific, and the China Sea 'as the probable scene of the future struggle for commercial supremacy'. Hence, while the first essential for defence of Australian interests was the supremacy of the Royal Navy, the second was the possession of a field force 'capable of undertaking military operations in whatever part of the world it may be desired by Australia to employ them'.

This second recommendation and the reasons given in its support ran completely counter to parliamentary sentiment, the strength of which cabinet recognized in its amendments of the 1901 Defence Bill. Ministers and backbenchers alike suspected that the actual size of the field force, perhaps the force itself, was designed less to defend Australia than to serve as an imperial reserve, the creation of which Hutton had long advocated. Collins, Defence Secretary, instructed Hutton that Forrest did not agree with any proposal to give control, or implied control, over Australian troops to any but the Commonwealth. Further, while it might be desirable to send volunteers abroad one day, present expenditure could not be incurred on troops maintained for external operations.[63]

Hutton's reply bristled with indignation. He demanded that Forrest point out the passages regarding control. The establishment was the minimum necessary for 'The Defence of Australian Soil'. Forrest remained unconvinced. In response to Hutton's refined scheme of June 1903, which called for a field force of 13 831, Forrest noted that the Colonial Defence Committee's memorandum 301R saw only a 'restricted' use of these troops for local defence, their main object being 'service beyond the limits of Australia'. Therefore, as the government had no such intention, the strength of the force now proposed would be in excess of requirements for a policy limited to local defence.[64]

Moreover, although Hutton based his initial minute on the number of troops existing in the States and on the 1901–2 estimates, his expectations for the near future were obvious. The estimates 'should be in the first instant sufficient'. An appendix pointedly drew attention to the low proportion of public expenditure devoted to defence in comparison with thirteen other western nations. Australia was at the bottom of the list in both *per capita* and percentage expenditure.[65]

But even as Forrest considered the minute he was again on the defensive, on this occasion in the Committee on Supply. His department was unpopular. It did not earn revenue. He understood 'those who are sent here specially to protect the taxpayers view any abnormal growth with some alarm'. But the defence estimate of £937 000 was not really his; the figure was the States' total at the time of transfer. Forrest's apologetic manner did not save him. Free Trade and Labor, whose own estimates committee recommended a reduction to £500 000, resumed the attack. Turner quickly promised a cut of £100 000. Batchelor, second to Watson in the Labor Party, suggested £400 000. Braddon and Watson moved a reduction of £200 000 but this was narrowly defeated.[66] But the message was clear. Two days later Forrest told Collins that the estimates had passed on the undertaking to reduce the next one by £131 000. He added: 'It was unmistakably shown during the debate that a still larger reduction was desired'. Collins immediately directed Hutton to stop all recruitment. Places of men selected for service in South Africa from the permanent artillery must 'not be filled'. This order must have pleased at least one Premier. On the same day Philp complained to Forrest about the cost of Queensland's permanent forces which were 'much too large'. Nearly half of the forces were in South Africa and 'if they can be spared temporarily they can surely be spared permanently'.[67]

Relations between federal administrators and Hutton rapidly

deteriorated as the government tried to fulfil its promises while the general conducted rearguard actions. These skirmishes were a constant theme in Deakin's letters to Barton, who was *en route* to London with Forrest for the Colonial Conference. On 14 May the acting Prime Minister wrote,

We are going to have a great deal of trouble about the Defence Retrenchments. The General objects to some details—the Cabinet to others—and the House to mine. We have to make the saving but just how it is to be done no one is agreed.[68]

A week later: 'Still worrying at the Defence Estimates for reductions. . . . Turner has been as usual immensely serviceable and is going through them line by line'. In June,

Turner is doing invaluable work with the Defence Estimates on which the General has been playing a deep game. . . . Forrest has reason to congratulate himself that he left it to others to find ways of saving £100,000. . . . without Turner none of us would have been able to cope with the military strategy of the General. He is absolutely 'slim'.[69]

'Strategy' notwithstanding, the general was on the retreat. Collins informed Hutton that the military estimates should be reduced to £600 000. Hutton was again indignant. He denied the charge by Lyne, then acting Minister of Defence, that defence establishments had not been cut. The permanent staff and artillery, he maintained, had decreased by 39 per cent: 'It was not too much to say that a reduction so summary and so drastic constitutes little less than destruction of the previously existing Military System of Australia.' Forrest, back from London, was still more ruthless; in view of the new Naval Agreement military expenditure should not exceed £500 000 a year.[70]

The outcome of the conflict was a victory for the parliamentarians over the general. In a statement on 30 July 1903 Forrest reviewed the battles with satisfaction. Defence estimates for the financial year 1902–3 were £175 198 below those in existence in the States on 1 March 1901; actual expenditure saved a further £84 525. Moreover as recruiting had stopped for the 'greater portion of the year', the strength of the forces was much under the establishment as provided in the estimates. Planned expenditure for 1903–4 was £84 435 down on 1902–3. This exceeded the amount promised to parliament. The total strength of the military forces on 30 June 1903 stood at 22 346 compared with the 25 844 provided for in the Commanding Officer's scheme of July.[71]

Despite this satisfactory outcome politicians continued to criticize Hutton and his plans in the second parliament. Forrest's successors—Protectionist Austin Chapman, Labor's Andrew Dawson, and Coalitionist James McCay—in turn bore the brunt of the general's temper. Like other men who did not suffer fools gladly Hutton believed he was surrounded by them. In March 1904 Chapman asked Hutton for his comments on criticisms of the scheme in the House and Senate. He retorted,

I will candidly confess that I find it difficult to reply to the comprehensive criticism by ill-informed Members of Parliament who have neither the training nor possess the Military instincts to qualify them as critics in so difficult a profession . . .[72]

In July Dawson rejected his suggestion to depart from the Imperial Service pattern for pistols for mounted troops. Hutton, a pioneer of mounted infantry, took this as a personal affront: in future the minister could ask for opinions elsewhere 'as I am not prepared to submit further recommendations'. In August he reiterated his opposition to the inclusion of naval officers on the proposed Commonwealth Defence Committee. The naval forces were 'insignificant' and part of 'Military Defence' he told McCay. Naval defence of Australia and her interests resided with the British navy 'and may be considered as a purely Imperial question'. Besides, no local officer possessed 'a high degree of practical experience in large Military or Naval strategical questions'.[73] Captain Creswell was appointed vice-president under Hutton.

Nonetheless despite the setbacks and enforced retrenchments Hutton looked back with some pride on his achievements. Though parliament never officially endorsed his minute of April 1902, he liked to believe that the principles it embraced had been unofficially accepted since 'the recommendations involved by these principles have been carried into effect almost in their entirety'. Hutton's second, and last, annual report noted the reorganization and reconstruction. In 1902 the Central and District Head-Quarters Staffs were created to control and administer the whole military forces. The Royal Australian Artillery Regiment was organized for garrison duties at defended ports and for instructional purposes. A general system of training was introduced. In 1903 the Commonwealth adopted a service uniform and converted State rifle clubs into one organization. Finally, in 1904, a military forces list, military regulations, and financial instructions were published. The Defence Bill, drafted in February and passed in October 1903, was proclaimed on 1 March 1904. Above all, in July the government approved the reorganization submitted in April 1902 and elaborated in May 1903. The scheme, which provided a field force of militia and a garrison force of volunteers, represented a 'complete reconstruction' and ensured the defence of the Commonwealth as a whole 'within the limitations imposed by the Defence Act 1903'.[74]

Others in positions of authority doubted that much of real value had been accomplished. Early in 1905, soon after Hutton's departure, McCay addressed a meeting of Commanding Officers in Melbourne: 'What I desire as Minister is not only that the new system of administration shall succeed but also that the Forces shall be as efficient as they were previously in any part of the Commonwealth.' Sir George Clarke, former secretary of the Colonial Defence Committee and first secretary of the newly formed Committee of Imperial Defence, told Deakin the fault of the scheme was that the reforms were 'largely of a paper character and therefore illusory'.[75]

Still, by 1905 some of the aims of the federalists had undoubtedly been fulfilled. The military forces were available for the defence of all parts of the continent regardless of internal boundaries. Economy had also resulted. Indeed expenditure did not exceed the colonial total until 1906–7. What was less certain was whether the greater efficiency expected of a central administration had actually taken place. But then what the federalists had wanted or had not wanted became increasingly less important in the second half of the decade.

The major event in naval affairs in the first five years of the Commonwealth was the Naval Agreement of 1903. The Agreement, negotiated by Barton and Forrest at the Colonial Conference of 1902, differed from the initial one of 1887 in three important respects. First, it introduced local training of Australian seamen; as far as possible Australians were to man one warship on active commission and three drillships as a branch of a Royal Naval Reserve. Secondly, it increased the subsidy from £106 000 to £200 000 a year. Thirdly, it abolished the distinction between the imperial and the Auxiliary Squadron (established by the 1887 scheme). Henceforth the new squadron was to operate in accord with the new doctrine of fleet concentration propounded in the early 1890s by Captain A. T. Mahan, the Clausewitz of naval warfare. Though based on Australian ports, the unit was to join with imperial ships of the China and East Indies stations to seek out and destroy the enemy wherever he might be within the bounds of the three stations. Therefore unlike the Auxiliary Squadron, which could only be removed from Australian waters with the consent of colonial governments, the unit was available for imperial duties over which the Commonwealth had no control.[76]

Barton and Forrest, who defended the scheme in federal parliament, received strong criticism. Opponents charged that they had failed to seize the opportunity to found an Australian navy and instead meekly gave in to British demands on strategy and control. The *Brisbane Courier* reviled Forrest as an ignorant, unpatriotic, British toady whose recommendations—'a gross misrepresentation of Australian public opinion'—frustrated the hopes of Australian navalists. Richard Jebb, a kinder and more responsible critic, suggested in his influential book *The Imperial Conference: A History and Study* that Barton must have returned from London 'with an uncomfortable feeling that the whole principle of the Agreement was antagonistic to the instinct of Australian nationalism which his own eloquence had helped to foster in the federal campaign'. Barton was in a difficult position as the standpoints of Australian nationalism were still unintelligible to the Admiralty. Hence,

For any Australian to explain and defend that standpoint in the London of May 1902 would have been difficult indeed. . . . Constrained by atmospheric pressure to yield, the Australian Premier could only try to yield as little as the situation would permit and make the best of it to his Parliament and people, who were intent on founding an Australian navy instead of continuing to subsidise the British navy. Had he felt free to follow his own inclination, he would probably have aligned himself with the Canadian Premier . . .[77]

Later Deakin commented to Jebb on his book:

In 1902 Barton was becoming over taxed and Forrest is a British and not an Austn Imperialist. The naval issue was the only one critical and meant hard fighting in one House to get it through. But at that time Barton's native dilatoriness and his position in Parlt combined to make us less effective in London . . .[78]

More recently C. Grimshaw speculated, like Jebb, that Barton disagreed with Forrest but was in a difficult position.[79]

Thus the picture emerges of a somewhat indolent, feeble and reluctant Barton and an excessively pro-British Forrest thwarting the great national demand for an Australian navy. Now whatever their deficiencies as administrators this interpretation of events is unfair to both. In the first place it exaggerates the level of interest in defence in general and naval affairs in particular in the late colonial and early Commonwealth period. Again, it attributes to Australians, especially 'nationalists', a burning desire for a navy not evident at the time. Finally, it misconstrues the motives and attitudes of the pair and the circumstances under which the Agreement was determined.

It is true, of course, that Barton and other federalists attempted to foster a spirit of nationalism in the federation campaigns of the 1890s. But there was no great demand for an Australian navy within the federation movement. Even Creswell's scheme of 1897, exhibited at the Colonial Conference of that year, contemplated not a navy but the training of seamen for a Royal Naval Reserve.[80] And this was in no way related to federation. Certainly once federation was brought about Creswell and others advocated a navy. 'Sea defence', he told Forrest in May 1901, was 'relegated to a secondary and very subordinate position' in the Defence Bill: an Australian navy was 'the proper course for the Commonwealth and the only one consistent with its dignity'.[81] The Melbourne *Age* also considered this a wise policy. With federation achieved the Naval Agreement and the subsidy should be abandoned: Australia could not avoid her 'destiny as a sea power'. But Jebb's implication that such sentiments were an integral part of the federation movement is incorrect. In fact the *Age*, which later led the navalist press attacks on the Agreement, was at best a late and lukewarm campaigner for federation. Deakin himself tells how before the end of the Melbourne Convention it 'had practically decided to defeat the Commonwealth Bill'. Shortly before polling day the paper retracted some of its censures 'almost in spite of itself' while 'sneering at the patriotic enthusiasm of the young members of the Australian Natives' Association'.[82]

Moreover expressions of navalist views were rare in the early days of federal parliament. In debates on the Defence Bill less than a handful of speakers opposed the New Naval Agreement. Quick and Crouch, a radical Protectionist, amidst heckling expressed doubts about the wisdom of relying upon England. McDonald, a Labor member from Queensland, attacked glib assumptions based on the supremacy of the British navy and vainly called upon members to 'be honest to the people who sent us here and tell them openly that it is necessary, for the efficient defence of the Commonwealth, to incur an enormous expenditure for the creation of a navy'. But in direct contrast, the leaders of both the Labor and Free Trade Parties opposed a local navy. Watson stressed the prohibitive cost and supported the subsidy to maintain the British fleet: 'All this emphasizes the fact that we cannot have anything like an Australian navy without incurring an expenditure that we dare not face'. Reid concurred. There was 'no necessity' yet to begin the founding of a navy. Even Hughes, who warned that invasion was no 'chimerical idea' and who almost alone had plans for defence, supported renewal: 'We shall soon have to make another agreement, when vessels of a more up-to-date character will have to be contracted for.'[83] Apparently Labor, supposedly the party of Australian nationalism, had so little interest in the subject that its special committee convened to examine the Defence Bill made no recommendation on naval defence.[84]

Further, in searching for a policy, Barton and Forrest showed an acute concern for parliamentary and public opinion and believed they were acting in harmony with it. They turned to Rear-Admiral Sir Lewis Beaumont, Commanding Officer of the Australian Station, for advice. Forrest told Barton that he should make it clear to Beaumont that 'public opinion would probably be adverse to the establishment and maintenance of a large Permanent Naval Defence Force'. Beaumont counselled the government to 'take no part in the creation or maintenance of Naval Reserves or State Naval Forces'. The future 'may see the creation of an Australian Navy, but for the present, the safety and welfare of the Commonwealth require that the Naval Force in Australian waters should be a sea-going fleet of modern ships'.[85]

Forrest, like many others, accepted the need for more modern ships and agreed that the federal government could not yet afford a navy. But he rejected the portions which denied navalist aspirations. Beaumont's proposals meant that the Commonwealth would subsidize the imperial government without any provision for the 'Sailors of Australia' to be 'a part of the Naval Defence Force of Australia'. If they were adopted the Commonwealth would not have for its object 'the gradual building up of an Australian Navy, but will depend entirely for its naval defence upon the Navy of the Motherland'. Any scheme which neglected this object 'will not meet with public approval'. If Australia merely contributed funds 'we would, in twenty years, be no more self reliant than we are today'. Therefore, the best course was to arrange that a certain number of ships be used for training so as to move in a direction 'which would eventually enable us to provide for and establish an Australian Navy'. It was imperative to secure an efficient system which at the same time was 'in accord with the wishes and aspirations of the Australian people'.[86]

Ultimately the policy Barton and Forrest took to London embraced these recommendations. Forrest, in his final minute of 15 March 1902, held an Australian navy impractical 'under existing conditions'. As the present Auxiliary Squadron was 'inadequate' a 'greater contribution' would be necessary. Until a more permanent basis for the naval defence of the Empire could be determined the existing agreement should be 'readjusted and extended for ten years'. The naval militia should be made effective for use in war, and two Royal Naval ships be allotted for training.[87]

Forrest's postscript stressed the identity of interests within the Empire.

If the British nation is at war, so are we; if it gains victories or suffers disasters, so do we. . . . There is only one sea to be supreme over, and we want one fleet to be mistress over that sea. . . . Our aim and object should be to make the Royal Navy the Empire's Navy, supported by the whole of the self-governing portions of the Empire . . .[88]

If this concept was ever adopted,

what a splendid idea would be consummated, and what a bulwark for peace throughout the world would be established! . . . I cannot think that for Canada and Australia to each have a few war ships and the Cape and New Zealand a few also, each independent of the other, is a plan suited to Empire . . .

Now the remarkable thing about the new Naval Agreement is how closely its terms followed Forrest's recommendations. It provided a new and relatively modern force of ocean-going ships which included one first-class and two second-class cruisers. Articles IV, V, and VII provided for the training of Australian seamen on board one warship and three drill ships supplied by the Admiralty, and a Royal Naval Reserve. The Agreement took a step towards the concept of 'one Empire one fleet' by enabling the new squadron to combine with imperial fleet units of the China and East Indies stations. It even cost the exact amount that Barton, Forrest and Beaumont decided the Commonwealth could afford for a slightly larger squadron. In short, despite differences in detail, Barton and Forrest got much of what they wanted. They may perhaps have misjudged Australian opinion but Jebb's idea that the Agreement and its terms were imposed on the unwilling Australians against their better judgement is as mistaken as his notion that the Australian parliament and people at this time were intent on founding a navy. Perhaps Deakin's description of

Forrest as a British imperialist is valid. But above all Forrest was a pragmatist, with the pragmatist's keen sense of the possible. His postscript may have expressed his philosophy of Empire and its defence, or it may have been a tactical move to enlist the support of freetraders, amongst whom such views were not uncommon. But even so it is a moot point whether for all that the rugged, self-made, exexplorer (or for that matter his companion the federal leader) was any less an Australian in 1902–3 than Deakin.

One further point needs to be mentioned. Leon Atkinson's detailed research exposes as myth the legend that Forrest alone was responsible for naval policy and the Agreement. But in discussing the naval doctrine of the concentration of capital ships in battle fleets for offensive operations he observes that the Colonial Conference of 1897 missed the opportunity of introducing the new theory to Australian statesmen, an omission rectified by Lord Selborne in 1902.[89] This statement is undoubtedly correct: the Admiralty failed to propound the theory in 1897 and lectured delegates in 1902; but the implication that Australian political leaders did not understand the new doctrine until 1902 is not. Forrest's support for one Empire fleet and strictures against independent local units—though perhaps inconsistent with his plans for an Australian navy—suggest he may have been aware of the strategy. But it is perfectly clear that Barton not only understood the doctrine, but actually approved it, well before the Conference of 1902. Part of his lecture late in 1900 could well have been drafted by Captain Mahan himself. Although the coming Australian Commonwealth would not be aggressive,

the true place of self-defence is not always to be found within artificial limits. . . . Our fleet, if we ever have one, may be better employed in assisting to destroy a powerful naval combination thousands of miles away, than it could be if distributed in the defence of separated ports, and so left in detail at the mercy of strong attacking squadrons. If concentration is powerful for aggression, it would be foolhardy to neglect it when defence is the only object.[90]

In 1902 Selborne and the Admiralty were preaching to the converted.

But despite their concern for what they believed to be Australian opinion Barton and Forrest had great difficulty in getting the Agreement ratified. Defence innovations were not expected of the Commonwealth, but the Agreement made three. The first change—the training of Australian seamen—did not upset many parliamentarians.

The other two did. The increased cost came at the very time when defence estimates were being scrutinized 'line by line'. In Barton's absence cabinet decided that any increase must be matched by a corresponding reduction in military expenditure. Deakin cabled Barton this 'unanimous' advice (only Kingston, O'Connor, and Deakin were present: Lyne, a supporter of the Agreement, was absent). He added a 'second axiom': the subsidy 'must always be unpopular and is merely a trifle towards the cost of the Royal navy'. He suggested an alternative: 'Commonwealth should establish Naval reserves our own men at own expense' trained on vessels lent by the Admiralty.[91] The merger of the auxiliary and imperial squadrons for service outside Australian waters ran counter to navalist sentiments expressed by the likes of Creswell, Collins, and the *Age*. It also aroused old fears of involvement in imperial wars. The new doctrine, critics such as Senator Matheson and Quick soon asserted, not only sanctioned offensive operations but could well deprive Australia of the squadron when it was most needed: it satisfied neither self-respect nor security.

Individually, therefore, each of these two innovations would have caused the government problems. Together they aroused resentment. Of the forty-five members who debated the issue only eight approved ratification without reservations.[92] Labor, and a small group of radicals from government ranks led by Crouch, solidly opposed the Bill. Had Barton not made the measure one of confidence the Agreement might possibly have been rejected.

On the other hand too much should not be made of these objections and of the alleged deficiencies of Barton and Forrest. After all parliament ratified the Agreement and it ran its full course. Like it or not, something had to be done as the 1887 Agreement was about to expire. In all probability whatever policy they had proposed would have caused at least as much outcry. Cabinet's suggestion of 'men instead of money', trained on borrowed ships, would not have fully satisfied navalist ambitions. Yet at the same time it would have provoked charges of disloyalty—'cutting the painter'—and of endangering security. Besides it was not a realistic alternative. The Admiralty was disinclined to encourage schemes not in accord with the 'blue-water school' and the doctrine of fleet concentration. In 1889 it had not responded to something similar proposed by a conference of naval commandants under Collins. But *The Times* no doubt reflected official policy: the 'deplorably mischievous proposals' were 'inadequate, inconsequent, and altogether inadmissible . . . The British Empire requires only one Navy, homogeneous, and obeying a common law'.[93] Even more decisively the imperial government, itself planning naval economy,[94] was utterly opposed to spending more on Australia's behalf. Australia, it rightly believed, was getting her security on the cheap and at the Colonial Conferences of 1887 and 1897 it had sought to redress the balance. In 1902 Selborne's full scheme would have cost the Commonwealth £387 490 a year.

In fact Barton and Forrest faced three alternatives. First, the Commonwealth could found a proper navy. But, other considerations apart, this would have been inordinately expensive and any increase, as cabinet recognized, had to be matched by a decrease in the military. Not only Hutton and his officers would have soon been aroused had this been attempted. Secondly, Australia could abandon the Agreement and rely upon military defence. This would have denied supporters of the existing arrangement, infuriated navalists, and endangered security. Thirdly, the government could negotiate a new Agreement to provide more modern ships on the best terms they could get. This Barton and Forrest did. Given the strident calls for, and expectations of, economy and the attitude of the British government and Admiralty they could scarcely have done otherwise. The actual terms did not satisfy everyone (and later they would satisfy less) but then no terms could. The circumstances of their determination and the conditions which prevailed were not as Jebb depicted them.

In the absence of public-opinion polls the exact popularity of the Agreement remains a matter for conjecture. Certainly, Deakin, Kingston (who probably suggested the alternative in 1902) and an increasing number of politicians disliked it. So did the navalist newspapers—the *Age, Bulletin, Brisbane Courier*, and the *South Australian Register*. But the free-trade papers of Victoria and New South Wales set the pattern for others in support of the Agreement. As Atkinson put it, 'The remainder of the Australian press followed the lead of the Melbourne *Argus* and the *Sydney Morning Herald*'.[95] Probably some of the criticism in parliament was designed more to embarrass the government than to discuss the merits of the Bill. Reid, for example, consistent in his inconsistencies, argued against it yet voted for it. Again, in a collection of official and semi-official documents on defence in the Deakin papers there is a memorandum, possibly written by Lyne, claiming that the dislike to the present Agreement is confined to a minority of the Australian people, and that if the Squadron were withdrawn, or even largely reduced, and a visiting Squadron of cruisers substituted, it would create a strong revulsion of feeling in favour of the Agreement being continued.[96]

In 1907 the *United Service Magazine* reported that the 'Sydney Correspondent' of a London paper telegraphed 'it is rumoured in that city [Sydney] that Sir W. Lyne's bitter opposition to Mr Deakin's proposal to cancel the naval subsidy is responsible for the fact of nothing appearing on the subject in the Governor-General's speech.'[97] As late as 1909 Deakin conceded the Agreement popular in Sydney (the squadron was based at Port Jackson) 'where our personal relations with the officers and men on the station have always been of the pleasantest character'.[98] Probably the Agreement was neither very popular nor very unpopular as the public at large was uninterested and was concerned only to get expenditure curbed.

Perhaps, with some allowance for military bias, the prevalent attitudes to military and naval defence in the period are best summed up in the words of Senator Lieutenant-Colonel J. C. Neild. In a paper presented in 1904 Neild argued that the Commonwealth 'must for many years to come rely upon Great Britain for naval defence'. He deplored the 'pernicious influence' of the Boer War and the national pride in 'horseflesh' in 'Horsetralia'. Together these had perverted defence thinking by inducing 'the propagation of a gospel of gallop-and-shoot that ignored organisation and derided discipline'. They gave rise to the mania shared and propagated by the members of parliament and ministers that 'an Australian, astride with four legs, is, if possessed of a rifle and a pillow-case full of cartridges, a match for an indefinite number of the best trained soldiers of any nation.' No defence journal existed and Australians did not 'seriously interest themselves in naval and military affairs'. They regarded a member of the permanent forces 'as one who does little for his living' and the militiaman and volunteer 'as rather a silly fellow, afflicted with a harmless craze for doing something utterly unnecessary, and upon whose vagaries a shocking amount of public money is thrown away.'[99]

5

THE DEFENCE OF
AUSTRALIA AND THE EMPIRE

The task of arousing parliamentarians and electors from their apathy
on defence questions and of changing British attitudes to Australian
naval ambitions was undertaken by certain politicians and organizations. Foremost among these were Hughes, the New South Wales
division of the National Defence League, the Labor Party, and
Deakin. They were greatly assisted and spurred by the intervention
of external events favourable to their cause, events without which
compulsory military training and the founding of the Australian
navy within the first decade would probably have proved unacceptable to parliament and public. But shrewd and ambitious men
skilfully exploited the fortuitous circumstances—chiefly the Russo-
Japanese War of 1904-5, the Dreadnought crisis of 1909, and the
changing Admiralty strategy during the period. Within a few years
widespread complacency as to Australia's security changed into deep
concern. Whereas individuals such as Hughes and Senators Neild,
Dobson and Matheson once despaired of success, by 1911 the anonymous Deakin could marvel at the

remarkable change in the attitude of our people generally towards
defence. Before Federation, and even in the first years after it, there
seemed to be a strong inclination on the part of Parliament, and particularly of the Labor members, to regard expenditure on preparations for
war as unnecessary extravagance. We have changed all that. . . . We
appear to have decided to secure something like an effective defence even
at a high cost.[1]

In June 1905 Deakin publicly expressed dissatisfaction with Australian indifference to defence issues in an interview in the Melbourne
Herald.[2] The statement received great publicity and the Senate

reprinted it as a paper. In September a number of prominent citizens and politicians formed the National Defence League in Sydney. But though the campaign began in earnest in 1905, Hughes started his personal crusade during the second reading of the Defence Bill of 1901. Despite later variations in detail he then gave the first outline of the theme which he later propounded at every opportunity.

Hughes concentrated his attack on the very basis of the existing military system. The volunteer system was a failure, permanent forces undesirable. The oft-mentioned example of the Boers was a false analogy; they were 'a people who live largely in the country, while we, unhappily . . . find that our civilization locates us principally in towns'. Australians should take the Swiss, not the Boers, as their model. The remedy, therefore, was compulsory military training of males in a 'national militia'. Universal service avoided the potential dangers that professional armies posed to fragile democracies. At the same time it would instil civic virtues and the duties of citizenship as in the Swiss democracy. National military service was the corollary of national manhood suffrage. Compulsory drill was not conscription in the manner of France and Germany. On the contrary, it was the very antithesis of despotic European militarism for it precluded the growth of a military caste and a shambling, unwilling soldiery. Civil and business life would suffer minimal disruption.[3]

In 1901 and again in 1903 when Hughes reiterated his scheme the plea for universal service was premature. Though many parliamentarians shared his distaste for a standing army, more believed that his compulsory cure was worse than the disease. Indeed in advocating military drill Hughes was out of step with his own comrades. Neither the Federal Labor Party nor its colonial antecedents believed in it and they took little more interest than their political rivals. Whatever prompted the formation of the Labor Party it was decidedly not anxiety for military security. In New South Wales, Hughes' stamping ground, the first platform supported federation but called for the abolition of the defence force, and the establishment of a military system upon a 'purely voluntary' basis. The first federal platform in 1896 ignored defence entirely, the second a year later included the plank 'Quarantine, lighthouses, and defence'. The 1899 platform excluded the subject as did the final pre-federation one of 1900.[4] 'There was a strong current of opinion among the rank and file', Watson later explained, 'that the whole question was negligible. This indifference was generally maintained until the colonies federated in 1901'.[5]

With federation accomplished Labor faced a new situation. The

Commonwealth possessed exclusive defence power and Forrest's Bill was imminent. Therefore it had to make a stand on the issue and in May 1901 caucus made a 'Citizen Army' a plank in its platform. Nonetheless interest in land defence remained essentially negative. In April 1902 caucus endorsed several committee recommendations. The defence estimate should be cut to £500 000, permanent forces reduced to the establishment of 1899, and one military staff created.[6]

Thus the growth of positive attitudes under the influence of Hughes was a post-federation development. Gradually he gained converts to the principle of compulsion. Delegates at the Third Commonwealth Labour Conference in 1905 only narrowly rejected universal service. At the fourth in Brisbane in 1908, Watson paid genuine tribute to the work of Hughes and moved to adopt the principle. The motion had few opponents. Senator Findley reminded delegates that before federation Labor was a 'Peace party'. Tudor attacked 'gold-lace glorification'. O'Malley wondered if the party had gone 'mad on militarism'. Sentiments such as these, orthodox in 1901, were becoming anachronistic by 1908. Fears of a military caste were as strong as ever but Hughes had demonstrated that the Swiss system avoided the evils of conscription yet conferred the benefits of military drill. Supporters ranged far and wide in their reasons—recent events in the east, the Asian hordes, an inevitably aggressive Germany or Japan. Watson warned of the fate of an earlier civilization caught unprepared: 'When Pizarro descended on Peru it was an ideal Socialistic community, peace-loving and carrying out some of the reforms aimed at to-day'. Delegates, overwhelmed with the lessons of history and contemporary events, approved a 'Citizens Defence Force with compulsory military training' by 24 votes to 7.[7] What started as the crusade of a dynamic individual, a sort of mad Mahdi of mass mobilization, in seven years had become official policy.

Hughes and a citizen officer, Lieutenant-Colonel G. R. Campbell, founded the National Defence League on the example of Lord Roberts' National Service League in Britain.[8] By 1910, when it disbanded, twenty one branches had been established. Membership reached a maximum of 1600 in 1908 as the result of a recruiting drive by Hughes. Though perhaps small in numbers, it included important personages from all parties and persuasions.

MacLaurin (now Sir Normand), conservative Member of the Legislative Council and Chancellor of Sydney University, was president. MacMillan, arch anti-socialist, Watson, Labor leader, and the Bishop of North Queensland served as vice-presidents. Senator

Walker, conservative free-trader and banker, sat on the General Council. Frank Fox, editor of the *Bulletin*, A. W. Jose, *The Times* correspondent, and W. A. Holman, deputy leader of New South Wales Labor, were members of the executive committee. Hughes and Campbell were joint secretaries.

The *Call*, the league's periodical, proclaimed the organization's aim 'To awaken Australians to realise that the defence of our country is the duty of all'. Its objects were to secure

(a) Universal compulsory training (military or naval) of the boyhood and manhood of Australia for purposes of National Defence, the military to be on the lines of the Swiss system, and the naval training on the lines of the British Royal Naval Reserve, modified to suit local circumstances.
(b) An adequate and effective system of National Defence.[9]

Deakin observed the league's advent with approval: it had 'struck a note higher than that hitherto heard in the Commonwealth parliament'.[10]

Although the objectives mentioned naval training, the league reflected the interests of Hughes and other officials, many of whom were citizen military officers. The second edition of the *Call* described the 'blue-water school of defence' as impractical. Australia was an island, but military defence should be considered first for only that could be made effective in the near future. 'No local navy within the bounds of possibility for many a long year to come can ensure our safety in this respect.'[11]

In addition to a propaganda campaign the league lobbied federal politicians and in 1906 it circularized members of parliament. 'Pressure of work' prevented most from answering but the sixteen who troubled to reply—sympathetic and otherwise—included prominent members of the three parties. Deakin, Ewing, and Dobson replied from Protectionist ranks; Reid, Bruce Smith, and Neild from Free Trade; Dr Maloney and Pearce from Labor. In May 1909 delegates met Deakin, by then a supporter of universal service, and Ewing, then a member of the league, to suggest improvements to their defence proposals. In August the league added 'direct political action on non-party lines' to its tactics and questioned federal candidates as to their soundness on its objects. On this occasion 'pressure of work' did not prevent a good response. The *Call* printed a list of seventy-nine candidates who proved their fitness to be endorsed for the election in April 1910. Later in the year the league ceased its activities, its work complete.[12]

Whereas Hughes and the National Defence League concentrated on military affairs, the proposed Naval Agreement soon forced Labor to discuss naval policy. Federal caucus itself did not consider the subsidy until July 1903 but delegates aired the subject at the second Labour Conference in December 1902. Pearce and Guthrie moved opposition to increasing the subsidy, and support for any available money for naval defence being 'used in the formation of a navy that would be owned and controlled by the Commonwealth.'[13] Apparently these views were controversial for delegates carried the motion 'after a long debate'. Nevertheless in so doing Labor became the first parliamentary party to advocate an 'Australian-owned Navy'. Possibly lack of expectations of having to implement the new policy strengthened the delegates' initiative. But in office for the first time in 1904 Labor proved willing to heed Creswell's advice and attempted to strengthen the local forces.

Nine days after Watson took office Creswell pressed his case on the new administration. Since federation the policy had been 'one of reduction, a destructive rather than constructive or reconstructive policy . . . and it is now at the lowest ebb possible to existence'.[14] The Commonwealth should acquire coastal defence vessels to protect local shipping and to serve as useful auxiliaries to the imperial fleet. Dawson was impressed and asked Watson to contact the Admiralty to arrange terms 'for loan of two or three Torpedo-boat Destroyers, new type, Commonwealth paying interest to cover cost of construction and sinking fund, and vessels to be manned and maintained locally'.[15] This modest step proved abortive. Dawson and Watson learned at first hand what colonial and federal ministers had already found out, and what Deakin was shortly to discover. The Admiralty was prepared neither to increase imperial costs nor to reverse its strategy. It had no such boats available; vessels of this type were inadvisable in Australian waters; enemy torpedo boats could not possibly appear appear off local ports in wartime and Australian ones would have 'very rare' opportunities.[16] Dawson contested the reply but in two weeks he was in opposition.

Labor remained out of office until the first Fisher government of November 1908 and from July 1905 Deakin occupied the stage. As such Labor could take no direct initiative, but in general it endorsed Deakin's sustained efforts to strengthen local naval and military forces. Back on the front benches Fisher used funds set aside by Deakin to order the first ships which later formed part of the fleet unit. Creswell was delighted and wrote Jebb: 'at last it is a Labour

Govt that makes a beginning to do something for Australia.
. . . Pearce our new Minister is a good man and has straight away
ordered 3 Destroyers with the £250,000'.[17] More importantly, perhaps,
Labor brought the defence question before the public and kept it
there. The party became increasingly identified with nationalistic
attitudes of self-help. The continent should be built into a white
fortress Australia with ships built, controlled and manned by Australians patrolling the moat. At federal elections from 1903 onwards
Labor made first the naval subsidy and then defence in general a
major issue, and one shrewd observer, Jose, attributed its electoral
success (and the decline of the ministry and the direct opposition) to
its stance on defence.[18] Hence, even as the party itself was undergoing
fundamental changes in its own attitudes, it seemed to show that a
positive defence programme need not be incompatible with winning
votes.

By mid-1905 the situation and Deakin's status had changed. The
Deakin had remained silent throughout the early years of federation while Hughes tried to secure universal service and Labor and
the navalist press challenged the Naval Agreement. He too disliked
the subsidy and privately he discussed defence with Sir George
Clarke. But as a cabinet minister Deakin was, of course, bound not to
oppose his colleagues publicly on a sensitive policy and he took no
part in the debate on the ratification. Further, Deakin was preoccupied with work for which he was directly responsible. As
Attorney-General he headed a department which was drafting foundation legislation and which was possibly subjected to greater pressure
than any other department during the first parliament.

By mid-1905 the situation and Deakin's status had changed. The
machinery of the Commonwealth had been set in motion. Barton had
retired thoughtfully to the High Court, and Deakin, now the established Protectionist leader, was about to become Prime Minister.
Therefore he was relatively free to pursue policies of his own choos-
ing and from this time until April 1910 he was 'continuously concerned' with the question of naval defence.[19] In June he gave his
interview to the *Herald*. He alluded to military questions but dwelt
on the limitations of naval defence under the Agreement. The forces
were 'inadequate in numbers, imperfectly supplied with war material,
and exceptionally weak on the naval side.' Coastal shipping and trade
were vulnerable, harbour forts 'antiquated'. The seaboard capitals
were 'by no means secure'. Though the squadron was the best protection against enemy fleets it might have to perform duties distant from
Australia. The Commonwealth could not afford sea-going ships, but

submarines, torpedo boats, and torpedo boat destroyers should be secured for defensive operations. In all, Australia must be prepared 'to spend more liberally than it had ever done on its defence and defence forces'. This could be done

Only by kindling a public interest and waking those who control our representatives, and who control them almost invariably in the direction of economy to the fact that in defence . . . to be penny wise is to be pound foolish.[20]

In August Deakin translated personal sentiments into official action. He seized upon criticisms of the Agreement by Admiral Fanshawe, the Naval Commander-in-Chief on the station, to air his grievances to the British government. The Agreement had never been popular. It did not stimulate patriotism. None of the subsidy was applied to any distinctively Australian purpose and the squadron was 'not specially Australian any more than it [was] Anglo-Indian or representative of the Straits Settlement, to which it may be called at any time'. He suggested either the construction of naval and coaling stations or a partnership to build a line of 'swift steamers' for the Australian run. The latter could follow the precedent of the arrangement between the British Government and the Cunard Company in 1903. The steamers would be available for use as war transports and the service would also benefit producers, travellers, British merchants, foster the spirit and resources of the Empire, and train crews in seamanship.[21]

Before the Admiralty could reply Deakin delivered another salvo. In a series of despatches carried on into 1906 he accused the Admiralty of breaching the Agreement. The number and type of ships in the squadron failed to comply with the articles, the training of Australian seamen was unsatisfactory. Considerable 'public disquietude' existed regarding the fighting and navigable qualities of the ships. While the Commonwealth had to pay the subsidy promptly the terms had 'from the first been loosely accepted by the Admiralty'.[22]

At the same time Deakin was acutely aware of his own lack of expertise and of the prime necessity of securing Admiralty cooperation if any scheme was to be effective. Dissatisfied with the results of federation, and supplied with conflicting advice, he accepted Clarke's suggestion and in November 1905 formally asked the Committee of Imperial Defence to prepare a 'general scheme of defence of the ports of the Commonwealth framed in light of present and future naval developments as far as can be judged adapted to any attacking forces which may be reasonably expected.' Privately he urged Clarke to use his knowledge of Australian efforts to make defence a national responsibility, 'a justification for speaking out as plainly as possible'.[23]

The Committee's report reached Australia in July 1906. It criticized aspects of Hutton's work on land defence but rejected outright the concept of a 'purely defensive' naval line within the defence line of the imperial fleet. Creswell's proposals were 'based upon an imperfect conception of the requirements of naval strategy'. Worst of all the report denied future development. Should strategy change so as to necessitate the provisions of local vessels then 'it would devolve upon the Admiralty to provide them as part of their general responsibility for the strategical distribution of the naval forces of the Empire'. The 'natural and legitimate aspiration' to furnish a distinctively Australian element to the sea power of the Empire would find satisfactory realization in the Naval Agreement when it had time to take full effect. Deakin hoped the Committee would enlarge upon the dangers of invasion so as to further his plans. Instead it adhered to the orthodox assessment. Hitherto Australian armaments had been based on the assumption that attacks would be limited to a maximum of three or four unarmoured cruisers: 'nothing has occurred in recent naval warfare to give ground for supposing that this is other than a liberal estimate'.[24]

Deakin was bitterly disappointed and told Jebb,

We have just received a Defence Scheme that is not a complete scheme by any means and is only emphatic in its condemnation of any and every plan of allowing Australia a floating defence of any kind in any terms—what can we do with such people ... ?[25]

Clarke attempted to placate him. The Admiralty simply could not justify the great expense involved in the creation of an Australian navy on strategic grounds and 'political' considerations were outside its orbit.[26] But the rebuff cut deep and strengthened Deakin's determination to make a start of some description.

In September 1906 Deakin commended Creswell's destroyer scheme to the House and declared the government's intention to purchase a few vessels as an experiment. At the Imperial Conference of 1907 the First Lord, Tweedmouth, recommended submarines as the most effective weapons for harbour defence.[27] Deakin, back in Melbourne and recovered from his breakdown, incorporated the results of London negotiations into his major speech on defence policy in December. The speech also contained the first ministerial scheme to introduce compulsory military service. Before the new naval and military policies could be implemented Deakin left office.

Hence these and earlier attempts to amend the Agreement ultimately failed. But although Deakin secured neither an alternative use for the subsidy nor vessels for the defence of harbours or coasts, his efforts served another purpose. Deakin made the original despatch of August 1905 and the subsequent correspondence public. Playford, Minister of Defence, leaked confidential information on the dispute with the Admiralty to newspapers. The navalist press, supplied with ammunition, resumed its attacks and from 1906 naval defence became a lively issue.[28] The submarine scheme provoked great controversy. For some it was too little, a false start—Deakin was being used by the British. For others it was too much, a step in the wrong direction— Deakin was being disloyal and weakening links with Britain. Moreover, if the British government and the Admiralty believed that their relationship with present and future Australian governments would be smooth, they were rapidly disillusioned. In short these efforts were an essential part in the campaign to stimulate public interest and to change opinion at home and abroad.

The invitation to the American fleet to call at Australian ports was part of the same process. The visit, arranged by Deakin during the protracted negotiations with Britain, was a great success. Deakin himself set the tone immediately after giving a speech on national defence in Sydney. A South African reporter caught the drama of the occasion. Deakin interrupted the speech of thanks with the news that the United States had accepted the invitation. As he spoke, 'face glowing' and 'trembling with excitement', his voice rose in a 'perfect crescendo of triumph': this was 'one of the greatest moments' in his life. It was a magnificent performance, a brilliant prologue. His audience—the public at large—rose to the occasion. An American correspondent on board the flagship of the Great White Fleet recorded the arrival in Sydney. The reception outdid those of San Francisco and New Zealand. The North and South Heads were 'black with people'. The enthusiasm and sentiment 'inspired a demonstration that simply overwhelmed not only those who received it but those who gave it'. Melbourne turned on a 'mad welcome'.[29]

By the time the Dreadnought crisis shook the antipodes in March 1909 innovation was already under way: Labor's destroyers, the first instalment of Creswell's defensive flotilla, were on order. But disclosures of German naval potential by the British Foreign Secretary,

Sir Edward Grey, and the First Lord of the Admiralty, Reginald McKenna, changed the course of events in Australia. Revelations of German capacity to build capital ships, especially the new Dreadnought type, and forecasts that German Dreadnoughts might soon even outnumber British ones, startled Australians. The 'navy scare' swept aside any remaining doubts about spending heavily on naval defence. Whereas colonial statesmen at the Conferences of 1887 and 1897, and Barton and Forrest in 1902, had resisted British pleas, politicians and electors now demanded that the Commonwealth act. The question became not whether public funds would be devoted to defence, but rather *how* should funds be spent. Should Australia give direct aid in the form of a Dreadnought, should she increase the subsidy, or should the Labor government proceed with its scheme and thereby indirectly aid the Empire?

The *Age*, long the champion of nationalism, sounded for once like its free-trade rivals. Was Australia 'rich enough and loyal enough' to give Britain a Dreadnought? Indeed it was. People 'will be eager to make the gift', and being a gift, 'our attitude on the issue of the naval subsidy would be in no way impaired'. The *Argus* pointed out that the British taxed themselves six times as heavily as Australians for local and imperial defence: 'We offer to shoulder some part of the burden'.[30] At the Sydney Town Hall, Cook and Reid, leader and former leader of the opposition, strongly favoured a Dreadnought. The public meeting resolved that the time had arrived for the Commonwealth to take an 'active share' in the naval defence of the Empire.[31]

C. G. Wade, Premier of New South Wales, telegraphed Fisher that the proper course would be to increase the subsidy, but if the Commonwealth decided on a Dreadnought, New South Wales and Victoria would pay their share.[32] Deakin, initially hesitant, played the opportunist and called for Australia to emulate New Zealand's offer of a battleship. Symon opposed the Dreadnought and supposed that while some people were apparently satisfied with Deakin's sincerity, he himself remembered that Deakin had 'posed' as a patriot and had been averse to continuing the paltry £200 000 a year subsidy.[33] Fisher was inundated with advice. Shire and town councils, mayors and town clerks forwarded pro-Dreadnought resolutions from public meetings. Political Labor Leagues, trade unions, and individual Labor supporters, suspected a jingoistic press plot and urged Fisher to stand firm. One perceptive correspondent warned him to tread warily as assistance to Britain was 'the ticket that will unite Cook and Deakin'.[34]

Pressure mounted. Only a week after Wade termed the offer of a Dreadnought 'inappropriate' he cabled the Secretary of State that New South Wales and Victoria would provide one if the Commonwealth did not.[35]

Fisher stood firm. He reassured the Governor-General that while Australian policy was to provide for its own defence 'in the event of any emergency the resources of the Commonwealth would be cheerfully placed at the disposal of the Mother Country.' At Gympie he reaffirmed Labor's policy. The Naval Agreement would be continued but the Commonwealth would establish its own naval force to operate around Australia's coast. In the event of war or emergency the force would automatically pass to Admiralty control, though Commonwealth approval had to be given to remove the vessels to 'remote' seas. Later Fisher proposed an early conference to consider definite lines of co-operation for the naval defence of the Empire.[36]

Before these intentions could be furthered the Fusion took place. Defence policy, namely

To develop the Australian naval and military forces, with the advice and assistance of the Admiralty and War Office, by means of universal training, commenced in the schools, and a Commonwealth coastal defence, and also to recognise our Imperial responsibilities.[37]

was one of only four policies the parties could agree upon. On the resumption of parliament the Deakin–Cook Party curtly ejected Labor from office. Deakin promptly offered 'the Empire an Australian Dreadnought or such addition to its naval strength as may be determined after consultation'.[38]

The final act was staged at the Imperial Defence Conference of 1909. As a full understanding of the Fusion's order of the fleet unit cannot be had without considering the setting for the Conference, it is first necessary to sketch the background in Britain.

The Dreadnought hysteria and the turn of events in Australia since 1905 had their counterparts in the United Kingdom. The Board of Admiralty reforms implemented from October 1904 by the First Sea Lord, Admiral 'Jackie' Fisher, had been a source of the bitterest naval and political controversy from the outset. The Dreadnought concept, the scrapping policy, the naval reductions of a new Liberal government 'bursting with unfulfilled plans for social reform' provoked unprecedented criticism and agitation. In 1906 the redistribution scheme and the concentration of the fleet in home waters aroused grave charges of sacrificing the security of the Empire: 'The din of protest in the Conservative press and among Conservative politicians was ear-shattering'. The fiery controversy—fanned by many naval and military journalists, retired admirals, Clarke, and high society, and inflamed by the Dreadnought scare—culminated in an official inquiry into the Board in April-July 1909. For the first time in history the Board was put on trial to defend itself against charges levelled by Admiral Lord Charles Beresford, leader of the 'Syndicate of Discontent'.[39]

Thus messages of anxiety and offers of Dreadnoughts from outposts of the Empire came at the very moment when the British government and the Admiralty were in a most vulnerable position. The Liberals, ever sensitive to cries of neglecting imperial affairs, and the Lords Commissioners, their new home fleet termed 'a fraud and a danger to the Empire', reconsidered their attitudes to Commonwealth attempts to establish a navy. In July Captain Collins, now the representative of the Australian government in London, told Deakin it was 'extraordinary how naval opinion has gone round in this country to favour the creation of an Australian Squadron. Almost every Admiral I meet seems to be in favour of it.'[40]

At the Imperial Conference McKenna, First Lord, suggested an Australian fleet of one armoured cruiser, three unarmoured cruisers, six destroyers, three submarines and auxiliaries as 'the smallest fleet unit which will offer both to officers and men a career in life'. The scale and nature of the proposal astonished the Australian delegates. Colonel Foxton believed the Commonwealth should begin with smaller vessels which could, if necessary, seek refuge from larger enemy ships in safe harbour. Captain Creswell, his destroyer flotilla sinking without trace, went down fighting. Provided there was 'no immediate danger', Australia should spend her money on 'the foundations of naval strength—naval schools, dockyards, gun factories, and other establishments'. A navy did not exist 'to provide careers for officers; moreover, there were outside appointments, such as harbour masterships'.[41]

The situation revealed by the secret report of the meeting at the Admiralty was full of irony. Admiralty spokesmen countered Foxton and Creswell with arguments that Australian navalists had themselves used for years on the Australian public. Admiral Fisher described vessels needing the protection of harbours as 'useless for

9 *Launching of the Parramatta, 1910*

Mrs Asquith, wife of the British Prime Minister, launches the first vessel built for the Australian fleet unit: 'First born of the Commonwealth Navy, I name you Parramatta.' She broke a bottle of Australian wine on the bow.

10   Deakin ministry, 1903–4
Standing, left to right: Drake, Playford, Fysh, Chapman. Seated: Turner,
Deakin, Lord Tennyson (Governor-General), Lyne, Forrest.

11   Deakin ministry, 1905–8
Standing, left to right: Ewing, Chapman, Playford, Keating, Groom.
Seated: Lyne, Deakin, Lord Northcote (Governor-General), Isaacs,
Forrest. Inset: Mauger, Hume Cook, Best.

war' and a 'waste of money'. Perhaps no immediate danger existed but 'the crisis would come in four or five years' time'. McKenna pointed out that the Anglo-Japanese Alliance might terminate in 1915:

By that time the Japanese and German fleets would be very formidable, and the position of Australia in the event of war might be one of some danger. . . . Australia was geographically isolated and remote from the centres of British naval strength . . .[42]

Foxton was quickly convinced. The proposals would be well received in Australia because 'people would realise that they were taking a share in their Imperial responsibilities'. He recommended the scheme to Deakin. The Commonwealth and the Empire would get a superior force for less money: the annual cost of the unit was an estimated £720 000 (of which Australia would pay £500 000) compared with the present squadron's £950 000. Creswell's advocacy of destroyers, he confided, 'only fell to pieces at once under the criticisms of Fisher, Ottley, and others'.[43]

Acceptance of the proposal by the Deakin–Cook ministry was a foregone conclusion. Indeed, given the earlier statements and activities of the two leaders it could scarcely have done otherwise. In a sense the Fusion was hoist with its own petard. Debate in parliament centred on whether the scheme should be financed by loans or direct taxation. Within two months parliament approved the proposal and the Naval Loan Bill. On 9 December the government asked the Admiralty to arrange for the construction of the cruisers 'without delay'. It was a good compromise. The Admiralty preserved its blue-water doctrine, Australia got a fleet, the Empire a Dreadnought.

These were the decisive stages in the campaign to alter Australian and British opinion, to introduce universal service, and to found a navy. Credit for the eventual success of the campaigns cannot, of course, be precisely apportioned between the various campaigners. Clearly the evolution of schemes of naval and military defence was the result of the collective efforts of many people and organizations. Nonetheless, prime responsibility for military innovation must surely be attributed to Hughes.

One informed verdict is that Hughes was able 'to impose' his beliefs 'on the Labor Party and on Australia at a most critical period'.[44] Perhaps in the manner of the biographer this slightly exaggerates the influence of the subject, but in the case of Hughes the view seems very near the truth. He was well placed within the party to propagate his opinions and he was quickly regarded as an authority on military affairs. He was the only member to sit on every party committee set up to deal with defence.[45] Outside party rooms as co-founder, joint secretary, and most active member of the National Defence League, he commanded an important public forum for his ideas. The *Call* bears the unmistakable imprint of his personal philosophy. He was a dedicated, forceful man possessing qualities supporters admired and opponents feared. Thus continuity as a member of federal parliament, Labor defence committees, and the league, together with sheer force of character, point to the impact of Hughes. In contrast Deakin regarded universal service as a remote ideal and waited until he sensed an acquiescent electorate before publicly adopting the principle in 1907. In November 1906 he agreed with a deputation from the Victorian division of the National Defence League in 'one important particular', namely that voluntary service must be tried first: 'Financial considerations, as well as others, dictated this course. In all the circumstances, a voluntary essay must precede any attempt at compulsory service.'[46] Compared to the determined Hughes, Deakin (who had the responsibility of office) was an affable Johnny-come-lately.

One thing is certain. When the Labor Party endorsed compulsory training at the Brisbane Conference a scheme of some description based on this became simply a matter of time. Shortly before Deakin's conversion and the Conference Hughes told Jebb: 'We are making headway here with the Universal Military Training: in five years I predict it will be law. Up to 18 years at any rate: if *we* get in again it will be sooner.'[47] In December 1907 when Deakin introduced the first ministerial scheme Jose eulogized Hughes, the *Call*, and the New South Wales division of the league, in which he observed that Labor leaders were prominent. When at last the principle was about to be incorporated in Fusion legislation *The Times* reported a tribute to Hughes by none other than Reid:

'He deserves the public thanks', said Mr Reid with obvious sincerity; 'I used to regard his motion for compulsory training as looking too far ahead, but in the light of what has since been made apparent, I congratulate Mr Hughes on his foresight'.[48]

The situation concerning naval developments is more difficult. Within the limits of practical politics and finance the Commonwealth was free to pursue whatever military policies it chose, but naval innovations involved complex technical and constitutional problems. British ministers and Admiralty Lords, as well as Australian tax-payers and politicians, needed to be convinced that a local navy was desirable. Ultimately the Admiralty itself suggested the actual nature of the scheme—a fleet unit capable of offensive operations in com-bination with the Royal Navy. Until the Conference of 1909, Deakin and Labor thought in terms of vessels for the defence of harbours and coasts—Deakin chiefly on practical grounds of cost, Labor on ideo-logy. The similarity of their ideas may be judged from Deakin's statement on Labor policy at the height of the Dreadnought scare. He congratulated Fisher

upon presenting a well-proportioned scheme for Australian defence. They were familiar with it. The naval portion was nearly on all fours with the report of the committee of naval officers in 1905, and which he presented to Parliament in 1906. It was not a new creation, therefore.[49]

In one sense neither Deakin nor Labor really created the fleet unit because neither planned it. Nonetheless their agitation probably determined the Admiralty's proposal. Without this agitation the British response to the crisis may well have been to increase the sub-sidy from Australia and to remove all limitations on the use of the squadron. Although newspapers like the *Age* and the *Brisbane Courier*, and later Labor, set the early pace, Deakin undoubtedly played the decisive role in conditioning the British government. Labor became the first party to advocate an Australian navy, but Deakin also educated local opinion. His inspired public conflict with the Admiralty and the visit of the American fleet were strokes of a master politician. The former aroused nationalistic sentiments. The latter showed Australians what powerful modern warships really looked like and reminded them of even further inroads into the formerly isolated Pacific with the imminent opening of the Panama Canal. Hence while the Fisher government actually ordered the first ships before the Dreadnought hysteria, it seems only fitting that Deakin had the good fortune to be in office when the Imperial Con-ference took place.

Irrespective of the merits of particular claimants it is evident that a great change had occurred within the decade. During the early years the mark of the good politician was the ability to limit defence spending. In 1903 McGregor boasted of Labor's role at a smoke concert of the Amalgamated Society of Engineers: 'In military expenditure the Federal Parliament had saved Australia more than £160,000, and so far the Federal expenditure had not come within a considerable amount of the lowest estimate given at the Adelaide convention.'[50] The major obstacle to innovation was always the pervading complacency, the near total indifference to defence issues reflected in the great outcries to slash defence estimates. Even as late as July 1907 Fox, editor of the *Bulletin* and the *Call*, could write Jebb,

At present we don't seem to be even making a beginning. The great stumbling block is that we have got into the way of paying practically nothing for defence, and the politicians are frightened to change that condition of affairs, which is delightful to the present interests of the taxpayer.[51]

Yet in 1909 Deakin complained bitterly about Labor's scheme to use the £250 000 for the purchase of destroyers as an attempt *to curry public favour*: 'it was only devised to defeat the bad impression of Fs [Fisher's] barren speech to the A.N.A. when contrasted with our programme.'[52] And in 1910 Fisher could reject Britain's offer to contribute to the cost of the fleet unit and declare that if the Commonwealth navy cost 'ten millions of money . . . the people were prepared to pay the price'.[53]

A number of questions naturally arise. What brought about the fundamental reversal of public and party attitudes? Why did various individuals and organizations really undertake their campaigns? What part did strategical considerations play in the whole process?

Some of the answers have been alluded to in the foregoing narrative. In the first place, much of the interest in defence, especially in Labor ranks, was the product of the proposed new Naval Agreement. The experience of the original Agreement should not be repeated. If the Commonwealth had to contribute £200 000 a year then there should be something tangible of her own to show for the money at the end of ten years. From reactions like this grew the demand for an 'Australian owned and controlled navy'. Secondly, federal union achieved one of its defence aims, economy, but only at the expense of another, efficiency. Men in positions of authority or specialists— ministers or experts like McCay, Neild, Creswell, Clarke—believed that the early years of federation and Hutton's reforms had had adverse effects.

But in the absence of a clear and present need these two factors galvanized neither widespread political nor public opinion. The turning point came with the Russo-Japanese War of 1904–5, and the Dreadnought crisis of 1909 underscored Australia's vulnerability and dispelled lingering doubts.

Australians viewed the war with mixed feelings. On the one hand Japan was Britain's ally in the Pacific; Russia—the gendarme of Europe and a traditional bogeyman—was a potential British enemy. On the other hand, the Russians were superior beings—white Europeans; the Japanese inferior yellow Asiatics. Most newspapers gave Japan a sympathetic press and welcomed both their victory and the extension of the Anglo-Japanese Treaty in 1905.[54] The *Sydney Morning Herald*, for example, praised the Japanese peace terms and applauded the renewal of the Treaty.[55] A few—the *Bulletin*, the *Worker*, *Tocsin*—commended neither. Until 1904 the *Bulletin* dismissed Japan as a military threat but on the outbreak of war it abandoned its traditional isolationism and predicted: 'A victorious Japan would bring within measurable distance the choice to Australia of abandoning its national aspirations or fighting for its very existence.'[56]

Although newspapers differed in their attitudes to Japan they generally agreed on some basic points. Japan had taught Australia a lesson. In a few short years since the Meiji restoration Japan had transformed itself into a modern nation by virtue of a proper sense of priorities and dedication; what Japan had done the new Commonwealth could emulate. The war also demonstrated that the Pacific was no longer a peaceful ocean. Australia had once led a 'dreamy existence far from the shout of strife and the friction of competing nations': the 'booming of the guns at Tsushima' had woken Australians from their 'sense of isolation'. The rise of a new force altered the balance of power in Europe and Asia. Even the *Sydney Morning Herald*, which saw in the defeat of Russia the removal of a menace to peace in the east, admitted:

For ourselves in Australia, it is only necessary to say that we lie open to be profoundly affected by the development of events in the Far East, and by the future shaping of Japanese and Chinese relations.[57]

Australians were 'no longer dwellers in the hollow lotus land, or like waifs marooned on a large isolated island in the South Pacific'.

Founders and supporters of the National Defence League drew similar conclusions. MacLaurin, in his opening presidential address, remarked: 'Once Australia had been looked upon as safe in her isolation, but recent events had shown us that nothing of the kind could give us safety.' McMillan termed federal defence a 'scandal'; Australia must be held for the British people. The *Call* featured Japan as the most likely enemy and in its first edition exhorted readers to

Call to mind the sudden and recent uprising of Japan to the forefront of military and naval power . . . and the danger in store for our half developed continent in the near future, unless we do our utmost to provide betimes an adequate system of defence, becomes apparent.[58]

As might be expected with Fox the editor and Hughes the driving force, much of the *Call*'s propaganda was blatantly racist. Several cartoons by Lionel and Norman Lindsay depicted Asiatics in the worst *Bulletin* tradition.

The war had the greatest and most important impact on members of the Labor Party and associated bodies. It gave the yellow peril a new dimension. In the 1890s exclusion was a technical or constitutional problem, a matter of finding the right 'form of words' to receive the Royal assent. Suddenly the Asian hordes were seen as a *military* threat to the White Australia policy. The success of the Japanese was doubly dangerous for it would inevitably render them as greedy and aggressive as the Huns or Goths. Victory would inevitably lead to diplomatic pressures on British and Australian governments to scrap or modify the policy. Labor distrusted middle-class Liberal ministers, British or Australian. Hence neither government could really be relied upon not to succumb. Moreover, Australia was doubly vulnerable. The navy which protected the continent from invasion was British, not Australian, and the locally controlled military forces were grossly inadequate. Therefore Australia must be self-reliant, acquire her own defensive flotilla, and strengthen land defence by means of compulsory military training for the reasons provided by Hughes. From 1905 these and similar arguments became commonplace. Other achievements besides a White Australia, such as a sense of an increasing share of the fruits of the fortunate country, made the task worthwhile. Watson, for instance, contended that the working class had something to defend in social reforms: 'Universal pensions in age; universal service in youth'. Anstey's taunt at Brisbane that 'property did not belong to the workers' found no support. But undoubtedly the decisive factor which convinced Labor and induced the party to undertake defence innovations was the threat to the White Australia policy.[59]

However, strategical considerations like those arising from the

Russo-Japanese War do not satisfactorily explain the motives of either Hughes or Deakin. Naturally they exploited the conflict and fears of Japan and other potential aggressors. After 1905 Hughes played upon the yellow peril at every pretext. Deakin astounded the *Herald* reporter with the news that Australia was within striking distance of no less than sixteen foreign naval bases and he doubted if the country was prepared to meet 'a dash at our weak spots delivered by two or three fast cruisers'. When, 'trembling with excitement', he announced the visit of the American fleet he declared: 'It means that our existence has been recognised by the other Great White Power of the Pacific, and that England, America, and Australia will be united to withstand yellow aggression.'[60] Probably Hughes was predisposed to believe his own propaganda, which was certainly consistent with other basic attitudes. But there are good grounds for believing that Deakin did not (at least until after the Dreadnought crisis) and that he used 'threats' to security to further policies which he advocated for different reasons.

Hughes began his campaign when Japanese and other undesirables threatened Australia only by infiltration through the education test. In the debate on the Defence Bill in 1901 Hughes mentioned the possibility of enemy bombardment or attack by a marauding expedition but this was not a major argument. In 1903 when he again moved to introduce universal service the notion was conspicuously absent. But Hughes needed no explicit danger to spur him on, for in his Darwinian world only the fittest could survive and the weakest would inevitably go to the wall. Thus the most persistent themes throughout his crusade were the development of his conception of good citizenship, and the moral and physical benefits conferred on the race by discipline. The 'average' Australian was a being 'to whom obedience and discipline [were] most irksome and disagreeable'; these qualities were 'amongst the most essential virtues of a good citizen'. He stressed the effects of physical training upon growing youths. Military drill would counter the growing 'curse of larrikinism' among youths who were becoming 'physical degenerates and a positive danger to society'. The physical decline of the British race was the inevitable result of town life. In Australia, as in England, life in towns was leading to 'degeneracy in the race'. One of the 'very great advantages' of military training would be the beneficial effect upon the 'mental, and moral' tone of youth. Also by adding to the attractions of country life the scheme would counter that 'most lamentable feature of civilized life, namely, the tendency of men to get into the large towns'. It might even reverse the drift and encourage large numbers 'to go back to the soil and get their living there'.[61]

Hughes was a genuine primitivist, a romantic who extolled the virtues of the yeoman and saw in his scheme the corrective for the vices of the townee. In this he was not alone. Charles Pearson, in his influential book *National Life and Character: A Forecast*, expressed similar sentiments. City life was 'neither physically sound nor morally complete'; conscripts gained 'habits of cleanliness, athletic frame, elements of knowledge, implicit obedience, traditions of honour and loyalty'.[62] The evils of town life and the social benefits of physical training were freely propounded by clerics, academics, and politicians in the *Call* and elsewhere. Clearly campaigners touched responsive chords, evidence of which can be found in strange places. *Faulding's Medical and Home Journal* advocated military service for the 'physical advantages to Australian youth . . . to say nothing of the improvement of his morals'.[63]

Furthermore, Hughes was an unashamed authoritarian who positively gloried in the principle of compulsion: 'Socialism lived by compulsion and civilization lived by compulsion.'[64] In a sense he and other middle-aged campaigners appealed to the authoritarianism of adult society. Youth was degenerate, the future for the race bleak. Regeneration could only be brought about by mortification of the flesh, which, as it happened, was someone else's. The *Call* reassured voters with this footnote to its objects:

> It is not intended that anyone who is *now over* the age of 18 shall be liable to *compulsory* training; only those now of 18 and under will come under the *compulsory* provisions, but they will continue subject to same for some subsequent years.[65]

Deakin was conscious of strategical considerations but his interest lacked the immediate urgency that the Russo-Japanese War gave to other campaigners. As Prime Minister he was well aware that experts —Clarke, the Committee of Imperial Defence, and leading Australian naval and military officers—continued to accept the orthodox assessment of possible attacks. In 1906 Clarke advised Deakin that 'all idea of the invasion of Australia can be dismissed'.[66] Creswell chaired the committee of local naval officers assembled to consider the imperial report. The committee specifically agreed that the maximum to be feared was a raid by four unarmoured cruisers with 1000 men.[67] As late as 1907 Creswell told Deakin: 'Up to this, attack from European

powers or European bases only had been considered. . . . Attack from
Extra-European powers must gradually enter more and more into
our defence calculations.'[68] The committee of military officers
which also examined the imperial report placed less faith in the
Royal Navy and was more alarmist. But the top brass, Colonel
Bridges, Chief of Intelligence, whom Deakin most respected, in 1908
still advocated a scheme based upon 'The strategical conditions laid
down in the memorandum of the Committee of Imperial Defence
of May, 1906'.[69] Hunt, nine years permanent head of External Affairs
and Deakin's adviser and confidant, in 1910 discounted suggestions
of possible Japanese aggression made by a London correspondent:

> But do you really think it is likely, if Japan and Great Britain do not
> renew their treaty, that the next step will necessarily be a Japanese-
> German rapprochement in active hostility to Great Britain? . . . I can
> hardly come to the same conclusion. It seems to me to be far more likely
> that Japan will decide, for a time at any rate, to go along quietly. With
> Korea to develop, and possibly Manchuria, I do not think she will be very
> keen on acquiring a part of our empty North.[70]

Deakin, *after* decisions to implement the new naval and military
policies had been taken, asked the Secretary of State if 'any modification in scale of probable attack on Australia, laid down by the
Committee of Imperial Defence in 1906' had become necessary.[71]

Thus Deakin's campaign from 1905 owed little to the war or
strategy. Asked in 1904 if a Japanese victory would endanger Australia he replied that that seemed 'rather a novel view to take':
absorbing territories on the Asian mainland would tax all Japan's
resources 'for a very long time and encourage expansion in a direction entirely opposite to Australia'.[72] In fact his sponsorship of
national defence just as the war ended was largely a coincidence. No
longer Attorney-General but Prime Minister, and with the High
Court established, he was both eager and able to adopt a great new
cause. In October 1905 he sought Clarke's advice 'upon a subject
[defence] which has been occupying my mind very much though
only at intervals as the pressure of other business permitted'.[73]
Because Deakin perceived no clear and present need, unlike others
he was never greatly concerned with the actual type of vessels for a
local navy so long as the Commonwealth made a small start of some
description. Indeed his first suggestion was 'swift steamers', not warships, and in 1908 he told Jebb 'I am not competent to fix the exact
craft to be selected and do not consider that essential'.[74] Publicly as

an astute politician he played upon fears of Australia's insecurity. Privately he was not deeply concerned.

For Deakin the truly vital issues were not directly strategical, but political and constitutional. He discussed the great questions at length with Jebb and Clarke. Imperial organization was the 'towering problem of the time'. Maintenance of the British Empire was the 'greatest national issue now before mankind'. Australia's contribution to the naval defence of the Empire must be 'visibly and concretely Australian in origin, but Imperial in end and value'. The Commonwealth had to recognize its imperial responsibility but the contribution 'must take a popular form in order to fulfil all its purpose'. Outside all naval and military 'lines of defence' came the ideal of the Swiss type of universal service. This should start with cadets who 'by and by . . . will be numerous enough to help us as electors to get universal service legalised'.[75] Large land forces could not be justified on grounds of military necessity, Clarke replied, but 'other considerations present themselves': the 'moral advantage, to which you and I attach importance of training and disciplining a people, which also has the effect of welding them together and promoting the sense of nationhood and the qualities of good citizenship.'[76]

The Commonwealth defence power therefore provided Deakin with a means to two related ends, one external the other internal. First he wanted to make Australia more self-reliant, especially in naval defence; a Commonwealth prepared to reduce Britain's burden and thereby share in the defence of the Empire, would be entitled to a voice in imperial policy. In his major speech in December 1907 he drew the attention of the House to the 'extremely pregnant' statement of the British Prime Minister at the Imperial Conference. Sir Henry Campbell-Bannerman had said 'Control of naval defence and foreign affairs must always go together'. The future implied 'with equal clearness, that when we do take a part in naval defence, we shall be entitled to a share in the direction of foreign affairs'.[77] The idea was not new to Deakin who had something similar in mind twenty years earlier when he said 'Surely in defending themselves they had made a great stride towards what was called Imperial Federation'.[78]

Secondly Deakin, like Clarke, advocated universal service as a means of fostering Australian nationalism and overcoming colonial parochialism. In the same speech he declared his policy of compulsory military training for youths: 'What we aim at is the maximum of good citizenship, with the spirit of patriotism as the chief motive power of a civic defence force.' There were, of course, authoritarian benefits in the manner of Hughes. Drill developed a manly character, discipline, loyalty and was 'an admirable antidote to the temptations of street life'. Rudyard Kipling envisaged military training as the most fascinating of sports and martial ambitions might 'take the place of those sports on which our young people look and speculate every Saturday'. Nor did Deakin neglect Australia's insecurity; Australia was no longer 'outside the area of the world's conflicts'. But the 'motive power' of the scheme was the 'everyday working patriotism, a sense of national unity'. Discipline in the service of the Commonwealth would be 'a potent factor in fostering that national spirit'.[79] In 1910 Fisher explained to South Africans that Australia had undertaken naval and military innovations 'for her defence and for the inculcation of national sentiment'.[80]

Hence the acquisition of a navy and the implementation of compulsory military service were for Deakin essential steps in the evolution from colony to nation within the British Empire. As such the policies were expressions of, and a means to, the enhanced status of the Commonwealth and nationhood. In 1907 Ewing told Bridges,

The Scheme for the Defence of Australia must be more in keeping with the wealth of the Commonwealth and the magnitude of its resources, and cannot be limited to the consideration of how best to defeat an expedition such as that postulated [the four unarmoured cruisers with 1000 men].[81]

But personal ambitions and idiosyncrasies cannot be ignored. The contrast between the Commonwealth Deakin, apparently concerned about the vulnerability of coastal trade, and the Victorian Deakin, apparently unconcerned at the first Colonial Conference, could not have been sharper. Had he remained in State politics he probably would have passionately resisted every attempt at federal aggrandizement. But rather as Cockburn anticipated in 1891, the natural tendency of all ministers was 'to augment their own importance and to act up to the full extent of their authority'.[82] Furthermore, if any single event ensured that Deakin would be preoccupied with naval defence it was the insensitive outright denial of all Australian naval aspirations by the Admiralty in the report of the Imperial Defence Committee. This was a challenge Deakin could not resist and it enabled him to partake in a pastime he relished and for which he was both experienced and endowed—taking on British officialdom.

The campaigners, whatever their motives, shared and appealed to a basic common belief. In stressing the need for self-reliance, in asserting their independence, they were demonstrating their British-ness. Deakin claimed that 'Those who say that we should sit still are not British, and are not worthy of the name of Briton. You cannot be content to expect defence at any other hands than your own.'[83] Fox believed the first duty of Australia was to defend herself, and the second to help defend India for the Empire:

Really, a very good working arrangement of that sort could be come to with a true conception of Imperialism—Australia making up for poor-ness in naval defence (which must exist for a long time yet) by keeping an organisation for an expeditionary force to India.[84]

Conscription was not an Anglo-Saxon characteristic, but then com-pulsory service on the Swiss model was not conscription. In this instance the Empire's sturdy sons should show old Mother England the way as they had with social legislation. For naval defence the campaigners extolled the Royal Navy, not the Swiss. The syllogism went: the British were a seafaring race; Australians were British; therefore Australians were seafarers—all they lacked were the ships. Creswell, on the Commonwealth's foundation day, urged Australia to follow Britain's example and concentrate on naval supremacy:

By training and organising sea defences we shall relieve the motherland of some anxiety on our own behalf and . . . by training a young navy we shall develop the arm of the greatest service to the motherland. . . . It is suited to the character of the Anglo-Saxon race before all other races.[85]

Fisher, Prime Minister in March 1909, announced that Labor's naval plan would 'give the help to the mother country that she has the right to expect from a wealthy and prosperous son.'[86] Pearce, Minister of Defence in November 1910, greeted the first Australian warships at Fremantle: there was no surer guarantee for attaining the high ideals of humanity than the

Union Jack, the symbol of the British Empire. . . . it would be a calamity to the world . . . if the Union Jack were humiliated by any foreign Power. They therefore had to look further afield than the mere defence of Australia and be prepared to defend that flag and all that it represented. . . . The British fleet must be one, and under the same control.[87]

The campaign and its results had repercussions far beyond the purely strategic. The apparent necessity for a vastly increased expenditure on defence became a standard argument in the battles over surplus revenue and the future Commonwealth-State financial relationship on the expiry of the Braddon clause. The use of the defence power ensured that the Commonwealth would try to retain the surplus and also that the States would fare less well under any new financial arrangement. In March 1908 a memorandum on the financial question circulated among cabinet contrasted the expected expenditure of the federal government at the time of federating with its increasing requirements and declared,

the situation is now changed. The Commonwealth is an expanding power. She requires very much more revenue than appears to have been anticipated by those who framed the Constitution. The air is vocal with schemes calling for Commonwealth action. . . . The monetary needs of the Commonwealth are great, and they are likely to be greater still.[88]

Foremost demanded of the Commonwealth was 'A complete system of Naval and Military Defence'.

The new situation disturbed the balance between the Commonwealth and the States in a second manner, tilting it again in favour of the central government. As the implications of the Russo-Japanese War sank in, as Australian isolation from Europe became more a liability than an asset, and as people realized that Britannia ruled the home waves (and perhaps not for ever) attention focused on the federal government. In their great hour of need State Premiers, politicians of all parties, and private citizens turned to the Commonwealth because it alone possessed the exclusive defence power. Just as the portfolio acquired an enhanced status under changed circumstances (Cook, joint leader of the Fusion with Deakin, became Minister of Defence), so too defence issues conferred a prestige and prominence on the Commonwealth that it had not enjoyed since the first year of federation with the White Australia policy. The 'special correspondent' of *The Times* saw the implications clearly in 1908. It was not apparently realized by many who contributed opinions on defence that 'considerations of economy or of strategy are really irrelevant to the main issue, which is one of morality and sentiment'. The real issue was the question of greater or smaller federal powers, the division between 'the modern national and the older colonial sentiment'.[89]

6

THE DEVELOPMENT OF
SOCIAL POLICIES IN THE COMMONWEALTH

In the first decade of federation successive federal governments enacted a substantial body of radical legislation in the field of social-industrial relations. Individually some of the statutes were similar to measures in existence in the United States, Germany, New Zealand, and several Australian States. Collectively, however, the legislation—together with payment of members and full adult suffrage—gave the young Commonwealth the reputation of being a national laboratory for social experimentation.

The promise of progressive measures came in Barton's Maitland speech in January 1901: Kingston was to prepare an early Conciliation and Arbitration Bill, federal legislation was to embrace a scheme for old-age pensions as soon as the financial position was clear. Fulfilment of the promises took considerable time and caused serious political crises. The process began inauspiciously in the second session of the first parliament after members had disposed of the tariff. In July 1903 Deakin introduced a Conciliation and Arbitration Bill because Kingston, who had fathered the Bill, had already left the ministry. Kingston resigned his portfolio of Trade and Customs because cabinet refused to extend the scope of the measure to all seamen engaged in the coastal trade. The principle of the Bill met with general approval, but its details gave rise to further conflict in committee. In September Fisher narrowly failed to bring Commonwealth and State public servants under its provisions. McDonald, another Queensland Labor member, succeeded in including State railway workers. Barton abandoned the Bill.[1]

Deakin's reconstructed ministry revived the Bill in the first session of the second parliament. In April 1904 Fisher's motion extended the Bill to State public servants. Deakin resigned and Labor found itself in office. Watson pushed the measure along until an amendment by J. W. McCay, a Protectionist, abruptly halted its progress. The amendment altered the government's clause to provide preference to unionists by requiring the prior approval of the majority of workers in the particular industry before the Arbitration Court could award preference. In August Watson tried to recommit the amended clause, but the House carried McCay's motion against recommittal. The Watson ministry resigned. Its successor, the Reid–McLean coalition, secured the passage of a compromise Commonwealth Conciliation and Arbitration Act in December.[2] In the fullness of time the measure had profound effects on social, economic, and political structures. It encouraged unions to develop on a national scale, influenced wage rates and hours, and caused periodical political crises through attempts to alter the system.

Barton's second promise for social legislation provoked less political turmoil but took longer to fulfil. A national system of old-age pensions, unlike an Arbitration Court, would necessarily involve the Commonwealth in massive expenditure. The central government had to manage on its quarter share of customs and excise duties for a minimum of ten years, unless it resorted to direct taxation. Clearly Barton had no such intention (he was publicly committed on this). Reid attacked the government's sincerity: members were not 'a collection of simple children'; the ministry's talk of a Commonwealth scheme was a 'monstrous absurdity'. Barton, in effect, feebly concurred: 'We cannot bring in an Old age Pensions Bill under the bookkeeping clauses of the Constitution.' O'Malley prophesied: 'The Government may be in heaven by that time.'[3]

More immediately, a Bill did not embrace a pension scheme until after Kingston had died and Barton and O'Connor had been elevated to the High Court. On 2 June 1908 Deakin introduced a Bill to provide invalid and old-age pensions. The next day Groom, Attorney-General, moved the second reading. By 4 June the measure had passed through all stages and it received the assent on 10 June. The Act incorporated recommendations of the Royal Commission of 1905–6 and features of existing schemes in Australian States and New Zealand.[4] The old-age pension provisions, which became effective on 1 July 1909, displaced similar schemes in Victoria, New South Wales, and Queensland, and provided pension rights to the inhabitants of South Australia, Tasmania, and Western Australia. The invalid pensions, which came into force on 5 December 1910, superseded legislation in New South Wales.

The Constitution conferred clear authority for Commonwealth legislation on arbitration and pensions. But while aged Australians awaited their pensions, federal parliament enacted statutes with provisions of doubtful validity. These measures, 'New Protection', attempted to extend benefits that 'Old Protection' had conferred on producers to workers in protected industries and to consumers at large.

New Protection evolved in stages. The Sugar Bounty Act 1905, as we have seen, made the award of the bounty to sugar growers conditional upon the recipients paying standard wage rates to their white labourers. The Trade Marks Act 1905 (part of an Australia-wide system on industrial property) contained elements of protection for employees. Part VII of the Act, 'Workers' Trade Marks', provided for the marking of goods made in establishments employing members of the trade unions that registered the labels:[5] part VIII, 'Commonwealth Trade Mark' enabled parliament to certify goods manufactured under 'fair and reasonable' conditions. A series of statutes offered direct incentives to Australian producers, safeguarded them against foreign 'dumping', and protected workers and consumers by suppressing local monopolies. The Australian Industries Preservation Act 1906 prohibited injurious combinations in restraint of trade in foreign and interstate commerce, and among trading or financial corporations formed in Australia. It also prohibited the dumping of foreign goods on the home market. The Bounties Act 1907 followed precedents set by the Sugar Bounty Acts, and gave bounties on 'white labour' and New Protection conditions to growers and processors of a wide range of agricultural products. The Manufacturers Encouragement Act 1908 awarded bounties on the production of iron, steel, and certain goods.

But the full New Protection, legislation directly involving the tariff and industrial conditions, came during the course of the second and third parliaments in the period of Deakin's second ministry. The Customs Tariff Act 1906 imposed high tariff duties on imported stripper-harvesters. But it empowered the Governor-General to reduce the duties if machines manufactured in Australia were sold at prices above those set out in the schedule of the Act. The complementary Excise Tariff (Agricultural Machinery) Act[6] imposed countervailing excise duties on agricultural machinery protected by the tariff. It enabled the remission of excise to manufacturers operating under approved awards or registered agreements. The Excise Tariff (Spirits) Act placed duties on spirits, and gave the Governor-

General power to impose additional duties on distillers who failed to observe fair labour standards. In 1908 the first extensive revision of the federal tariff established full-scale protection, but before Lyne, Minister of Trade and Customs, could incorporate the new technique into the complementary Excise Act, the High Court declared the 1906 attempt unconstitutional.

Special problems have confronted historians trying to account for this radical legislation. The protection of native industries from foreign competition by the erection of high tariff walls was, of course, common practice in Australia and other countries. But the principle of extending benefits to workers and consumers by direct government intervention was more novel. New Protection, invalid and old-age pensions, and compulsory conciliation and arbitration, attempted in various ways to assist worker organizations and underprivileged sectors of the community. But the Federal Labor Party, which drew its main support from the new beneficiaries of government action, held office but briefly during the period when parliament placed the progressive legislation on the statute books. Until the election of 1910 Labor was either a minor party, or merely one of three elevens. Liberal-Protectionists formed only minority governments in the first three parliaments, while in the productive era from the end of 1906 to 1909 (and Fusion) Deakin led a minority party.

Possible explanations fall into two broad categories. First, progressive legislation of this general character on a nation-wide basis was to be expected from the national parliament because the federation movement which created the Commonwealth was a progressive force. The thesis which will be considered is that federation was promoted by radical liberals, opposed by parochial conservatives, and approved by nationalistic Labor (and/or its followers) who expected to influence the policies of progressive Liberal governments. Secondly, the origin of the legislation was independent of the forces making for federation as such: rather, the origin is explained chiefly in terms of the strategy of the Labor Party in exploiting its balance of power by extracting concessions in return for its support. In this sense Labor held the initiative, and hence this interpretation neatly dovetails into the complementary one which accounts for social welfare legislation over the whole span of federation. Labor, though out of office for most of the period, has been the 'party of movement' or initiative: non-Labor or anti-Labor parties have generally been the 'parties of resistance'.[7] Both categories of explanation (which need not be mutually exclusive) necessarily raise important questions concerning the nature of the federation movement, the political process, and Australian society at the turn of the century.

Brian Fitzpatrick depicted the federation movement as politically progressive. In dealing with socio-economic factors making for federation he noted that individual colonial governments and intercolonial employer organizations had ruthlessly suppressed the great strikes of the early 1890s. Labour troubles, which had the incidental consequences of laying the foundations of an Australian Labor Party, might therefore have strengthened pro-federation forces. The 'liberal and progressive personages, who, in fact . . . would control the political machinery of the Commonwealth until 1913' were the 'prime advocates' of federal union. Hence,

If federation came, such people might be expected to control the disposition of the coercive forces of organized society, and the states might discard their strike-breaking rôle. Surely Labour politics could so influence a Liberal Commonwealth leadership as to prevent official suppression of strikes by force, and would not that be a great gain? It may have been with some such notion in mind that Labour opinion generally was not unfavourable to federation.[8]

Labor's apparent indifference to practical schemes was really a matter of tactics: federation was not a cause 'in which "support in return for concessions"' could readily be brought to bear in the colonial parliament.

Vere Gordon Childe and Russel Ward provide indirect support for this conception of the nature of the federation movement. Childe observed that 'nationalistic sentiment' focused itself on the banner of the Labor Party partly because the labour movement had long been continental in scope and had not been bounded in outlook by arbitrary divisions into States. Trade unions overleapt colonial boundaries and artificial barriers and Labor parties acquired 'a broad Australian outlook which made them ardent supporters of Federation, while the old middle-class parties, having a vested interest in the State Governments, were narrow "State-righters"'. Labor, for economic reasons, also 'desired to encourage Australian industry which would provide increased employment'.[9] Ward stressed the clear 'rising tide of nationalist sentiment' which increasingly spilt over into the federation movement. It was less clear, 'but probably equally true, that federation sentiment was strongest among working-class and middle-of-the-road citizens and weakest among conservatives'. Though Labor political leaders themselves were generally at best lukewarm towards union, the lead came from liberal middle-class politicians such as Parkes, Deakin, and Kingston.[10]

Some corroborative evidence—though not much (and Fitzpatrick, Childe, Ward, provide none)—can be found in contemporary sources. In 1891 the first Labor platform in New South Wales included 'the federation of the Australian Colonies on a National as opposed to an imperial basis'.[11] In 1895 D. M. Charleston, a direct Labor representative in the South Australian Legislative Council, told fellow delegates at the inaugural meeting of the Federation League what he and 'labouring classes' thought of federation:

The question was chiefly viewed from the commercial and sentimental aspects, but the greater were the commercial. From the standpoint of economy nothing but good could result. (Applause). Anything that would increase wealth production and decrease the discomforts attending labour should be hailed with satisfaction. Whilst admitting that federation under present industrial systems was impotent to produce any great change among the masses, he saw in federation a growth capable of such expansion as would ultimately conquer and destroy the anarchy now in our industrial and social life—(applause)—and promote individual and collective prosperity.[12]

Watson caused the appointment of a committee to draft a federation scheme at the Annual Conference in 1896. In March of that year the *Australian Workman* asserted that pending federation 'the development of the giant resources of the interior by the aid of water conservation and irrigation must wait'; the union of Australia would 'mark the first great step in our national development'.[13] In June 1899 Kingston recommended the Constitution to Kirwan as 'not only a magnificent instrument of democratic government . . . but also as an example on the basis of which provincial Constitutions must some day be fashioned and reformed'.[14] Victor S. Clark, an American scholar commissioned by the United States government, visited Australia in 1903–4 and reported that the Labor Party

had consistently supported federation, so they were sympathetically disposed towards the new government. Meantime the measures chiefly sought by the working people could be most effectively secured through a central government. This had been sufficiently foreseen to determine the federal policy of their leaders.[15]

Other historians and contemporary commentators have observed the identical phenomena and drawn opposite conclusions. According to H. V. Evatt, opponents of Labor wanted federation because they calculated that under a conservative Constitution the political power of workers concentrated in New South Wales 'would be diluted and weakened over the larger electoral field of Australia where the voting power of New South Wales could be counterbalanced by industrially backward States'. The motive of 'many supporters of Federation . . . was to "dish" the Labour Party'. Cardinal Moran had regarded federation 'as the only means of preventing one or other of the colonies from jumping over to extreme Socialism'. In 1897 Bruce Smith, a reactionary free-trader, had said of Labor: 'This growth upon our body politic can now be removed for all time by the proposed union of the colonies.' (Evatt cited George Black, Labor politician and historian, for these statements of Moran and Smith.)[16]

Crisp, in the best-argued case for the essentially conservative nature of the federation movement, also quoted Moran and Smith (again from Black). Crisp analysed the composition of the Federal Conventions and remarked that for the most part 'the big men of the established political and economic order, the men of property . . . moulded the federal Constitution Bill'. The 1890–1 strikes, the rise of Labor, engendered 'fear of the "masses" in the minds of many Australian men of property which inclined them to take the plunge into the federal experiment'. Conservatives did not explicitly enshrine 'rights of property' in the Constitution, but as they shaped its provisions they were 'undoubtedly guided by their conservative philosophies'. They intended the national government to accommodate further economic and social developments 'along essentially established and accepted lines'. The great majority of federal leaders perceived union as 'an expedient provision of extended governmental machinery and in no sense as a facilitation of major social change, much less of social revolution'. Labor politicians such as Black opposed the 1891 Draft Bill partly because they knew that some of the men of property openly sought federation as a measure to counter their growing power. J. A. McPherson, South Australian Labor leader, in 1897 termed federation a 'check on the democratic movement. The masses think it is an attempt to get advantages for the classes'. The truth was that Labor, though mildly interested in federation (but not at any price) was 'more deeply concerned with social reform than with federation, and was not altogether free of confusions about the interconnection of the two'.[17]

More evidence exists to support the view that some radicals suspected federation as a conservative plot to 'dish' Labor than exists to
sustain the notion that they perceived it as a progressive scheme to
advance social reforms. In 1891 H. Valentine Haynes, in a radical
pamphlet (quoted by Crisp), saw a *sinister* connection between the
great strikes and the advent of the federation movement. Haynes
remarked on the coincidence of the Federal Convention having been
called together immediately after the labour troubles. Parkes had
declared the principal object as the creation of a federal army. Federal
troops would be used to suppress workers. Federation was 'a design
on the part of the rich, for the oppression of the poor: a mighty
engine in the hands of employers for the coercion of labour'.[18]
Holman described the federal proposition as 'a distinctly restrictive
and delaying force against reform'. Another labourite believed that
conservatives 'who saw themselves played out' wanted to create a
new parliament of their own to block colonial radicalism. In 1899
the Brisbane *Worker* suspected a conspiracy of conservatives and
capitalists. The new Constitution ensured that 'forward' States would
be hampered in their progressive tendencies by the backward. This
explained why subjects such as 'arbitration and conciliation, old age
pensions, which are really matters of domestic concern, have been
removed from the control of the more advanced colonies'. Monopoly
capitalism threatened economic reforms and local Labor with its
'political hand upon the throat of Capital', would inevitably lose
influence.[19]

But suspicion of a conservative scheme is not the same thing as
there being one. Significantly, despite the existence of a vast quantity
of federation literature, apparently the only available evidence of a
deliberate intention of the kind is the statements by two unsuccessful
candidates—Moran and Smith—for the second Convention. Neither
received publicity at the time and the two papers which printed
Smith's private advertisement—the *Sydney Morning Herald* (a supporter of federation) and the *Daily Telegraph* (an opponent)—both
reviewed his manifesto but ignored the particular remark.[20]
Curiously Black himself did not mention either statement in numerous early editions of his history.[21]

Perhaps then members of the labour movement and others can be
excused their confusion about the relationship between federation
and social reform when perceptive writers such as Fitzpatrick and
Crisp (with the advantages of hindsight) reach diametrically opposite conclusions on the same question. Confusion surely existed, and

exists, because there was no direct or deliberate connection for be-wildered contemporaries to discern. The federation movement was neither a subtle radical scheme nor a Machiavellian conservative plot. The convening of the first Convention in March 1891 shortly after the outbreak of the great strikes in August 1890 was precisely what Haynes derided—a coincidence. The Convention resulted from the Federal Conference of February 1890 which *preceded* the labour troubles. Clearly the origin of the federation movement in 1889–90 had nothing to do with the strike or the advent of the Labor Party as these came *after* the opening moves had been made. The strikes proved a disaster for the unions and a triumph for the employers and the colonial governments which backed them. Why then should the 'big men of the established political and economic order' disturb a *status quo* (which had served them so admirably) and plunge into the federal experiment? Fledgling Labor parties might well have had good reason to promote the new federation movement, but initially they were generally indifferent to it. As the *Australian Workman* remarked when Watson raised the issue in 1896:

In the past the Labor Party have consistently ignored the great national movement towards a United Australia. . . . to their shame be it said, the Labor Party have materially assisted in retarding progress. A silly idea that the democracy of Australia cannot be trusted . . . has been respon-sible for this unprogressive attitude.[22]

This new-found interest rapidly evaporated in 1897 after the demo-crats of south-eastern Australia failed to elect Labor candidates to the second Convention. The *Workman* then argued that federal par-liament should possess only those powers that the colonies 'may be pleased to entrust to it from time to time. . . . It should be the work of the separate States to raise revenue, and the Federal Government should depend upon them for its income'.[23]

Therefore, while Australia-minded Labor parties endorsed federa-tion in the abstract, none officially supported the practical scheme which brought about the Commonwealth. On the contrary, Labor actually led the anti-Billite forces in New South Wales and South Australia, and in Victoria and Queensland members were sharply divided. At the same time—and to compound the confusion—con-servatives entrenched in their Upper Houses in New South Wales and Western Australia also vigorously opposed the Constitution Bill, while their counterparts in Victoria ardently supported it. In New South Wales (where Labor was strongest), the Legislative Council disapproved of federation and in 1899 Reid found it necessary to 'swamp' the chamber.[24] In Victoria (where Labor was relatively weak) the Legislative Council approved of federation. The emphasis placed on the 'threat' posed by the new Labor parties to the old-established parties overstresses the strength and influence of Labor in the 1890s. Then, if not later, they were comparatively minor third parties more to be courted than thwarted. The term 'Labor Party' does not appear to have been even used at the Federal Conventions (though 'socialism' and 'socialistic' were on rare occasions). Politicians of the same persuasion fought on opposing sides on the issue of federal union under the Bill because the federation movement was basically apolitical, being neither progressive nor regressive.

Nonetheless, in terms of *expectations* of and *potential* for social-industrial reform, the weight of evidence strongly supports Crisp, not Fitzpatrick. Progressive liberals such as Deakin and Kingston were leading advocates of federation, but there can be no doubt that they were far outnumbered by the Symons, Bakers, and other conservative men of property. Labor men would have needed quite extraordinary prescience to have expected that 'liberal and progressive personages' would control the political machinery of the Commonwealth. The fact is that the majority had no such foresight or expectations, and nor did they expect their own party to be strongly represented in the federal sphere. According to *Tocsin*, the few radicals such as Deakin and Kingston were genuine, but regrettably they were 'careless of the future' and could not see 'the trap towards which they are leading their generation, and certainly the next'. The Constitution itself provided few outlets for social reform and—in the unlikely event of the Commonwealth Parliament being so inclined—those it had would be ineffective. The central government had authority to legislate on old-age pensions but no means. It possessed a bounty power, but free-traders would prevent its exercise. It had no power to impose 'decent' factory conditions.[25]

Clearly the radically oriented social-industrial legislation of the first decade cannot be explained as the deliberate or inevitable outcome of a progressively inspired federation movement.

Historians have commonly attributed much of the legislative output of the new federal machine, especially its socio-economic products, to the tactics of the Federal Labor Party in exploiting its balance of power. Labor adopted the policy of 'support in return for concessions' proven by the party in New South Wales during the

1890s. Black announced the now famous tactics in 1891. Labor held the 'only sensible position' in supporting neither free trade nor protection:

The motto of the labour party in this House is, 'Support in return for concessions'. If you give us concessions, then our votes will circulate on the Government benches, and if you do not give us concessions then we shall withdraw our votes from circulation there. That is the position we hold. . . . We have not come into this House to support governments or oppositions. We have come into this House to make and unmake social conditions . . .[26]

In 1930 Hancock quoted Black and observed that the 'period of profitable bargaining' in the Commonwealth ended in 1908. At the turn of the century Labor was 'united on everything except the fiscal issue', and though it came to outnumber Deakin it was 'content that Liberalism should do its work'. In the *Cambridge History of the British Empire* Hancock returned to the theme and elaborated. The Federal Labor Party was the smallest of three returned at the election of 1901, but it 'possessed the organisation and the programme most likely to turn this situation to its advantage'. Ten years' experience in New South Wales had indicated the most effective tactics for such a situation. Labor was divided on the fiscal issue but on all other important questions it voted as one body: 'Thus it was able to offer "support in return for concessions", and to exact from unstable ministries the measures which it had at heart.' From May 1905 to December 1908 the Labor and Protectionist parties 'collaborated' in the task of developing the 'economic and social forms in which Australian nationalism made itself determinate'. It would be misleading to say that one dominated the other, that Deakin was the instrument of Watson or Watson of Deakin. However, Labor 'influence' was particularly apparent in industrial legislation. The Trade Marks Act included the 'union label' clause but in return for concessions of this kind Deakin might claim the triumph of converting Labor to his own special policy of protection. If Deakin could convince Labor members that the benefits of protection could be extended to workers, free trade would be less attractive. Deakin elaborated New Protection to supply this 'special guarantee'.[27] In 1933 Maurice Blackburn, a prominent Labor politician, stressed the role of pledge, platform, and caucus in fashioning a disciplined Labor Party into the 'real rulers' of New South Wales in the 1890s. The Federal Labor Party followed

suit, and hence its control of the Commonwealth in the first decade
of federation was 'undisturbed' except for short intervals.[28]

Later generations of politicians and historians have generally
endorsed the interpretation of their mentors. The Australian Labor
Party, Evatt believed, confounded its adversaries by employing
the balance-of-power technique pioneered in New South Wales.
A. A. Calwell asserted that Labor 'whether in or out of office' had
been the 'basic dynamic force' in politics since federation. Fitzhardinge held that this 'compact and disciplined' body played a part
out of proportion to its numerical strength: caucus made decisions
and members were pledged to obey. Social questions divided the
ranks of both traditional parties: this brought Labor to the front 'for
this was the division for which they were organised'. Crisp argued
that other parties constantly solicited, consulted, and cajoled Labor
for its approval of measures, connivance in strategy, support in office.
The initiative was not one-sided: Labor had a 'large and growing
programme and was willing to "auction" its support in return for
concessions' on priorities and details in legislation. The party's votes
were for sale—'payment had to be in Labour currency'. Partridge
noted that Labor held, and exploited, its balance in the early years of
federation. To regard Labor as the only initiating force was an 'over-
simplification': nonetheless, it was true that Labor had 'most influenced the course of social legislation' in the Commonwealth. Greenwood described Labor entering federal parliament in 1901 as a
compact group committed to a 'definite platform of social reform'.
Labor members, heartened by the colonial example and impressed
with the prospect of continuous concessions, pursued the successful
bargaining tactics with the broadly sympathetic and like-minded
Deakinite liberals.[29]

Labor and non-Labor contemporaries expressed this familiar interpretation more forcibly. In 1906 Clark (the American scholar)
believed that the achievements of Labor were so great that it was
'gradually driving its opponents into a single organisation'. Hitherto
'conservative' ministers had endorsed Labor's legislation to retain
office. Federal voters could say 'a direct yes, but not a direct no' to
Labor's positive programme 'because however they voted, they put in
power a party that could carry out its [own] policy only by making
concessions to the workingmen in parliament.'[30] In 1909 W. G. Spence
proclaimed the success of the strategy: until recently Labor had held
the balance and had therefore 'more or less directly controlled legis-

lation'. Committees would discuss important Bills, and, if caucus approved, proposed amendments would be taken to the minister in charge: 'Many would be accepted, others would be left to the House to decide.' New Protection was a proposal which 'entirely originated with the Labor Party'.[31] In the same year Senator A. St Ledger, a virulent Anti-Socialist, gave a similar assessment.

The great bulk of Australian legislation since 1901 must be studied closely and directly in its relation to the position of political parties and the balance of power held by the Socialists. The New Protection is the result of a new form of auction. As a result of the Commonwealth elections of 1906 the Socialist offered to subsidise the Victorian and New South Wales tariff prohibitionists by political support in return for a Commonwealth Law controlling wages in industries affected by the Tariff. . . . This was the price of the Socialist support to Mr. Deakin during his second term of office.[32]

H. G. Turner, a biased conservative, at the end of the decade stressed that only Labor had 'the power, the organisation, and, above all, the courage to state their position in plain language': parliament had experienced the 'thrall of Labor domination, under which the so-called Liberal Party was alone permitted to exist'.[33]

Perhaps the major points, which (despite qualifications and inconsistencies) together make up a persistent and persuasive theme, may now be summarized. Labor politicians believed that support in return for concessions had operated effectively in New South Wales: the Federal Labor Party openly adopted the successful tactics. Labor, armed with the weapons of caucus, platform, and pledge, entered the new parliament as a disciplined phalanx dedicated to fighting social injustice with federal legislation. Conversely, Free-Traders and Protectionists were united only on their respective attitudes to tariff questions and both—especially the Protectionists—were sharply divided on social issues. Therefore, with Labor holding and exploiting its balance, progressive social measures came to the fore. In short, the Federal Labor Party fairly dominated early Commonwealth parliaments and Liberal-Protectionist governments, extracted concessions, and exerted a great initiative and creative influence on the course of legislation in the social-industrial field.

Most of these points are undoubtedly valid, but one at least is not. Labor did not enter federal parliament united on everything except the fiscal issue. On the contrary, the first Commonwealth Labor Conference agreed on a platform of a mere four planks. The initial federal platform embraced only adult franchise, exclusion of coloured and other undesirable races, old-age pensions, and amendment of the Constitution to provide for the 'initiative' and national referendum. In May 1901 federal caucus expanded the platform to five planks by adding a citizen army and compulsory arbitration, and dropping the amendment plank because members from small States opposed the national referendum.[34] Still, Labor did openly declare its tactics of support in return for concessions. McGregor, Labor leader in the Senate, outlined party policy in order to give the government 'an idea of the support which they may expect and the Opposition an idea of the magnitude of the bait they can offer in the future'. Senator Higgs, in a later debate, explained Labor's position:

> We find ourselves in a minority. We have a certain programme. We say to the two great parties here—'We are anxious to get the best we can. Give us such reforms as we believe will be for the benefit of the people, and we will support you so long as you try to do something for the people of the Commonwealth.'[35]

The party sat on the cross benches in each House, and gave a general support to Liberal-Protectionist ministries until Fisher took office in November 1908. Compared to other *contemporary* parties, Labor was highly organized, especially on an extra-parliamentary basis. Their organization was so perfect, Kirwan told Groom after his defeat in Western Australia in 1903, that Labor there 'could return a lamp post if they liked against any non-Labor man in the Commonwealth'.[36] Dedicated opponents (such as St Ledger and Turner) feared this new phenomenon and strongly urged other parties to adopt similar techniques in order to survive.

Nevertheless, the conclusion drawn from these valid points remains dubious. Few actual examples are given of concessions successfully extorted, except by contemporaries whose claims are of questionable value. On the one hand, Labor politicians such as Black and Spence had every reason to magnify the success of their tactics: the parliamentary wing was frequently attacked by the industrial wing for achieving little. Some of the claims made by Spence take on a note of special pleading. For instance, he cited Deakin's 1905 programme 'which itself was the outcome of Mr. Watson's interview' with Deakin a few days earlier, as evident of Labor influence on the business of parliament. In fact the programme was almost identical to the one Deakin gave in his policy speech at Ballarat in October 1903.[37] On the other hand, conservatives such as St Ledger and H. G. Turner emphasized Labor domination not to praise Labor and give it due credit, but rather to damn Deakin and deny him credit.

Therefore, we will now consider the bargaining position which allegedly enabled Labor to exert influence and extract concessions, before turning to the evolution of the specific socio-economic policies.

The bargaining strength of Labor as a third party depended partly on its usefulness to the other two parties (assuming for the moment that Labor could have given its support to Free Trade). The party was, of course, in a position to refuse to keep a particular ministry in office. But on the particular issues which the Protectionist and Free Trade parties *most* wanted their support—the fiscal ones—Labor was unable to command its own votes. Hancock's statement that at the beginning of the century Labor was 'content' to treat the fiscal issue as a matter for individual judgement is misleading. Labor members were less content than divided on the tariff question, and any attempt to have forced a decision would have irrevocably split the party. Hence the fiscal issue was specifically exempt from the federal pledge, which in any case only bound members to decisions on items in the platform.[38] Ironically, caucus did take action once by opposing, not supporting, duties proposed by the Barton ministry: in November 1901 Labor caused some seventeen items to be reduced, or freed from duties. Again, the party could not guarantee immunity to the candidates of the other parties in the elections. In June 1904 the Queensland Central Political Executive informed federal caucus that they refused to be bound by any agreement to aid in the elections liberals who had supported the Watson government. In September the Central Executive of the Victorian Political Labor Council refused to promise immunity to any candidate not pledged to its own federal platform.[39] In June 1906 federal caucus approved immunity to Higgins, but a Labor candidate in Victoria still opposed Higgins, the most progressive liberal in federal parliament, a radical who had been their own Attorney-General. Deakin, with this incident in mind, pointed out to Watson that facts were 'dead against' his theory that Protectionists had only to adopt radical planks to discourage Labor opposition: 'How can you expect men to take part of your programmes when those who take it all are threatened with opposition.'[40] The 'Labor machine', Fox informed Jebb, 'has broken away from Watson to a great extent & gone on the rampage.'[41]

But the bargaining strength of Labor largely depended on the range of alternatives open to it should the party on whom the pressure was being applied refuse to make the desired concessions. In theory Labor members had two. They could either turn out the Protectionists and seek office themselves, or they could switch support to Free Trade and play the game of concessions with them. In practice the alternatives were closely circumscribed. Labor was reluctant to take office (and Deakin knew it) and Reid (especially after 1905) was not a credible alternative to Deakin. Forrest soundly argued that an alliance between 'Reidites' and Laborites was a contingency Protectionists could 'well afford to risk'.[42] Apparently neither Free Trade nor Labor contemplated negotiating or bargaining one with the other.

In 1904 when Labor persisted in extending the scope of the Conciliation and Arbitration Bill and Deakin resigned (not, incidentally, a good example for concessions), Labor members were astonished to find themselves asked to form a government. The experience proved an unhappy one, and the Bill did not reach the statute book during Labor's barren period of office. The Watson ministry, the president of the Labour-in-Politics Convention of 1905 explained, 'was unable to accomplish anything in way of legislation'.[43] On assuming office in April 1904 some members immediately moved for Watson to form a coalition with Deakin. Watson sympathized with the suggestion and revived it himself in May. Caucus empowered the leader to negotiate an alliance, but the attempt was abortive as Deakin rejected the proposal.[44] Clearly Deakin and his party were happier with the consequence of Labor's action on the Arbitration Bill than Watson and his party.

Labor's action also led to an unproductive round of unstable ministries and resulted in the formation of the Reid–McLean coalition of Free-Traders and conservative Protectionists: this was the very combination Labor could expect to influence least. In September Watson arranged an alliance with Isaacs and the progressive wing of the Protectionist Party. The alliance split federal caucus and State parties, giving rise to an acrimonious public conflict. In July 1905 Labor decided to give a general support to Deakin for the remainder of the second parliament, but the Commonwealth Labor Conference of 1905 restricted Watson's ability to manoeuvre by resolving that he could enter no alliance extending beyond the existing parliament. About this time Reid reared, and then rode, his socialist tiger. After the general election in December 1906 for the third parliament Watson privately advised Deakin:

our party is not anxious for office unless a programme worth having could be carried through, and I'm not too sure that in the Parliament as at present constituted there is much chance of carrying much of the Labor party's programme. . . . At least you can rely that we shall do nothing against your Ministry while engaged in altering the tariff and in carrying other matters of a Democratic nature.[45]

Therefore, taken in all, when, as Spence assured us, his leader approached ministers with suggestions or demands he bargained from a position of relative weakness, not strength. The tactical situation, it should be noted, contrasted with that in New South Wales in the 1890s. There the colonial Labor Party had an extensive platform, it controlled its own candidates, and above all Lyne was a credible alternative to Reid. It seems reasonable to believe that Barton and Deakin in fact 'conceded' very little of substance that they themselves did not want.

Deakin said as much in an exchange with Forrest, who early in 1907 urged an alliance with Reid. There had been only one 'tough problem'—the union label—and that had been resolved to Forrest's satisfaction. Despite their position as a minority party they were still in a 'more independent and commanding role than either of our rivals are or can hope to be without our help'. They should simply continue in office without an understanding or alliance with any one. If he were forced to choose he would prefer to be in the power of Watson, but why take 'either road' until compelled.[46]

Doubtless Deakin could be expected to assert claims of independence, but on this occasion there is good reason to believe him as the replies of Forrest and the fate of distinct or exclusive Labor policies suggest. The best Forrest could reply was that he feared the Protectionists would get into their former situation and Labor would be *'thought to be'* their masters: Deakin had missed the difficulty of being even 'supposed to be' under Labor domination.[47] When Forrest resigned in July because his constituents would consider him dishonourable if he continued in a position which *they* considered an alliance, Deakin justly retorted: 'there's not a shred of fact justifying this implication'.[48]

Only a few policies—direct exclusion of coloured races, preference to unionists in the Arbitration Act, referendum on the tariff, nationalization of monopolies, land tax—fell into category of being peculiarly Labor. It seems fair to argue that Labor's presence in parliament ensured that the White Australia policy could not be neglected (if the Barton ministry had been so inclined) and that the Kanakas would have to depart with a minimum delay. But the mechanism of exclusion of immigrants, despite Labor's battle, remained the indirect education test. The Arbitration Act did not include preference to unionists in the form Labor had insisted on; it did embrace State railway workers, but this was not a concession from Deakin as the Reid–McLean ministry passed the measure. Labor did not secure a referendum on the tariff, a land tax, or nationalization of monopolies. When in 1905 a Queensland correspondent asked what action Deakin was going to take on nationalizing the iron industry, caucus replied 'there was nothing likely to be done this Session and that this Party were not in the confidence of the Govt.'[49]

As to the one 'tough problem', the one specific case cited as a concession, the circumstances were these. The first Deakin ministry drafted the Trade Marks Bill without a union label clause, but it left office before the Bill could be introduced. McGregor, leader of the Watson government in the Senate, introduced the same Bill in July 1904 and received the congratulations of Best, a Protectionist, for bringing it forward. Pearce suggested 'trade union labels' on his own initiative (caucus had not considered the idea) and Senators accepted the new clause without much opposition. Caucus supported the provision, but Labor lost office before the Bill passed through all stages in the Senate. Symon, Attorney-General and leader of Free Trade in the Senate, reintroduced the measure and a group of Free-Traders moved to recommit Pearce's clause. The attempt narrowly failed and the Bill received its third reading in the hands of Symon on 30 November. The next day Reid moved the first reading in the House but he resigned early in the next session after Deakin's 'notice to quit'. Isaacs, the new Attorney-General, resumed the Bill in July-August 1905 with a modified clause. Thereupon Reid attacked Deakin for being under the dictation of Labor by including a clause that Deakin had earlier refused: Deakin had said that he would take up his programme of 1903-4 but his former Attorney-General had not thought it proper to include the clause. Deakin was abusing the power of parliament to secure 'a large number of the constituents' of Labor. Forrest, Mauger, Watson, and Higgins asserted that Deakin had not refused the clause in 1903—it was simply that no one had thought of it then.[50]

Was the union label provision a 'concession'? Deakin, in the *Morning Post*, considered the possibility and the general charge of Liberal 'obsequiousness' to Labor. The 'only trace' of such was the union label where the Prime Minister met Watson 'half way', though 'whether this implied any sacrifice on the part of Ministers is not known'. Certainly Lyne, Minister of Customs, and Isaacs, Attorney-General, needed no pressing and if there was a concession then the amendment of the Immigration Restriction Act more than compensated. The Prime Minister had brought Labor members to such a position 'that they must either accept most of his proposals or face the country'. He ruled the House 'because the Labour members follow his flag with what is really an amazing docility'.[51] Watson (normally an honest man) repelled Reid's charge on the union label by claiming that he had not exchanged a word on the provision with any member of the ministry 'until it was actually in print'.[52] In 1914 he described Labor as 'one of the dominant forces in Australian politics', which 'even where not in power has helped to colour the proposals of its opponents'.[53] This statement seems unexceptionable. But it does not suggest a degree of influence or initiative usually associated with the term 'support in return for concessions'. Apparently the concept is of limited value in explaining the progressive social-industrial legislation of the first decade.

In a sense the concept was a device to account for a number of undeniable facts. The sharpest contrast between the Convention delegates, who framed the Constitution, and the Commonwealth politicians, who came to implement it, was the presence in parliament of a Labor Party, which, as it happened, held the balance between Free Trade and Protection. The Federal Conventions and the federation movement neglected social issues but federal parliament stressed them shortly after the foundation of the Commonwealth. The two specific social powers—arbitration and pensions—became part of the Constitution only after persistent attempts on the part of their sponsors, and considerable reluctance on the part of the majority of delegates. Yet federal legislation soon strained the Constitution to its limits, and beyond, according to three High Court Justices—Griffith, Barton, O'Connor—who as Convention delegates had done most to draft its provisions. Therefore, Labor, 'committed to a definite platform of social reform', directly and indirectly influenced the orientation and course of legislation by 'auctioning' its votes to obtain measures close to its interests. Social issues came to the fore.

The unexpected and rapid emergence of the Labor Party in both Houses of the Commonwealth Parliament was an event of great significance. Labor members undoubtedly 'coloured' legislation. But some of the inadequacies of the concept as a fully acceptable explanation for Labor's mode of influence and for the preoccupation of parliament with socio-economic reforms have been suggested. Moreover the hypothesis ignores, or at least underrates, other important but perhaps less obvious changes in circumstances. These in themselves must have led federal politicians to concentrate on social questions, if not precisely in the same manner.

Progressive liberals such as Deakin and Kingston were but a handful of relatively powerless men among the fifty delegates of the second Convention. Even had they then wanted a radically different Constitution—and this is by no means certain—they could not have got one. By contrast, in federal parliament they occupied positions of power as prominent ministers in governments which could, and indeed were obliged to, formulate policies and legislate. Deakin soon came to head cabinets wherein, despite theory, he was manifestly not merely first among equals. Deakin the Convention delegate was a different being to Deakin the federal politician and Prime Minister of Australia.

The composition of federal parliaments as a whole—partly but not solely because of the Labor segment—was decidedly less conservative than either Convention. Federal voters, drawn from electoral rolls very similar to those which had served for the election of delegates in 1897, returned politicians of a more progressive turn of mind to represent them in 1901 and at subsequent Commonwealth elections. The reason for this is obscure. Perhaps electors demanded something different from men who had been selected to frame a Constitution, than from politicians who were to put it into effect. Perhaps the division into electorates in most States for the return of members of the House of Representatives partly explains the variation. Different electors might have tended to poll on the separate occasions. But whatever the reason, Deakin as Prime Minister had with him on ministerial benches and behind him on the government side, not only the former Conventionists Kingston, Higgins, Isaacs, and Lyne, but other progressive members such as Hume Cook, Groom, Ewing, Bonython, Chanter, Crouch, Storrer, and Mauger. Labor sat on the cross benches, and the opposition Free Trade Party numbered politicians such as Reid, whose term in office in New South Wales was not devoid of social reforms, and Neild, whose record on social questions like old-age pensions was unimpeachable. The Senate, elected on the same franchise but on a State-wide basis, unexpectedly contained men of similar political persuasions and interests as those in the House, whose possible excesses it was supposed to check. Whereas radicals had once derided the 'fat men' of the Conventions and suspected their motives, they could now look with favour upon the new national parliament with expectations of measures as enlightened (Constitution permitting) as those emanating from advanced States. Contemporaries were appalled or delighted at the prospect, depending on their viewpoints. The fact that early federal parliaments assembled in progressive and democratic Victoria heightened the contrast for some politicians from less advanced States.

Rapid changes had also taken place within the separate colonies during the decade leading to federation, and colonial and then State governments responded to new demands. The bank and financial crashes and their aftermath taught many thrifty, hard-working, sober middle-class citizens lessons which less fortunate people had long known. Poverty was not necessarily the consequence of wasted opportunities, the just reward for the spendthrift, the idler, the drunkard. One did not always get what one deserved after all. Financial hardship, unemployment, decimation of unions, bad seasons, combined to sharpen social problems which had existed in less acute forms in better days. State electors demanded government remedies for the evils of sweating, exploitation, unemployment, and the like—evils which inevitably told hardest on the most vulnerable sectors of society—the aged, the infirm, and the working class. State governments and politicians—given manhood or adult suffrage—could ignore such calls at their peril and they attempted to provide remedies. But the self-same voters, unaware of the legal subtleties of the Constitution, also elected candidates to the central parliament. Therefore federal governments and politicians could ill afford to neglect social problems which demanded attention and occupied the thoughts of their electors.

Finally, provisions of the Constitution itself provoked questions concerning social issues. The Constitution provided that within two years the Commonwealth had to enact a uniform external tariff and introduce internal free trade. But the individual colonial economies had been constructed around, and fostered by, a wide range of tariffs. The federal tariff was a compromise between the high protection of Victoria and the low tariff of New South Wales. Manufacturers and workers, especially in Victoria where they had become accustomed to high duties, naturally cried hardship and campaigned for greater protection. Federal politicians from all States, ensconced in Melbourne, could not escape the full blast of the *Age*. Different conditions of labour had also grown up within the separate colonial economic units. The Constitution introduced equal conditions of marketing throughout Australia, but left untouched unequal conditions of production. Therefore workers and manufacturers inevitably demanded uniformity, a levelling up, or perhaps down, as the case might be.

The influence of factors such as these quickly became apparent. Barton, Deakin, and Kingston planned their election platform and strategy late in 1900. They recognized that they needed a programme with mass appeal to get them elected and broaden their support in the electorates and parliament. Hence Kingston's original suggestions included adult suffrage, old-age pensions, and industrial conciliation and arbitration: Deakin urged the necessity of a 'popular' or 'progressive' platform for the general election.[54] In this way, although these subjects had not been prominent in the Federal Conventions or the federation referenda, they became part of Barton's Maitland speech in January 1901.

The subject of old-age pensions developed into a live issue in Australia at the end of the century as the inability of existing asylums and institutions to cope with new circumstances became increasingly apparent. In 1895 Neild and Canon Boyce began public campaigns for old-age pensions. In September Neild moved the first resolution in New South Wales (and probably in any local parliament) to establish such a system:

(1) That, in the opinion of this House, asylums for the aged and infirm should be superseded by a system of old age pensions.
(2) That this House requests the Government to introduce during the present session a bill to give effect to the foregoing resolution.[55]

Pensions for the unfortunate needy in the community would be more rational, humane, and Christian than 'herding' aged poor into 'penal-like establishments'. The movement for pensions in England was being promoted by the 'extremes of political parties', pensions being the policy of both the Conservative Party and the 'great' Labor Party. In the same month Canon Boyce advocated a scheme in the *Daily Telegraph* and in February 1896 he sponsored an Old-Age Pension League. In January the Labor Party made 'State Pensions for old age and the infirm' a new plank in its platform.[56] In June Neild moved a second resolution out of which came a select committee. Reid appointed Neild Old-Age Pension Commissioner, he sailed for Europe in August, and on his return presented a 600-page report to parliament.

In 1897 the Victorian government established a Royal Commission to investigate the question. Testimony of witnesses revealed the extent of the problem. The Reverend A. R. Edgar of the Methodist Central Mission told the Commissioners of a new class of poor. Clerks in warehouses and business places were thrown out of work when prosperity ceased and depression came: these thrifty and deserving men, being unfitted for manual relief work, were among the 'most helpless and hopeless of the community'. Machinery and 'young fellows' had replaced skilled older workers; a man past fifty years of age 'ought to keep a bottle of hair dye in his bedroom'. The mining industry produced destitute old men (even though most Cornish miners were Methodists—'a particularly economical and temperate class of men') and the wool industry the itinerant 'poor old swagman'. A series on poverty in the *Argus* in 1896, Edgar said, had estimated that some 12 000 old people existed on less than 10 shillings a week. A second witness, Herbert Henry Booth, head of the Salvation Army in Australasia, said that in twelve months the Army had provided 33 482 beds and 103 013 meals in Melbourne. The Victorian Commissioners considered that the conditions of modern industry were the most prolific cause of aged poverty:

> The potent agency of steam and the fecundity of the inventor have not only displaced labour, but 'one generation of masters wears out three generations of men'; but worst of all, 'the race is to the swift, and battle to the strong'. . . . preference is given to the younger and more vigorous competitor, and the inevitable result is that the physically weak—and not only the aged, but even the elderly—are unable to obtain a sufficiency of employment. . . . The Pauline injunction—'He that will not work, neither shall he eat' does not apply to this class. They are involuntarily manufactured idlers, and the inability of the State to arrest the march of industrial tendency in no way relieves it of its responsibility to these victims.[57]

In 1897 Kingston also set up a Royal Commission to investigate the problem of the aged poor. The Commissioners were impressed by the Victorian experience and the financial disasters of 1891–4, 'in which the savings of the thrifty were dissipated by fraud or mismanagement'. The existing methods in South Australia—destitute asylums, benevolent and friendly societies—were 'confessedly inadequate'. Old age itself stood first as the 'immediate cause of distress' in the country, city, and suburbs; in the fight for survival young men pressed out older and less active workers. The Commission recommended a contributory pension fund, controlled and subsidized by the State.[58]

Colonial governments, made aware of these acute problems by the campaigns of private members of parliament, citizens, religious bodies, and reports of their own committees and commissions, responded to agitation for pensions. Moreover, persons of sixty years and over were becoming an increasingly larger proportion of the community. In New South Wales this age group increased from 3.04 per cent of the population in 1861 to 5.58 in 1901: in Victoria it rose from 1.47 to 7.96 (probably as survivors from the gold-rush immigration of the fifties aged).[59] Presumably then there were both social evils to rectify and vital votes to be had. Even as the Commonwealth came into existence pension schemes in Victoria and New South Wales were about to come into operation. Therefore, though all Australian citizens were to be treated equally under the Commonwealth's tariff and electoral laws, some were more equal than others in their state of old age.

These were circumstances that aspiring federal politicians could not fail to exploit. Barton himself admitted when pressed in parliament about his mention of pensions in his campaign: 'It was demanded of us to make some reference'.[60] Once Protectionists had raised the issues and taken the initiative, Free Trade and Labor candidates generally endorsed a national scheme, even if some were more explicit about the financial obstacles. Symon approved of pensions, but denounced Barton's plank as 'an electioneering placard'.[61] J. S. Clemons, soon to be opposition whip in the Senate, believed that pensions 'appealed to the humane side of every elector' and were 'eminently desirable', but doubted their immediate practicability.[62]

These were also circumstances that successful candidates of all three parties could not ignore in federal parliament. Senator Fraser (Protectionist, Victoria) who as the oldest member moved the address-in-reply, alluded to malfunctioning of the Victorian scheme, and advocated a national one which would be fairer to people not resident in the State for the obligatory twenty years. McGregor (Labor, South Australia) pointed out that the great majority of candidates had called for a federal system: it was disgraceful to have 'old men and old women at the corners of our streets in the State capitals selling newspapers and matches—men and women who are monuments of misery.' Walker (Free Trade, New South Wales) stressed the unfairness of State residential qualifications and suggested that the States hand over payments for old-age pensions to the federal government. In August 1901 O'Malley moved for the government to formulate a scheme 'without unnecessary delay': progressive income tax and succession duties could provide the funds. Kirwan (Free Trade, Western Australia) seconded the motion and McLean, a 'reactionary' Victorian Protectionist, suggested repealing the Braddon clause (this would have required a constitutional amendment). Later in August Neild moved to invite State governments to authorize the Commonwealth to 'deduct from the sums payable to the States under section 87 of the Commonwealth Constitution Act the amounts required to provide such pensions.' In October 1904 the Reid–McLean government set up a Select Committee, which was converted into a Royal Commission in February 1905. O'Malley proposed federal pensions financed by special duties on tea, kerosene, champagne, and silk.[63] Deakin took up the suggestion with a Constitution (Special Duties) Bill but the Premiers refused to exempt these duties from the financial provisions of the Constitution. At the Premiers' Conference of 1906 they firmly resolved that it was 'incumbent' on the Commonwealth to fund pensions without 'trenching' upon customs revenue returned to the States.[64] Senator Dobson, a conservative Free-Trader, in 1907 called upon the government to establish a compulsory fund to provide pensions for contributors when they reached pensionable age. In March 1908 Fisher moved a motion of urgency, noting that electors, who knew 'nothing about the restrictions of the Constitution', had thrice returned a 'large majority' of candidates pledged to federal old-age pensions. Deakin for the government, and Cook for the opposition, endorsed the motion.[65] The Bill, Deakin informed Forrest in August, would have been hurried in by himself because 'the Fleet rendered its passage impossible after September without taking up the whole Session', which he wanted for defence and financial issues.[66]

In sum, a general consensus of opinion existed within federal parliament on the desirability of a national system: the question was not should the Commonwealth exercise its power, but when and how could it afford to legislate. Pressing objective situations confronted State and Commonwealth politicians at the turn of the century and during the first decade of federation. Citizens demanded action and were not over-concerned about which government should provide it. Humanitarian and religious sentiments were outraged by the all too manifest social injustice and inequality. Practical federal politicians, cynics might claim, eagerly took up the good cause mainly to attract votes at general elections. Fisher's urgency motion anticipated the Surplus Revenue Bill (intended to set aside funds for naval defence and pensions) by a matter of weeks. He forced the pace on an issue (which was drawing to a successful conclusion) in a field of legislation that Free-Traders, Protectionists, and Labor men had long tilled.

Similar considerations applied to the issue of conciliation and arbitration. Victoria had taken tentative steps with voluntary boards and councils of conciliation as early as 1884 and 1886.[67] In 1889 the Intercolonial Congress of Trade Unions had decided (though not unanimously) that the time had arrived for the creation of boards to settle disputes, and prevent strikes and lock-outs. In 1890 Kingston had introduced the first Bill to provide for compulsory Conciliation and Arbitration. But the great strikes and events of the early nineties supplied (as with pensions) the impetus which placed effective measures on colonial statute books. The New South Wales government, as a result of the maritime strike, established a Royal Commission and in 1892 enacted the Trades Dispute Conciliation and Arbitration Act. In 1894 the South Australian Legislative Council passed a mutilated version of Kingston's 1890 Bill, and in 1896 Turner created a system of wages boards in Victoria. Trade unionists, in an era of defeat and employers' conditions, became more interested in the question. The foundation platform of the Progressive Political League of Victoria included a plank for courts of conciliation, and the New South Wales Labor Party added compulsory arbitration to its platform in 1895. In Western Australia Forrest passed an Industrial Conciliation and Arbitration Act in 1900, and in New South Wales Lyne introduced the Industrial Arbitration Bill, which became law in 1901.

Again, therefore, even as the Commonwealth was founded, popular measures—the result of agitation and necessity—were coming into operation in the States. Given Kingston's record as pioneer of compulsory arbitration in the colonies and of the federal power in the Constitution, nothing was more certain than that he would press the issue on his colleagues. The fact that Deakin had given Kingston reluctant support at the first Federal Convention, and that Barton had consistently voted against the subject as a federal function at both Conventions no longer mattered. The potential for the exercise of a federal power now existed. Given the urgent requirement of a popular, progressive programme there was no doubt that Barton would agree to Kingston's suggestion to include conciliation and arbitration in his Maitland address. Turner, Forrest, and Lyne— members of the first ministry—had all found it convenient to pass similar measures in their own colonies.

Conciliation and arbitration had the great advantage over pensions of costing relatively little to implement, and thus a Bill could be expected once the tariff was out of the way. Deakin moved the first and second readings in July 1903. His eloquent plea that the Bill marked the start of a new era and phase of civilization, a 'People's Peace, under which the conduct of industrial affairs in the future may be guided' fell upon a responsive House. Reid termed its introduction 'justified', its object 'so excellent'.[68] But although members of all parties endorsed the principle of compulsory conciliation and arbitration, the scope of the measure—largely because of the Labor Party —proved highly controversial.

Initially Labor had no official federal policy on the subject as the first Commonwealth Labour Conference failed to place it in the federal platform. Federal caucus (after the Barton ministry had announced its policy at Maitland and in the Governor-General's speech) partly rectified the omission by adding the plank 'Compulsory Arbitration'. The party disapproved of conciliation. At the second Commonwealth Labour Conference delegates carried a motion for 'a Compulsory Arbitration Act, with due regard to the conditions obtaining in each State', but rejected an amendment to add conciliation. Trade unionists remained unconvinced about the wisdom of any federal legislation. At the Commonwealth Trades Union Congress in November 1902, McGrath, of the Melbourne Trades Hall Council, advocated a Commonwealth Arbitration Act. Pearce urged caution: 'It should be framed so that due regard would be paid to the interests of the different States.' A second West Australian, J. W. Croft of the Central Trades and Labor Council, opposed a federal measure unless it could be shown that 'it would not clash with the arbitration legislation at present in operation. If the State rights were trenched upon by such an Act the West Australian workers would oppose it.' Congress considered it prudent to proceed no further.[69]

But once Liberal-Protectionist initiative had raised the question, then trade unionists and the Labor Party tried to influence the shape of the forthcoming measure and to enlarge the scope of the Bill. In

August 1902 Kingston furnished R. S. Guthrie, the 'Plimsoll' of
South Australia, with a letter of introduction to Deakin (then acting
Prime Minister): Guthrie was 'a very old & good friend. . . . I wish
you could give him a good hearing. . . . It is a seamen's matter & he is
the seamen's friend'.[70] No doubt the matter was the place of seamen
in the Arbitration and Navigation Bills. In May 1903 events inter-
vened to convince waverers in the labour movement of the necessity
for a Commonwealth Act, and for an all-embracing one. In that
month engine drivers and firemen employed by the Victorian railways struck because of a government directive to disaffiliate from the
Trades Hall Council. The Irvine ministry immediately introduced a
coercive measure, the Railway Employees Strike Bill, which provided
for the dismissal of strikers and the deprivation of their pension
rights. The Bill also empowered the Commissioner of Railways to
engage strike breakers on a permanent basis and to promote non-
strikers. Within nine days the railwaymen returned unconditionally,
but the ministry still passed the Act. The 'whole community', said
Stephen Barker (secretary of the Trades Hall) 'was plunged into
almost an industrial war'.[71]

Had the strike not occurred, it seems probable that the Conciliation and Arbitration Bill would have had a smooth passage through
parliament, Kingston's resignation notwithstanding. Certainly the
issue of State railway employees had not been raised in caucus before
the strike, and nor indeed had the subject of arbitration. Now, however, Labor members and radical Protectionists determined that the
Bill should embrace State servants. On the day before the second
reading, Batchelor, a former railway employee and union leader,
moved in caucus 'that the Commonwealth and State employees be
brought under the provisions of the measure'.[72] When Fisher moved
his amendment to the Bill the rail strike was clearly uppermost in
his mind. But the brutal use of State power did not escape the notice
of other federal parliamentarians, who returned to Melbourne for the
second session a few days after the strike had been 'settled'. In fact
Kirwan (Free Trade) first raised the issue of State railway workers
by giving notice of two questions on 30 May 1903:

1. Whether the Government are aware that the railway associations of
all the Australian States are desirous of having all the railway employes
brought within the scope of the proposed Federal Arbitration and Conciliation Act.
2. Whether the Bill now in preparation for Conciliation and Arbitration
will be framed with due regard to the wish of the associations.[73]

Clearly Kirwan's questions prompted the ministry because Kingston, asked by Barton for information, scribbled: 'This matter had better be discussed in cabinet'. When the House narrowly carried Labor's amendment to include railway servants, Kirwan's vote numbered amongst the 'Ayes': not all Free Trade support was cynical opportunism to defeat the government.

In the event Barton and Deakin argued that the proposal offended the spirit and letter of the Constitution. Barton, shortly after his elevation to the High Court, informed Hunt that he hoped Deakin would win the row as the opposite meant 'chaos, & such a provision will anyhow never become law': it would be a 'pleasant little question' for the High Court.[74] The Federal Labor Party, under great pressure from labour organizations, could not afford to compromise even if it wanted to: the Arbitration Bill had become a great public issue. In this instance, as it happened, Labor served to retard rather than advance the passage of a social measure. Ultimately, the Reid–McLean coalition passed the Bill, a fact sometimes conveniently overlooked (by Spence, for example).

The eagerness of federal politicians to involve themselves directly in the States' field of industrial relations became evident very early in the life of federal parliament. On 28 June 1901 Higgins moved the first motion by a private member: the Commonwealth should acquire, subject to the concurrence of the States, 'full power to make laws for Australia as to wages and hours and conditions of labour'. The central government had responsibility for the tariff, whose problems were 'so inextricably intertwined' with these questions that federal parliament could not fulfil its functions in one respect without power to deal with the other. Internal free trade would prevail yet different factory standards existed. It would not do to permit 'sweating' in one State while others paid reasonable wages. Australians had declared for 'one economic area' and for 'experimental legislation', and the national parliament ought to give it 'fair play' under 'fair conditions'.[75]

This attitude of Higgins was consistent with his stand at the Convention, but the conversion of some other members was remarkably sudden. In 1898 McMillan had maintained that 'the whole industrial life, the inner life of each community' should be left entirely to the States. Now the acting Free Trade leader hailed the motion 'with delight'. He was convinced of the 'necessity of including certain powers in the Commonwealth which we decided to leave in the States': he believed that 'everything that affects the rights and liberties—especially the industrial life of the community—ought to be in the hands of the national Parliament'. It would 'repair the initial fault which we made when framing this Constitution, and when we ought to have taken those powers to ourselves': anything that 'may affect a man's liberty or his industrial interests, ought to be relegated to this Parliament'. Barton, a persistent opponent of federal powers in the field of social-industrial relations at the Conventions, echoed McMillan. The Prime Minister confessed that he had had doubts when Higgins first submitted the motion, but now he had second thoughts (as well he might in view of McMillan's warm response). The more he considered the question the less his doubts impressed him: the effects of internal free trade and the uniform tariff would be 'crippled' unless the national parliament also had 'power to deal uniformly with the conditions of employment throughout Australia'. One member, a self-described 'outsider', marvelled at the miraculous conversion: it was 'exhilarating to know that three members of the Federal Convention agree . . . that this question should have been dealt with during the time that the Constitution was under consideration'.[76]

Barton forwarded a copy of the resolution to State Premiers in July. His ministry and the House had no wish to 'arrogate to themselves any power in this direction'. But in view of the importance of general legislation on the subject and the impending interstate free trade, the government wished to give 'official intimation' that any action on the part of the States—'in the friendly spirit of the resolution'—would be welcomed. The Premiers did not favour the proposal. Neil Lewis believed it undesirable for the Tasmanian Parliament 'to surrender its rights to make its own laws upon the important subjects named in the resolution'. J. G. Jenkins considered it inexpedient for South Australia to take any action. John See held that the question should be left to the States, and Walter James, Western Australia, thought the idea 'not advisable'. Apparently the Premiers of Victoria and Queensland did not reply.[77]

One interesting feature of the debate on Higgins' motion was the total silence of Labor members. Watson had drawn the attention of caucus to the notice of motion, but after a short discussion Labor, which supposedly 'sought to fight the decisive battles on Commonwealth ground', decided to take no action.[78] Presumably caucus took this course because the labour movement was divided on this issue, as on federal conciliation and arbitration. In September 1901, Samuel Mauger, after consulting Deakin and Batchelor, convened an interstate conference of Anti-Sweating Leagues and Trades Hall Councils. The conference discussed the role of government in regulating working conditions and wages. Delegates agreed on the right of the 'third party' to intervene, but disagreed on whether the State or Commonwealth governments would be the more effective. Labor's Pearce and Higgs moved that 'industrial regulation rightly belongs to the State Legislatures'. Pearce argued that to entrust the subject to the Commonwealth meant appointing a new set of officials and

He did not believe in extending the powers of the Federal Parliament to the social concerns of the States. He hoped the conference would pause before it handed over to the Federal Government a function which it could not so well perform as the State Legislatures.[79]

Batchelor, on instructions from the South Australian Trades and Labor Council, termed the time 'inopportune' for federal factory legislation though he himself thought it was the natural corollary of internal free trade. McGregor, Stewart, and McDonald, all Labor parliamentarians, favoured federal powers. When at the second Commonwealth Labour Conference in December 1902 the party finally resolved that 'all industrial legislation' should be taken over by federal parliament it did so with some misgivings. Delegates rejected Higgs' counter-motion in favour of State legislation by 13 votes to 11 'after a long debate'. They placed the new plank in only the general platform and Labor in New South Wales refused to put it in its federal platform.[80]

Apparently, therefore, Labor adapted more slowly to the changed circumstances and the new political environment than 'conservative' Free-Traders and Protectionists such as McMillan and Barton. They also reacted more cautiously than some employers. In August 1901 a mass meeting of Victorian employers met in the Athenaeum Hall under the chairmanship of Sir Malcolm McEacharn, shipping magnate and federal politician. McEacharn protested against the activity of wages boards, which threatened to stop capital investment, drive away employers, and give manufacturers elsewhere an unfair advantage: uniform factory legislation throughout all the States of the Commonwealth was a 'grave' necessity. F. T. Derham, president of the Chamber of Manufactures, warmly endorsed these remarks: 'All would agree with the chairman that the subject should be dealt with by the Federal Parliament, so that conditions of labour throughout Australia might be equal.'[81]

But, of course, statements and resolutions of this kind could not be translated into direct action by compliant federal politicians. The national government had no direct power and the States were unwilling to surrender theirs. If the Commonwealth Parliament was to have its way and link its control of the tariff with industrial conditions, then it would have to be by some indirect method. Nevertheless, New Protection was neither a Liberal bait to convert Labor to protection nor a Labor demand to concede the policy in return for its support. Rather than being a deliberate course on either part, New Protection evolved haphazardly as the Commonwealth grew into Old Protection.

In one respect the expectations of the founding fathers were entirely fulfilled: the federal tariff was indeed the great issue of the first Commonwealth Parliament. Federation brought together into a common political arena for the first time the great advocates of the two fiscal faiths. Gifted orators and skilled debaters such as Reid, Symon, and Hughes—disciples of free trade—and Deakin, Kingston, and Watson—disciples of protection—related at length the virtues of their own particular faith and the vices of the other with a passion bordering on religious fanaticism.

The fiscal odds were tilted against free trade from the outset. The financial provisions of the Constitution, especially the Braddon clause, meant that there could be no true free trade, only a revenue or a protectionist tariff: in a sense, the very name 'Free Trade Party' became anachronistic on the inception of the Commonwealth. The gradual development of central functions and the natural desire of ambitious federal politicians to exercise power ensured that the financial requirements of the Commonwealth would increase. The fact also that the first federal tariff was a compromise meant that many industries, especially in Victoria, were more exposed to foreign competition than before federation. Barker informed the Protectionist Association that his own enquiries had revealed the 'most disastrous' effects of the federal tariff on Victorian industries. Commonwealth and State politicians, protectionist newspapers, and powerful pressure groups such as the Protectionist Association, demanded higher protective duties. In the 'fiscal peace' election campaign of 1903 the Association distributed some 280 000 leaflets and manifestoes and held twenty-six public meetings.[82]

Although both traditional parties, more especially the Protectionist, lost ground to Labor in 1903 and 1906, Reid could draw no comfort from the election results. Clearly the protectionist tide was rising throughout the country and Labor was being increasingly drawn into

the protectionist net. On the one hand, Australians apparently preferred the immediate guarantee of employment to the promise of
cheaper food and goods. On the other hand, rejecting cheap labour at
home was but one step from protection against the produce of cheap
labour abroad. Labor's ardent support for a White Australian sugar
industry necessitated approving protective duties on sugar and
rebates or bounties to the growers. Though Hughes no doubt disagreed, there was surely much truth in the *Age*'s unkind taunt: 'Mr
Hughes is that most contradictory of all inconsequential things—a
Labor Free-trader. The term is equivalent to "Yes-No", to the idea
of a white black man.'[83] Protection could also be related to a growing
preoccupation of Labor—the defence of Australia. Watson pointed
out in 1905 that protection could foster and diversify Australian
industry and help populate the nation, especially the empty north,
which was a temptation to the yellow hordes. The motion by Senator
O'Keefe at the third Commonwealth Labour Conference in 1905 to
place protection in the fighting platform was a measure of the
strength and confidence of Labor protectionists, even though delegates decided to forgo a fiscal plank until 1908.[84]

The doctrine of free trade, which had only been applied in recent
times in one colony (and even there Lyne took office in 1899), was a
declining force. Reid's anti-socialist campaign in 1906 was less an
expression of concern about Labor's alleged socialism than a desperate
search for a new election catch-cry: whipping a socialist tiger was a
tacit admission that he could no longer flog a dead free-trade horse.
After the election, though the Anti-Socialist Party polled well compared to the Protectionist, Reid acknowledged the government's
'mandate' for a new tariff. He owed it to the 'manifest truth' to
concede 'that at the last election, there was a majority of honourable
members returned here pledged to increase the duties collected under
the existing Tariff.'[85]

At the same time the greatest flaw in the protectionist system had
been thoroughly exposed during the interminable debates on the
fiscal issue: protection did nothing directly for workers in protected
industries. Enlightened protectionists, Liberal and Labor, had long
sought to remedy this great defect: to do so was both *humane* and
sensible in electoral terms. Deakin himself had pioneered social legislation in Australia with his Factories and Shops Act of 1885. As an
active member of the National Anti-Sweating League since its foundation in 1895, he had continued to press for just and equitable wages
and conditions in protected, but sweated Victoria (a 'perfect Turkish

bath' according to Symon in 1901). Although Deakin does not seem to have used the actual term 'New Protection' until April 1906, the idea was implied in earlier speeches. In his election address at Ballarat in October 1903, for instance, he spoke of protection and the 'old economy' which had but one measure, 'price': the 'new economy looks at the nation being national as well as humane, with fair wages for the makers and the profits of barter distributed as far as possible amongst one's fellow citizens.'[86] Mauger, foundation Secretary of the Anti-Sweating League and the Protectionist Association, had promulgated similar policies. The Association (an organization of employers and employees) since 1901 had openly campaigned for the 'social side' of protection:

Protection is a system of philosophy and a matter of social condition, rather than a mere question of trade preference or commercial supremacy. Ethics and morals must therefore have a prominent place in what has been happily termed "the New Protection" . . .[87]

The Association bracketed early the Commonwealth's control of the tariff with uniform industrial legislation throughout Australia and New Protection. W. T. C. Kelly, chairman of the first annual general meeting in 1902, said in his address:

A most important question of the day was that known as the new protection. It was recognised that if the manufacturer was to be protected the workmen should be protected also. . . . The whole question of factory legislation should be placed in the hands of the Federal Government.[88]

For Labor protectionists the *raison d'être* of the system of protection was to benefit workers: less a principle with some than an 'expedient', protection was useless if it could do no better for employees than free trade. The Political Labor Council of Victoria early required all federal candidates to be 'pledged to the new protectionist policy'. A persistent theme of Labor members from all States, protectionist and free trade alike, was that where protection was applied the worker should 'get his share'. Liberal and Labor protectionists then had much in common. The Protectionist Conference of Australasia in 1903 numbered delegates as 'diverse' on social issues as Lyne, Forrest, Groom, Kingston, McGregor, and Higgs. In its message to Commonwealth electors it declared: 'The day of the worker is coming. The "New Protection" protects both the employer and worker. It makes possible fair profits for the manufacturer, and fair wages and reasonable hours for the workers.'[89]

Therefore, when manufacturers, workers, and delegates of the United Trades Conference, demanded higher duties for agricultural machinery 'threatened' by the 'dumping' of American machines[90] a general consensus existed in parliament that factory owners were not to be the sole beneficiaries. Indeed, none were more determined than members of the Free Trade Party. In 1901 Reid, in his censure motion on the tariff, had insisted that wages boards were an 'absolute corollary', an 'absolute necessity', for any system of protection (Poynton, a Labor member, interjected: 'That is the new protection'). In 1903 Neild had made the first attempt to tie a fiscal measure to the working condition of white labour. When parliament changed the rebate on sugar to the bounty, Neild tried to add a proviso that the bonus could not be granted 'in respect of any sugar-cane grown or produced by or with the labour of females, or of persons under the age of 21 years'. He had no 'sinister object', he insisted, but his recent tour of Queensland had left him disturbed about the health and welfare of women and children exploited in the cane fields.[91] Now, in 1906 in the tariff debate, Free-Traders demanded that selfish Victorian manufacturers such as McKay should not simply pocket the increased profits. McKay, they (and Labor) alleged, had moved his factory to Braybrook outside the range of the wages boards in order to escape 'fair and reasonable conditions of employment'. The Tariff Commissioners had heard irrefutable evidence of this 'den of sweaters'. Tariff duties, W. E. Johnson claimed, should only be raised provided that 'every manufacturing firm engaged in industries within the Commonwealth, the products of which are protected by duties, shall distribute in increased numeration to their employés the full amount of duties imposed.' Two Labor members immediately accepted the challenge. The opposition, Fisher observed, had frequently pointed to the 'great advantages' enjoyed by sugar growers in Queensland as the result of Commonwealth legislation. He would extend manufacturers of harvesters 'even more generous treatment' and would support a proposal under which the government would be enabled

to levy an Excise upon these machines equal to half the amount of Customs duty, and . . . to legislate in the direction of securing the return of the whole of that Excise duty to the employers who will conform to the awards of Wages Boards and Arbitration Courts.[92]

Batchelor supported his colleague. Johnson's proposal was impractical but his intention that workmen in protected industries should share the benefits derived from duties was 'an object with which all honorable members must be in sympathy'.

Here then was a Labor 'solution' to a problem which had first vexed Free-Traders and Protectionists in federal parliament in June 1901: how to relate the Commonwealth's control of the tariff with the 'inviolate' States' control of industrial conditions. The answer had apparently existed since the customs-excise-rebate mechanism devised in 1901–2 to speed the departure of the Kanakas and preserve the sugar industry with white labour. Now all that remained was to incorporate the technique in the first extensive revision of the tariff in 1907–9 (for which the government had its 'mandate') and for the High Court to approve the method, which was by then under challenge. Alas the High Court disapproved. Old Protection triumphed: New Protection was still-born.

The progressive legislation enacted in the early years of federation placed the Commonwealth of Australia briefly in the vanguard of social welfare states: concepts like 'fair and reasonable' industrial conditions and minimum basic wages were peculiarly Australian. But it is difficult to discern any coherent overall policy or plan, or to supply any simple explanation for a confused and complex situation. There is perhaps but one constant theme. For some reason—great strikes, financial crashes and depression, mechanization and urbanization—social issues became prominent in the Australian colonies towards the end of the century: the emergence of Labor parties was part cause and part effect of the socio-politico dynamism of the period. Great social injustices became manifest. The swagman was not jolly, but poor and pathetic. The match-girl of the fairy tale was likely to be a miserable old woman. Workers toiled in sweated factories for ruthless employers. Hence even as the Commonwealth was about to experience labour pains and birth pangs, there came into existence problems, from which, as it happened, the Constitution largely insulated the federal government. But adult citizens who experienced the ill-effects of these problems, and wanted solutions, elected aspiring candidates to the national parliament. And once the federal machinery had been created and the tariff formulated, federal politicians had to justify their existence and secure re-election. The few direct outlets (and perhaps some indirect ones also) for federal action in the social field had therefore to be fully exploited. How could astute politicians such as Deakin, Reid, and Watson stump the country on 'popular' and 'pressing' issues such as uniform marriage and divorce laws, decimal currency, metric weights and measures? How could even brilliant orators such as Kingston and Symon attract and hold audiences, and sustain election campaigns, on topics such as census and statistics, quarantine laws, bills of exchange?

In short, social issues came to the fore in the Commonwealth because social issues had come to the fore in the States. Federal politicians became preoccupied with these questions, it seems fair and reasonable to conclude, because these questions preoccupied their electors. In the new political environment, as experienced politicians instinctively knew, only the attractive and adaptable political animals could survive.

7

PROSPER THE COMMONWEALTH

The founding fathers apparently believed that the duties of the Commonwealth Parliament would be less demanding than those of State legislatures. Once federal members had disposed of the tariff they would probably meet infrequently and proceed leisurely lest they soon exhaust the enumerated powers and be left with the mere process of amendment. Higgins, a 'centralist', expected federal parliament to sit no more than two months in the year. The new governmental machine would not cost much because it would not do much. Perhaps one day (but not in the foreseeable future) the Commonwealth might use up the surplus revenue, but it was unlikely ever to resort to direct taxation.

The federal government could have little direct impact on Australian citizens or industry because of the nature of its prescribed powers. It could interfere little with the residual, undefined (and therefore unlimited) functions of the States. Convention delegates, though generally co-ordinate federalists, intended the Senate to inhibit the national government in the exercise of its delegated powers. They expected the States Assembly to safeguard State rights should their representatives be outvoted in the lower House, or should Senators (though few seemed to believe it) divide on party lines. In 1891 Baker, seeking to strengthen the Senate, had asked:

what chance is there that men of character and position . . . will seek to become members of the senate? Will not all the most experienced, all the most energetic men, all the most able men become members of that house which has the power concentrated in it?[1]

In 1901 Baker, Downer, Symon—three of the staunchest advocates of a powerful States House—nominated for the Senate. Presumably

Baker did not believe himself lacking in character, position, energy, and ability: Downer was no fool, Symon was not simple (the Webbs considered Symon the only man they had met in Australia possessing that 'indescribable quality of "distinction"').[2] The High Court would serve as an additional independent check to undesirable federal excesses.

Federationists propagated notions such as these at conventions, conferences, and referenda campaigns. So far as they looked to late nineteenth-century America as the best example of a working federation, they perceived (despite development of the Constitution since 1787) a limited central government and a decentralized system which preserved the theory of residual State sovereignty. Representatives of broad regional or financial interests, not national political parties, controlled a relatively strong American Senate. The Supreme Court restricted government and gave lattitude to *laissez-faire* capitalism. The apparently limited powers and power of the proposed Commonwealth were virtues, not vices, of the Australian Constitution. Antifederationists challenged many of the claims and expectations of their opponents and viewed the future with misgiving. In the event, the people of the several colonies placed more confidence in the federalists.

The genesis and development of what are now called 'settled policies' exposed the limitation of some of these assumptions. The legislative process proved much more demanding and dynamic than most had expected. The first policy legislation of the Commonwealth —the Immigration Restriction and Pacific Island Labourers Acts— required complementary and dependent measures. This satellite legislation, as well as the initial Acts, soon proved deficient: administrative difficulties, changed circumstances, fresh problems, soon led to their amendment. The amending process provided opportunities for the introduction of principles envisaged by neither Convention delegates nor cabinet ministers who sponsored the Bills. Pearce's new clause in the Sugar Bounty Bill 1905 is a good example. That a member of the Labor Party (none of whom by most accounts should have emerged as Senators) suggested the provision adds force to the point. The amendment of the Immigration Restriction Act in 1905 resulted in the Contract Immigrants Act, itself the direct progeny of another novel provision introduced by a 'private' Labor member. Had anyone told Convention delegates that the seemingly innocuous immigration power could be exploited in this fashion, they would surely have been astounded. Most would have been appalled. Debating and shaping legislation for a changing White Australia, and policing its administration provided federal parliamentarians with much work throughout the decade.

So also did questions related to defence. Initially members closely checked and rejected the ambitious schemes of Hutton; as expected, they severely restricted defence expenditure. Later they reviewed a range of plans devised by servicemen and politicians such as Creswell, Deakin, and Hughes. Ultimately they considered and approved measures which few Australians had apparently contemplated in the nineties or the early years of federation. Whereas federal ministers and politicians once prided themselves on curbing expenditure, by the end of the decade they boasted about expensive innovations.

The founders, in granting the Commonwealth full rights of taxation and exclusive control of defence, had provided in principle for innovation in times of emergency. But delegates were not alone in believing that they, unlike historical counterparts, were attempting to federate under uniquely peaceful circumstances. In 1891 Professor Edward Jenks, Dean of the Melbourne Law Faculty, claimed that if the Australian colonies actually federated, they would

succeed in a political experiment for which there [was] practically no precedent in modern times. All through modern history there has been one and but one determining cause of political union between communities—physical force, or the fear of physical force. In Switzerland, Germany, Austro-Hungary, Sweden and Norway, the United States of America, Canada, Mexico, Central America, the tale has been always the same. No community has consented to link its fortunes with the fortunes of another, save when instigated by fear of violence from that other or a third power.[3]

In 1897, during the Adelaide session of the second Convention, Chief Justice Onslow wrote pessimistically to Symon from isolated Western Australia. He did not expect to see a united Australia: 'Federation in cold blood [was] a mighty difficult matter.' It could only come about when people desired it at 'all costs', but was 'it reasonable to expect them to nurse actually such views in days of peace when no danger [was] impending and when the sole object of every man [was] to turn his sixpence into a shilling?'[4] On 1 January 1901, Creswell argued that defeat for Nelson at Trafalgar would have meant a French Australia:

And since 1805? Well, we have not had a care or anxiety. A mere handful of people, we have been conserved in our right to the whole island continent, and no colony-hunting Power has ever dreamed of threatening it.[5]

Ironically, many of the men who most exploited the ambitions of service officers and post-federation developments (the Russo-Japanese War, new naval doctrines and German naval designs) fought against federation. In 1901 Hughes asked: 'For what reasons, other than a Customs union and union for defence, had we to federate at all?'[6] Labor in the south-eastern colonies generally led the democratic anti-Billite forces, and Hughes himself was particularly active. There appears to be no overt evidence that Hughes was interested in defence questions before federation, and we have Watson's word that Labor regarded the whole subject as 'negligible'. MacLaurin headed conservative opposition to federation in the New South Wales Legislative Council. In 1897 he attacked the Federal Enabling Bill and ridiculed the idea of united defence: why incur the 'enormous' expense of federal government,

which, after all, would not be likely to have to do with defence at all, and could not do more than we could do well for ourselves, if we put our hands into our pockets, at very much less expense . . . ?[7]

As it happened, after federation Labor members played a prominent part on defence issues, Hughes became the driving force in the Australian National Defence League, of which MacLaurin was foundation president. Deakin and Kingston were great figures in the federation movement. But their correspondence late in 1900 reveals that they had not considered possibilities such as compulsory military training (nor indeed had politicians in other British communities). Barton, Parkes' heir and Australia's 'noblest son', clearly had no thoughts of an Australian navy.

Social issues exhibited dynamics similar to White Australia and defence. Deakin predicted that the federal parliament was unlikely to exercise its conciliation and arbitration power for 'many years': Deakin introduced a Commonwealth Conciliation and Arbitration Bill in 1903. Debates on the Bill and subsequent measures dealing with the subject exhausted parliamentarians and hampered the functioning of parliament. Billites had commonly advised electors that their local parliaments seldom legislated on matters surrendered to the central body, and that no colonial government had ever lost office on such issues. Yet within four years of federating the Bill occasioned the downfall of two federal governments and brought about an unprofitable round of musical ministries. When it eventually passed, Symon received congratulations: 'You must feel like a man who has reached the top of a steep hill after a long climb . . . and meets a cool breeze'.[8] Within seven years Justice Higgins had given his Harvester Judgment, which was to reverberate throughout the Australian continent and Australian history.[9] Had anyone prophesied that this federal power would have these repercussions, he would surely have been denounced as a false prophet.

By the end of the decade, therefore, it was apparent that the Commonwealth Parliament would manage to keep itself fully occupied even without the addition of new powers. The legislative process was, in a sense, self-generating: the solution to every problem created new problems. Uniform immigration restriction settled one question but stirred others. No sooner had the federal government finally disposed of Queensland's Protocol to the Treaty of 1894 than Britain concluded two more treaties with Japan. Should Australia adhere to the Anglo-Japanese Agreement and the Treaty of Commerce and Navigation of 1911? The whole process was set in motion once again. The full force of the defence power was not to be experienced until the Great War. But it was already evident that the Commonwealth possessed a powerful weapon, which could be used to overcome 'colonial' parochialism and glorify the Commonwealth. The measures embracing conciliation and arbitration, and invalid and old-age pensions, were but first steps into a field wherein the Commonwealth was increasingly to trespass. The High Court, in declaring sections of the Conciliation and Arbitration Act and New Protection invalid, undoubtedly acted in accord with the pre-federation spirit of the makers of the Constitution. But the dissenting judgments of Higgins and Isaacs, and the Court's approval of the Surplus Revenue Act, suggested that the composition of the Court, and the letter of the Constitution, were to be of greater importance than any problematical intentions of the founders.

Federal politicians soon learned to relish their duties. In June 1901 conservatives and liberals sought to enlarge Commonwealth powers so as to 'repair the initial fault' which they themselves had made when framing the Constitution. But nowhere was the transformation more apparent than with Labor members. Caucus took no action on Higgins' motion to accept industrial powers from the States. Senator Higgs, at the September conference prompted by Mauger, asked what would become of State Labor men if federal parliamentarians took up 'questions of this kind?'[10] But at the Commonwealth Labor

Conference in 1908 federal members strongly endorsed the motion of Senator Givens to elevate 'Uniform Industrial Legislation, amendment of Constitution' to the fighting platform. Senator De Largie confessed the error of his earlier ways. Federal Labor and State Labor came into conflict. Hughes and Holman (who as it happened fought Givens' motion along with McGowen) feuded on the proper functions of Commonwealth and State Parliaments.[11] In 1911 and 1913 Fisher attempted sweeping amendments of the Constitution.

The actual implementation of policies evoked similar dynamics within the administration. In 1902 Hunt told Barton that the Immigration Restriction Act continued to 'develop new features': new problems had to be overcome, precedents set, procedures formulated and adopted. Hunt also took delight in his tasks: 'We continue to eject the industrious Jap and the wily Chow . . . the I. R. Act has not yet exhausted its possibilities'.[12] Underlings found their duties more onerous: the Act was always raising problems, Deakin informed Barton, 'but gradually we are knocking its principles into the Customs men who administer it'.[13] Initially Barton decided minute points; inevitably Hunt acquired expertise and became a recognized source of power whom supplicants solicited. While Prime Ministers and cabinets might come and go, Permanent Secretaries such as Hunt went on, and on . . . The first heads of the seven departments established in the decade served an average of fifteen years in their posts.[14] Collins, who as Secretary of Defence had the briefest career, outlived nine Ministers of Defence—Forrest, Drake, Chapman, Dawson, McCay, Playford, Ewing, Pearce, Cook—in his nine years' service. Just as fresh problems continually confronted legislators, so too new problems faced administrators. In the process they gained more expertise, more power, and more staff: a sort of Parkinson's law operated. The Commonwealth began with 1408 public servants on 1 January 1901, when only State customs officers were transferred. Four years later, by which time all seven departments were functioning, the public service employed 22 296. On 1 January 1911 Commonwealth public servants numbered 34 459. In the financial year 1901–2 the departments, and the policies administered by them, cost £3 565 840; in 1910–11 the cost was £8 635 952. The Attorney-General's Department, which drafted Bills and supplied legal opinions, had the greatest rate of growth—1218 per cent (£2680 to £35 329). Treasury had the greatest absolute cost increase—£10 466 to £1 960 318. Commonwealth expenditure per head of population rose from £1 0s. 7d.

in 1901–2 to £2 19s. 6d. in 1910–11. Up to 1908 the federal government returned £6 059 095 (or 11 per cent) of its own one-quarter share of the net customs and excise revenue to the States.[15] In 1908 it passed the Surplus Revenue Act to meet its accruing obligations.

The Senate, in direct contrast to expectations, was clearly destined to be an inferior party chamber, not a superior States House. The first policy legislation—the Pacific Island Labourers Bill—immediately raised a State-rights issue. The duly elected government of Queensland strongly opposed the measure, and brought a variety of pressures to bear on Barton. But in 1901 the majority of Queensland Senators—most of them by some mischance Labor men—supported the Bill. Again, in 1903, the South Australian government objected to the change from sugar rebate to sugar bounty. Only two of the State's Senators, Baker and Downer, mustered to vote against the Sugar Rebate Abolition Bill: McGregor, a Labor Senator, voted for it. Paradoxically, Baker and Downer fought on principle for Glassey's amendment, which by extending the bounty to more growers in Queensland and New South Wales, would cost South Australians still more. Senators Drake (Queensland) and O'Connor (New South Wales) opposed the amendment which would have increased benefits to growers in their States. As it happened, both were members of the ministry which sponsored the clause in its original form. Responsible government may not have killed federation, but it was going to make what Baker understood by the term federation difficult to live with. Carruthers, in his sustained campaign to secure Commonwealth adherence to the Treaty of 1894, does not seem to have tried to use his State's Senators. The Senate did amend tariff items, but it acted less as a States Assembly than a party House. In 1902 Downer, a Protectionist, complained about the activities of fellow South Australian States-righter, Symon, a Free-Trader: the opposition leader had been 'playing the fool pretty well with some of the smaller terms of the tariff'.[16]

Generally, however, the Senate failed to live up to expectations in either of its dual roles. In 1903 the issue of the form of Glassey's amendment provoked a direct confrontation between the chambers. The Senate, led by Baker, may or may not have had the right to amend the Bill, but seemingly it realized it did not have the power. Put to the test Senators backed down. Their subservience, and the dominance of party, came to be widely recognized. In 1907 the *Even-*

ing News recalled that 'eminent jurists' had believed that the Senate would be 'strongly conservative' and 'pre-eminently' the States House:

The distinguished framers of the Australian Constitution overlooked the possibilities of machine politics when they indulged in such bright hopes for Federation, for no sooner had the first polls been declared than it was evident that the Upper House ... was to be very much like the Lower one, only more so. Instead of acting as a check upon the crude and crackbrained measures which come up from below, the Senate has become a mere registry office ...[17]

In 1908 the *Daily Telegraph* deplored the Senate's inability to block the Surplus Revenue Bill in the common interest of the States. The Bill's passage through the Senate was certain 'because its treatment there was covered by the party arrangements which had been made for it in the Representatives': the Senate had no more concern for the States as such 'than if we had unification instead of federation'.[18] The dismal record of the Senate as guardian of State interests, and the election of Labor candidates to all eighteen of the vacancies in 1910, led H. G. Turner, now a disillusioned conservative, to deride the Upper House as 'merely an appendage' of the Lower.[19] Symon, in 1912, refused on principle to pledge himself to the platform of the Liberal Union for the forthcoming election and received no party endorsement. He appealed to the electors, *his* masters, to 'Choose at least some free men—men independent of caucus and party tyranny'.[20] At the elections in 1901 and 1906 Symon had topped the State polls: the self-styled 'Champion of the Small States' (now the only Senate candidate in Australia to have been a delegate at the Federal Conventions) lost his deposit.

In external affairs the Commonwealth fulfilled, indeed exceeded, its promise. In 1907 the federal government finally established its authority to represent Australia at imperial conferences. The States, prompted by Carruthers, vigorously denied Deakin's right to discuss subjects not specifically included in the Commonwealth's enumerated powers and claimed individual participation. The Australian States, unlike the Canadian Provinces, Tom Price, Premier of South Australia argued, were 'independent of the Federal Government, and [were] in no way subordinate to it': the Commonwealth was an 'agency' for the management of customs, posts, and defence.[21] Elgin firmly rejected these submissions and similar protests: apparently the

Colonial Secretary was as anxious as Deakin to have but one government represent Australia in the councils of Empire. While both sides
in the dispute—Deakin on the one hand, State Premiers and Governors on the other—made exaggerated claims, this outcome unquestionably met the intentions of the founders. But during the first
federal campaign Barton was fond of explaining: 'There could be no
foreign policy of the Commonwealth. The foreign policy belonged to
the Empire. (Cheers). They could not affect that policy except by
such representations as they could make to the Imperial Government.'[22] The Australian Prime Minister complained to the Colonial
Secretary in 1902 that the French Consul-General appeared to assume
there was

> some analogy between his functions and those of an Ambassador. No
> such assumption can be admitted on the part of the Commonwealth, the
> Government of which [was], of course, precluded from the discussion
> with external authorities representing Foreign Nations, of matters involv-
> ing the relations between the Empire and those Nations, excepting with
> the express authority of His Majesty's Imperial Government.[23]

His Majesty's government, Chamberlain replied, agreed 'with the
views held by Mr Barton'.[24] Yet Barton himself negotiated directly
with the Japanese Consul-General on an issue (the Treaty of 1894)
which was really a question for the Crown, and neatly presented the
British government with an accomplished fact. In 1904 Deakin dealt
directly with the Japanese government on the passport arrangement
(clearly the Crown's prerogative) and was censured by the Colonial
Secretary, who learned of the agreement from a report in the *Daily
Chronicle*.[25] Strictly, Barton and Deakin should have used the
indirect channel of communication (Governor-General, Colonial
Secretary, Foreign Secretary, Japanese government) which may well
have produced different results.

British and Australian views on 'foreign' issues diverged considerably during the decade. The operation of White Australia legislation
and the new Naval Agreement, and above all different perspectives
on Japan—Britain's ally—produced friction and dissension. Australian
nationalism grew apace under the impetus of haphazard external
events and deliberate internal policies of federal governments. The
rapid development of something approaching a national identity was
reflected in a new attitude towards protection for the sugar industry.
In 1901–2 its preservation had been a politico-social issue, and Barton
had been willing to risk depopulating northern Queensland. But as

the continent seemed to become an increasingly vulnerable ' "white man's outpost in the Pacific" ',[26] the conception of the nature of the problem underwent a dramatic change. The issue became one of national survival for an Australia under siege. In 1911–12 the Royal Commissioners on the industry assumed 'loyal adherence' to White Australia and the national importance of settling tropical and semi-tropical areas of the continent for defence purposes:

Responsible persons will scarcely impugn the validity of these assumptions. . . . Their acceptance implies no more than a due consciousness of the progress of Australia towards nationhood—the recognition of the ideal of a Commonwealth which shall be socially coherent, and politically self supporting. While this ideal has been held in times past by an isolated few, the progress of recent events, both within Australia and beyond its borders, has given to the idea a new validity and significance, and a virtually universal acceptance.[27]

So long as these regions remained unoccupied they were 'an invitation to invasion, as well as a source of strategic weakness': the 'supreme justification' for continued protection for the local sugar industry was its contribution to the 'settlement and defence of the northern portion of the Australian continent'.

Although Australia could 'never have a foreign policy', something that looked very much like one was beginning to emerge by the end of the decade. These sentiments of independent Australian-Britons would soon have to be accommodated in London and at Versailles.

Many of the expectations of the founding fathers had been disproved within the decade. The Commonwealth did not yet 'dwarf' the States, but its potential was evident. The position of the States was not unlike that of the separate colonies in relation to Britain before federation: they would probably be unwilling or unable to present a united front against the Commonwealth on many issues. At the initial Premiers' Conference in 1901 Philp appealed in vain for support from fellow Premiers against Barton on the sugar issue: 'At some day', he warned, 'it may be a question affecting the other States'.[28] The decision of the High Court on the Surplus Revenue Act and the limitation of the Braddon clause to ten years rendered the States impotent on the vital subject of finance, on which they displayed some unity. The Commonwealth absorbed the surplus within eight years of federating. Forrest, chief architect of the financial arrangement which superseded the Braddon clause, recognized that the States were 'absolutely at the mercy of the Commonwealth'.[29] Fisher introduced the Commonwealth into the field of direct taxation with the land tax of 1910, something which most delegates believed would probably never happen. Electors, perhaps sensing where power resided, perhaps experiencing the impact of federal legislation, began to take more interest in federal affairs. In the election of 1910 more than 50 per cent voted in every State, and Victorian and Queensland electors polled more heavily than in State elections: the federal election of 1913 attracted more voters in every State than the State elections of 1912–14.

The federal machine operated in a manner that few people appeared to have foreseen and functioned more powerfully than expected. It was gaining an independent momentum, not slowing down, its powers running out. A new political animal, the federal politician, manipulated the machine. These creatures, originally descended from the colonial variety, quickly adapted to the new environment and evolved into a distinct alien species. They were not unambitious, and desired to survive and thrive. They herded together and hunted in packs or parties, their quarry votes, their weapons popular policies. They competed for attention, support, and power with each other and with their rival species.

Colonial politicians drew up the Constitution. Federal politicians put it into effect. They discovered that the makers had fashioned not a sealed compact, but a Pandora's box.

ABBREVIATIONS

AG	Attorney-General
ANL	National Library of Australia, Canberra
BPP	*British Parliamentary Papers*
CAO	Commonwealth Archives Office (Australian Archives)
CPD	*Commonwealth Parliamentary Debates*
CPP	*Commonwealth Parliamentary Papers*
CRS	Commonwealth Record Series
1890 MC	Federation Conference, *Proceedings and Debates*, Melbourne, 1890
1891 SC	Federal Convention, *Debates*, Sydney, 1891
1897 AC	Federal Convention, *Debates*, Adelaide, 1897
1897 SC	Federal Convention, *Debates*, Sydney, 1897
1898 MC	Federal Convention, *Debates*, Melbourne, 1898
GG	Governor-General
MHA	Member of House of Assembly
MHR	Member of House of Representatives
MLA	Member of Legislative Assembly
MLC	Member of Legislative Council
NSW	New South Wales
PM	Prime Minister
Qld	Queensland
SA	South Australia
SAR	*South Australian Register*, Adelaide
SMH	*Sydney Morning Herald*
S. of S.	Secretary of State for Colonies
Tas.	Tasmania
Vic.	Victoria
WA	Western Australia

APPENDIX 1

BIOGRAPHICAL NOTES ON DELEGATES TO THE NATIONAL AUSTRALASIAN CONVENTION, SYDNEY, 1891

New South Wales

ABBOTT, Joseph Palmer: b. Muswellbrook 1842, d. 15 September 1901. Ed. C. of E. School, Muswellbrook; John Armstrong School, Redfern; J. R. Huston's Surry Hills Academy; King's School, Parramatta. Pastoralist; solicitor; chairman of directors of Australian Mutual Provident Society; governor of King's School, Parramatta. KB 1892. KCMG 1895.
MLA Gunnedah 1880–7, Wentworth 1887–1901. Secretary for mines 1883–5; secretary for lands 1885; speaker 1890–1900.

BARTON, Edmund: b. Sydney 1849, d. 7 January 1920. Ed. Sydney Grammar School; Sydney University. NSW Bar 1871; justice High Court 1903–20. QC 1889. PC 1901. GCMG 1902.
MLA Sydney University 1879–80, Wellington 1880–2, East Sydney 1882–7 and 1891–4, Hastings and McLeay 1898–1900. MLC 1887–91, 1897–8. Speaker 1883–7; AG 1889, 1891–3; opposition leader 1897–8. MHR Hunter 1901–3. First PM of Aust. 1901–3.

DIBBS, George Richard: b. Sydney 1834, d. 5 August 1904. Ed. St Phillip's C. of E. School; Australian College under Dr Lang. Wine merchant and commission agent in brother's firm J. C. Dibbs & Co.; corn factor Chile 1865–7; managing trustee Savings Bank of NSW. KCMG 1892.
MLA West Sydney 1874–7, St Leonards 1882–5, Murrumbidgee 1885–94, Tamworth 1894–5. Treasurer 1883–5; premier and col. sec. 1885; premier and treasurer 1885; premier and col. sec. 1886–7, 1889, 1891–4.

JENNINGS, Patrick Alfred: b. Ireland 1831, arr. Vic. 1852, arr. NSW 1862, d. 11 July 1897. Ed. Newry; high school, Exeter. Mercantile career in Eng.; gold miner Vic. 1852; large pastoral interests Riverina 1862. KCMG 1880.
MLC 1867–70, 1890–7. MLA Murray 1869–72, Bogan 1880–7. Vice-president executive council 1883; col. sec. 1885; premier and treasurer 1886–7.

McMILLAN, William: b. Ireland 1850, arr. NSW 1869, d. 21 December 1926. Ed. Wesley College, Dublin; privately in London. Resident partner in W. & A. McArthur Ltd., merchants and importers 1876; president of Sydney Chamber of Commerce 1886. KCMG 1901.
MLA East Sydney 1887–94, Burwood 1894–8. Treasurer and minister of railways 1889–91.
MHR Wentworth 1901–3. Deputy leader of Free Trade Party.

PARKES, Henry: b. Eng. 1815, arr. NSW 1839, d. 27 April 1896. Elementary schooling in Kenilworth and Gloucester. Ropemaker and apprentice ivory turner in Eng.; farm labourer, employed in ironmongers and brass founders in Sydney; customs-house officer 1840–4; established business as toy-seller and ivory turner 1844; founder and editor of *Empire* newspaper 1850–8; importer; representative of financial company 1884–7. KCMG 1877. GCMG 1885.
MLA Sydney 1856, Cumberland 1858, East Sydney 1859–61, Kiama 1864–9, East Sydney 1869–70, Mudgee 1872, East Sydney 1872–7, Canterbury 1877–80, East Sydney 1880–2, Tenterfield 1882–4, Argyle 1885, St Leonards 1885–95. Commissioner of immigration 1861; col. sec. 1866–8; premier and col. sec. 1872–5, 1877–83, 1887–9; secretary for lands 1888; premier and col. sec. 1889–91.

SUTTOR, William Henry: b. Bathurst 1834, d. 2 October 1905. Ed. Parramatta under Dr Woolls. Manager father's cattle station at Lachlan; pastoralist Bathurst 1875.
MLA East Macquarie 1875–9. MLC 1880–1900. Secretary for mines 1877–8; vice-president executive council 1889–91, 1894–5.

Victoria

CUTHBERT, Henry: b. Ireland 1829, arr. Vic. 1854, d. 5 April 1907. Ed. Drogheda Grammar School. Admitted as solicitor Ireland 1852; legal practice Melbourne and Ballarat from 1855; formed Buninyong Gold Mining Co. 1857; pastoral lease on Lachlan River 1877; director Permewan Wright & Co. QC 1899. KCMG 1897.

MLC South West Province 1874–84, Wellington Province 1884–1907. Minister of justice 1886–90; postmaster-general 1877–80; commissioner of trade and customs 1880, 1889; solicitor-general 1894–9; minister of health 1894–5.

DEAKIN, Alfred: b. Melbourne 1856, d. 7 October 1919. Ed. C. of E. Grammar School; Melbourne University. Vic. Bar 1877; journalist with *Age* and *Leader* 1878–83.

MLA West Bourke 1879, 1880–9, Essendon and Flemington 1889–1900. AG, vice-president board of land and works, commissioner of water supply 1883–6; chief sec. and commissioner of water supply 1886–90; minister of health 1890.

MHR Ballarat 1901–13. AG 1901–3; acting PM 1902; PM 1903–4, 1905–8, 1909–10.

FITZGERALD, Nicholas: b. Ireland 1829, arr. Vic. 1859, d. 17 August 1908. Ed. Trinity College, Dublin; Queen's College, Galway. Commercial pursuits India and Ceylon 1852; established Castlemaine Brewery 1859; founder and director of SA Brewing Co.; pastoral interests in NSW and Qld; chairman and managing director of National Trustees, Executors and Agency Co. of Australasia. Papal Knight.

MLC North West Province 1864-74, North Central Province 1874-80. Chairman of committees 1903-8.

GILLIES, Duncan: b. Scot. 1834, arr. Vic. 1852, d. 12 September 1903. Ed. Glasgow High School and Academy. Office worker Glasgow; storekeeper Geelong; digger Ballarat 1853; member first Ballarat Mining Board 1858; working partner in Great Republic Mining Co.; agent-general for Vic. 1894-7.

MLA West Ballarat 1861–8, Maryborough 1870–7, Rodney 1877, 1877–89, Eastern Suburbs 1889–94, Toorak 1897–1903. President of board of land and works and commissioner of crown lands and survey 1868; commissioner of railways and roads and vice-president of board of land and works 1872–5; commissioner of crown lands and surveys, president of board of land and works, and minister of agriculture 1875–7; commissioner of railways and vice-president of board of land and works 1880, 1883–6; minister of public instruction 1884–6; premier, treasurer, minister of railways, and minister of mines 1886–90; speaker 1902–3.

MUNRO, James: b. Scot. 1832, arr. Vic. 1858, d. 25 February 1908. Elementary schooling. Printer in Edinburgh and Melbourne to 1865; founded various companies, notably Victorian Permanent Building

Society, Federal Banking Co., Real Estate Bank; large interests in other companies, especially Melbourne Woollen Mill Co.; agent-general for Vic. 1892–3.
MLA North Melbourne 1874–7, Carlton 1877–80, North Melbourne 1881–3, Geelong 1886–92. Minister of public instruction 1875; opposition leader 1886; premier and treasurer 1890–2.

SHIELS, William: b. Ireland 1848, arr. Vic. *c.* 1852, d. 17 December 1904. Ed. Scotch College; Melbourne University. Vic. Bar 1873; tutor briefly SA; practised in Melbourne to *c.* 1885.
MLA Normanby 1880–1904. AG and minister of railways 1890–2; premier and AG 1892–3; AG and treasurer 1899–1900; treasurer 1902–3; vice-president board of land and works and minister of railways 1903–4.

SMITH, William Collard: b. Eng. 1830, arr. Vic. 1852, d. 20 October 1894. Mining speculator; land agent and auctioneer Ballarat 1855; pastoral interests Riverina; manufacturing interests Vic.; lt-col. in volunteer forces; member Ballarat City Council 1857–64, 1870, and mayor 1875.
MLA Ballarat West 1861–4, 1871–92, 1894. Minister of mines 1875; minister of mines and minister of public instruction 1877–80; treasurer 1878–9; minister of education 1880–1.

WRIXON, Henry John: b. Ireland 1839, arr. Vic. 1850, d. 9 April 1913. Ed. Trinity College, Dublin. Irish Bar 1861; Vic. Bar 1863; vice-chancellor Melbourne University 1897–1910. QC 1890. KCMG 1892.
MLA Belfast 1868–77, Portland 1880–94. MLC South West Province 1896–1910. Solicitor-general 1870–1; AG 1886–90; president LC 1901–10.

South Australia

BAKER, Richard Chaffey: b. Adelaide 1842, d. 18 March 1911. Ed. Eton; Trinity College, Cambridge. Lincoln's Inn Bar 1864; legal partnership, Adelaide; chairman of directors of Qld Investment and Land Mortgage Co.; director Wallaroo and Moonta Mining & Smelting Co.; large pastoral interests. QC 1900. CMG 1886. KCMG 1895.
MHA Barossa 1868–71, the Province 1877–85, Southern District 1885–1901. Minister of education 1884–5; president LC 1893–1901.
Senator 1901–6. First president of Senate 1901–6.

BRAY, John Cox: b. Adelaide 1842, d. 13 June 1894. Ed. St Peter's College, Adelaide; Eng. SA Bar 1870; agent-general for SA 1892–4. KCMG 1890.

MHA East Adelaide 1871–92. Minister of justice and education 1875; AG 1876–7; premier and chief sec. 1881–4; treasurer 1884; chief sec. 1855–6; treasurer 1886–7; speaker 1888–90; chief sec. 1890–2.

COCKBURN, John Alexander: b. Scot. 1850, arr. S.A. 1875, d. 26 November 1929. Ed. Chamely School, Highgate; King's College, London. Medical practitioner; chairman various public bodies; agent-general for SA 1898–1901; director, in UK, of English Scottish and Australian Bank, Mt Lyell Mining and Railway Co., Central Insurance Co. KCMG 1900.

MHA Burra 1884–7, Mt Barker 1887–98. Minister of education and agriculture 1893–8.

DOWNER, John William: b. Adelaide 1844, d. 2 August 1915. Ed. St Peter's College, Adelaide. SA Bar 1867; legal partner G. & J. Downer. QC 1878. KCMG 1887.

MHA Barossa 1878–1901. MLC Southern District 1905–15. AG 1881–4; premier and AG 1885–7; premier and chief sec. 1892–3; treasurer 1893.

Senator 1901–3.

GORDON, John Hannah: b. Scot. 1850, arr. SA 1859, d. 23 December 1923. Ed. private schools. SA Bar 1876; legal practice Strathalbyn. QC 1900. KB 1908.

MLC Southern Districts 1888–92, 1893–1903. Minister of education 1889–90, 1892; chief sec. 1893–6; AG 1899–1903; minister of education 1902–3.

KINGSTON, Charles Cameron: b. Adelaide 1850, d. 11 May 1908. Ed. J. L. Young's Educational Institution, Adelaide. SA Bar 1873. QC 1888. PC 1897.

MHA West Adelaide 1881–1900. MLC Central District 1900. AG 1884–5, 1887–9; chief sec. 1892; premier and AG 1893–9.

MHR Adelaide 1901–8. Minister of trade and customs 1901–3.

PLAYFORD, Thomas: b. Eng. 1837, arr. SA 1843, d. 19 Apr. 1915. Ed. Thomas Mugg's School, Mitcham. Farmer; market gardener; orchardist; chairman East Torrens District Council 1861–82; agent-general for SA 1894–8.

MHA Onkaparinga 1868–71, East Torrens 1875–87, Newcastle 1887–90, East Torrens 1890–4, Gumeracha 1899–1901. Commissioner of crown lands 1876, 1877–8, 1878–81, 1885; commissioner of public works 1884–5; premier and treasurer 1887–9, 1890–2; commissioner of crown lands 1892; treasurer and minister controlling the Northern Territory 1893–4.

Senator 1901-7. Vice-president and senate leader 1903-4; minister of defence 1905-7.

Tasmania

BIRD, Bolton Stafford: b. Eng. 1840, arr. Vic. 1852, arr. Tas. 1874, d. 15 December 1924. Ed. private academy in Northumberland and by private tuition. Wesleyan minister 1865; Congregationalist minister Ballarat and Hobart to 1879; farmer, fruit grower and fruit exporter, Huon; mining interests. CMG 1919.
MHA Franklin 1882-1903, South Hobart 1904-9. MLC 1909-24. Postmaster-general and treasurer 1887-92; postmaster-general 1899-1901; treasurer 1899-1903; speaker 1894-6; chairman of committees LC 1919-21.

BROWN, Nicholas John: b. Hobart 1838, d. 22 September 1903. Ed. St Andrew's School and Hutchin's School. Large pastoral interests Tas. and Vic.; legal manager, mining and general agent for companies and estates, especially Mt Lyell Mining and Railway Co., the Lyell Tharsis, the Tasma Lyell; magistrate.
MHA Cumberland 1875-1903. Minister of lands and works 1877-8, 1882-7; speaker 1891-4, 1897-1903.

BURGESS, William Henry: b. Hobart 1847, d. 1 May 1917. Ed. Hobart High School. Wholesale and retail grocer in father's firm; founded Burgess Bros Wine, Spirit and General Merchants, Importers and Commission Agents 1884; director Elwich Railway Co.; adjutant in artillery; one-time chairman Hobart Chamber of Commerce; Hobart alderman 1876-81, mayor 1879-80; consular agent for France 1889.
MHA West Hobart 1881-91, Denison 1916-17. Treasurer 1884-7.

CLARK, Andrew Inglis: b. Hobart 1848, d. 14 November 1907. Ed. Hobart High School. Office worker in father's iron foundry; Tas. Bar 1877; judge Supreme Court of Tas. 1898-1907.
MHA Norfolk Plains 1878-82, South Hobart 1887-98. AG 1887-92, 1894-7; opposition leader 1898.

DOUGLAS, Adye: b. Eng. 1815, arr. Tas. 1839, d. 10 April 1906. Ed. England and France. Articled law clerk Southampton; admitted as solicitor Tas. 1839 and later established legal firm; squatter in Tas. and Vic. 1840-2; Launceston alderman 1853-84 and mayor 1865-6; 1880-2; agent-general for Tas. 1886-7. KB 1902.
MLC Launceston 1855, Esk 1884-6, Launceston 1890-1904. MHA

Launceston 1856–7 and 1862–84. Premier and chief sec. 1884–6; chief sec. 1892–4.

FYSH, Philip Oakley: b. Eng. 1835, arr. Tas. 1859, d. 20 December 1919. Ed. privately, London; Denmark Hill School. Clerk in merchant firm London; founded P. O. Fysh & Co., general merchants and wholesalers Hobart 1862–94; chairman of board of directors of AMP; agent-general for Tas. 1898–1901; hop grower and orchardist Derwent Valley 1910–19. KCMG 1896.
MLC Hobart 1866–9, Buckingham 1870–3, 1884–94. MHA East Hobart 1873–8, North Hobart 1894–8. Treasurer 1873–5; premier 1877–8; premier and chief sec. 1887–92; opposition leader LC 1892–4; treasurer 1894–9.
MHR Denison 1901–10. Minister without portfolio 1901–3; postmaster-general 1903–4.

MOORE, William: b. Isle of Man 1823, arr. Tas. 1853, d. 9 August 1914. Timber merchant; landowner.
MHA Wellington 1871–7. MLC Merser (later Russell) 1877–1909. Minister of land and works 1873–6, 1877; col. sec. 1877–8; chief sec. 1879–84; president LC 1889–94; chief sec. 1894–9, 1904–6; minister without portfolio 1906–7.

Western Australia

FORREST, Alexander: b. Bunbury 1849, d. 20 June 1901. Ed. Bishop Hale's School, Perth. Surveyor in survey department 1869–70; contract surveyor 1871–80; explorer in WA 1870s; land agent 1880; agent to Anthony Hordern in land grant railway schemes 1883–6; pastoralist and stock agent 1890s; mayor Perth 1892–5, 1897–1900. CMG 1901.
MLC Kimberley 1887–90. MLA West Kimberley 1890–1901. Government whip 1890–1901.

FORREST, John: b. Bunbury 1847, d. 3 September 1918. Ed. Bishop Hale's School, Perth. Surveyor in survey department 1865; explorer and expedition leader 1860s and 1870s; deputy surveyor-general 1876; acting commissioner of crown lands 1879; acting comptroller of government expenditure 1880–1; surveyor-general and commissioner of crown lands 1883–90. PC 1897. CMG 1882. KCMG 1891. GCMG 1901. Baron 1918.
MLC 1883–90. MLA Bunbury 1890–1901. Premier and treasurer 1890–1901; col. sec. 1894–8.
MHR Swan 1901–18. Postmaster-general 1901; minister of defence

1901–3; minister of home affairs 1903–4; treasurer 1905–7; acting PM 1907; treasurer 1909–10, 1913–14, and 1917–18.

HACKETT, John Winthrop: b. Ireland 1848, arr. NSW 1875, arr. WA 1882, d. 19 February 1916. Ed. Trinity College, Dublin. Irish Bar 1874; station manager 1882; WA Bar 1883; founded *Western Mail* 1885; editor and part owner *West Australian* 1887–1916; chairman Perth Public Library 1893; first chancellor University WA 1912–16; chancellor C. of E. diocese of Perth; governor of Perth High School. KB 1911. KCMG 1913.
MLC 1890–4. MLC South West Province 1894–1916.

LEE STEERE, James George: b. Eng. 1830, arr. WA 1860, d. 1 December 1903. Ed. Thames Ditton and Clapham Grammar School. Merchant Marine 1843–58; commanded East Indiaman 1854–8; large pastoral interests WA 1860; chairman WA Trustee Executive and Agency Co. KB 1888. KCMG 1897.
MLC Wellington 1870–80, Swan 1880–4, MLC 1885–90. MLA Nelson 1890–1903. Unofficial member executive council 1885–90; speaker LC 1886–90; speaker LA 1890–3.

LOTON, William Thorley: b. Eng. 1839, arr. WA 1863, d. 22 October 1924. Ed. privately. Employed in mercantile house, London; co-founder of merchant firm Padbury Loton & Co.; large pastoral interests; director of WA Bank 1882–1924, chairman from 1909; director WA Trustee, Executive and Agency Co.; mayor of Perth 1901–2. KB 1923.
MLC 1884–7. MLC Greenough 1889–90. MLA Swan 1890–7.
MLC Central Province 1898–1900, East Province 1902–8.

MARMION, William Edward: b. Fremantle 1845, d. 4 July 1896. Ed. Fremantle and Perth. Master in mercantile marine 1866; founded W. E. Marmion & Co.; pastoral, pearling, and maritime interests; established mining companies on the Yilgarn; JP 1872; member Central Board of Education; consul for Netherlands.
MLC 1870–2. MLC Fremantle 1872–90. MLA Fremantle 1890–6. Commissioner of crown lands 1890–4.

WRIGHT, John Arthur: b. Eng. 1841, arr. WA 1885, d. 24 February 1920. Ed. privately and Queen Elizabeth School, Crambrook. Civil engineer in Eng., Spain, America, France, and Russia; manager WA Land Co. 1889; general manager Great Southern Railway; consulting engineer to WA government; government resident at Albany 1896–1908.

MLC 1885–94. Director of public works and commissioner of railways 1885–91.

Queensland

DONALDSON, John: b. Mt Rouse, Vic. 1841, arr. NSW 1876, arr. Qld 1881, d. 25 July 1896. Pastoralist and businessman NSW 1876; managing partner Mt Margaret Station *c.* 1881; manager Union Mortgage Co. 1886–96, director to 1889; director Qld Deposit Bank 1886–92.
MLA Warrego 1883–8, Bulloo 1888–93. Postmaster-general and secretary for public instruction 1888–9; treasurer 1889–90.

GRIFFITH, Samuel Walker: b. Wales 1845, arr. NSW 1854, arr. Qld 1860, d. 9 August 1920. Ed. private school, Sydney; Maitland High School. Articled law clerk 1863–5; Qld Bar 1867; legal business and land speculator; chief justice Qld 1893–1903; lt-governor 1899–1903; chief justice High Court 1903–19. QC 1876. KCMG 1886. GCMG 1895.
MLA East Moreton 1872–3, Oxley 1873–8, Brisbane 1878–93. AG 1874–8; secretary for public instruction 1876–9; secretary for public works 1878–9; premier and col. sec. 1883–6; secretary for public instruction 1883–5; postmaster-general 1885; treasurer 1887–8; premier, chief sec. and AG 1890–3.

MACDONALD-PATERSON, Thomas: b. Scot. 1844, arr. Qld 1861, d. 21 March 1906. Ed. private academy, Glasgow. Butcher 1863; Brisbane solicitor; pastoral and mining interests, especially Mt Morgan; Rockhampton alderman 1867, mayor 1870.
MLA Rockhampton 1878–83, Moreton 1883–5, North Brisbane 1896–1901. MLC 1885–96. Postmaster-general 1885–7.
MHR Brisbane 1901–3.

McILWRAITH, Thomas: b. Scot. 1835, arr. Vic. 1854, arr. Qld 1862, d. 17 July 1900. Ed. Ayr Academy; Glasgow University. Civil engineer with Victorian railways and contractors; large pastoral, mining, banking, and commercial interests; director Qld National Bank and Qld Investment and Land Mortgage Co. KCMG 1882.
MLA Warrego 1870–1, Maranoa 1873–8, Mulgrave 1878–86, North Brisbane 1888–96. Secretary for public works and mines 1874; premier and treasurer 1879–82; premier, chief sec., and treasurer 1888; minister without portfolio 1888–9; treasurer 1890–3; premier, chief sec., and secretary for railways 1893; chief. sec. and secretary for railways 1893–5; minister without portfolio 1895–7.

MACROSSAN, John Murtagh: b. Ireland 1832, arr. Vic. 1853, arr. Qld 1865, d. 30 March 1891. Ed. private and Catholic schools, Glasgow. Miner in Vic., New Zealand, NSW; miner and mining speculations Qld 1865.
MLA Kennedy 1873–8, Townsville 1879–91. Secretary for public works and mines 1879–83; col. sec. and secretary for mines 1888–90.

RUTLEDGE, Arthur: b. Penrith 1843, arr. Qld 1851, d. 8 February 1917. Ed. NSW. Legal and mercantile experience Sydney 1859; Qld Bar 1878; judge of Qld District Court 1906. QC 1899. KCMG 1902.
MLA Enoggera 1878–83, Kennedy 1883–8, Charters Towers 1888–93, Maranoa 1899–1904. AG 1883–8, 1899, 1899–1903.

THYNNE, Andrew Joseph: b. Ireland 1847, arr. Qld 1864, d. 27 February 1927. Ed. Christian Bros School, Ennistymon; Queen's College, Galway. Public servant 1864–7; admitted as solicitor 1873; founded legal firm Thynne and Macartney; director Financial Guarantee and Agency Co.; lt-col. in volunteer rifles; a founder of Qld University, vice-chancellor 1916 and chancellor 1926.
MLC 1882–1927. Minister of justice 1888–90; minister without portfolio 1893–4; postmaster-general 1894–6; postmaster-general and secretary for agriculture 1896–7.

New Zealand

ATKINSON, Harry Albert: b. Eng. 1831, arr. NZ 1853, d. 28 June 1892. Ed. Rochester School and Blackheath. Farmer; deputy-superintendent, provincial secretary and council member of Taranaki province; major in volunteer rifles. KCMG 1888.
MHR 1861–6 Grey and Bell, New Plymouth 1867–8, Egmont 1873–91. MLC 1891. Minister of defence 1864–5; secretary for crown lands and minister of immigration 1874–5; treasurer 1875–6; commissioner of customs 1876; premier, secretary of crown lands and minister of immigration 1876–7; treasurer 1879–82, 1882–3; premier 1883–4; premier and treasurer 1887–90; speaker LC 1891–2.

GREY, George: b. Portugal 1812, arr. NZ 1845, d. 20 September 1898. Ed Guildford, Surrey; Royal Military College, Sandhurst, 1826. Captain in regular army, serving in Scot. and Ireland; explored WA 1830s; governor of SA 1840–5; lt-governor of NZ 1845–53; governor of Cape Colony and high commissioner for South Africa 1854–61; lt-governor of NZ 1861–8. KCB 1848.
MHR Auckland West 1874–8, Thames 1878–90, Newton 1891–3, Auckland City 1893–5. Premier 1877–9.

RUSSELL, William Russell: b. Eng. 1838, arr. NZ 1857, d. 24 September 1913. Ed. Royal Military College, Sandhurst. Captain in regular army; pastoralist Hawkes Bay; racehorse owner and breeder; first president NZ Racing Club. KB 1902.
MHR Napier 1875–81, Hawkes Bay 1884–1905. MLC 1913. Postmaster-general and commissioner of telegraphs 1884; col. sec., minister of defence, and minister of justice 1889–90; opposition leader 1894–1903.

APPENDIX 2

BIOGRAPHICAL NOTES ON DELEGATES TO THE AUSTRALASIAN FEDERAL CONVENTION, 1897-8

New South Wales

ABBOTT: see appendix 1.

BARTON: see appendix 1.

BRUNKER, James Nixon: b. Newcastle 1832, d. 5 June 1910: Ed. Christ Church School, Newcastle; Sydney College. Trained as solicitor in Sydney; established stock and station agency, Maitland, 1856, later with branches in Sydney and Newcastle; mining interests; established Hunter River Farmers Association; director Mutual Life Association of Australasia 1890.
MLA East Maitland 1880-1904. MLC 1905-9. Secretary for land 1888-9, 1889-91; col. sec. 1894-9; minister without portfolio 1905-7.

CARRUTHERS, Joseph Hector McNeil: b. Kiama 1857, d. 10 December 1932. Ed. Williams St and Fort St public schools; Goulburn High School; Sydney University. Articled law clerk; NSW Bar 1879; property owner southwest NSW. KCMG 1908.
MLA Canterbury 1887-94, St George 1894-1908. MLC 1908-32. Minister of public instruction 1889-91; secretary for lands 1894-9; treasurer 1899; opposition leader 1902-4; premier and treasurer 1904-7; vice-president executive council 1921, 1922-5.

LYNE, William John: b. Apslawn, Tas. 1844, arr. NSW 1875, d. 3 August 1913. Ed. Horton College, Ross, and privately. Pioneer settler Gulf of Carpentaria 1864; clerk in Glamorgan Council 1865-74; pastoralist near Albany 1875. KCMG 1900.
MLA Hume 1880-1901. Secretary for public works 1885, 1886-7;

secretary for lands 1889; secretary for public works 1891–4; opposition leader 1895–9; premier and treasurer 1899–1901.
MHR Hume 1901–13. Minister of home affairs 1901–3; acting minister of defence 1902; minister of trade and customs 1903–4, 1905–7; treasurer 1907–8.

McMILLAN: see appendix 1.

O'CONNOR, Richard Edward: b. Sydney 1851, d. 18 November 1912. Ed. Sydney Grammar School; Sydney University. Clerk in NSW Legislative Council 1871–3; leader writer for Sydney *Echo* and connected with *Freeman's Journal*; NSW Bar 1876; justice High Court 1903; first president Commonwealth Court of Conciliation and Arbitration 1905–7. QC 1896.
MLC 1887–98. Minister of justice 1891–3; solicitor-general 1893.
Senator 1901–3. Vice-president executive council and government Senate leader 1901–3.

REID, George Houstoun: b. Scot. 1845, arr. Vic. 1852, arr. NSW 1858, d. 12 September 1918. Merchant's clerk 1856–64; clerk in treasury department 1864–78; secretary to AG 1878–90; NSW Bar 1879; high commissioner in London 1910–16; conservative member of House of Commons 1916–18. PC 1897. QC 1898. KCMG 1909. GCMG 1911. GCB 1916.
MLA East Sydney 1880–4 and 1885–94, Sydney-King 1894–1901. Minister of public instruction 1883–4; opposition leader 1891–4; premier and treasurer 1894–9; premier and AG 1899.
MHR East Sydney 1901–10. Opposition leader 1901–4; PM 1904–5.

WALKER, James Thomas: b. Scot. 1841, arr. NSW 1862, d. 18 January 1923. Ed. in Edinburgh and King's College, London. Branch manager Bank of NSW 1862, later director and president 1900; general manager Royal Bank of Qld; part owner Mt Ubi, Qld; director numerous companies, especially AMP Society, Burns, Philp, & Co., Harrison, Jones and Devlin.
Senator 1901–12.

WISE, Bernhard Ringrose: b. Sydney 1858, d. 19 September 1916. Ed. Rugby; Queen's College, Oxford. Middle Temple Bar 1883; NSW Bar 1883; agent-general for NSW 1915–16. QC 1898.
MLA South Sydney 1887–9, 1891–4, Sydney-Flinders 1894–5, Ashfield 1898–1900.
MLC 1900–8. AG 1887–8, 1889–1904; minister of justice 1901–4; acting premier 1904.

Victoria

BERRY, Graham: b. Eng. 1822, arr. Vic. 1852, d. 25 January 1904. Elementary schooling until 11. Apprentice draper; storekeeper and wine merchant, Melbourne; manager mining company 1862; proprietor *Collingwood Observer*; acting editor *Geelong Advertiser*; part proprietor, and later editor, *Geelong Register*; agent-general for Vic. 1886–92. KCMG 1886.
MLA East Melbourne 1861, Collingwood 1861–6, Geelong West 1869–77, Geelong 1877–86. Treasurer 1870, 1871–2; commissioner of trade and customs 1871; premier and treasurer 1875; premier and chief sec. 1877–80; premier, treasurer, and chief sec. 1880–1; chief sec. 1883–6; postmaster-general 1883–4; treasurer 1892–3; speaker 1894–7.

DEAKIN: see appendix 1.

FRASER, Simon: b. Canada 1832, arr. Vic. 1853, d. 30 July 1919. Ed. Pictou Academy. Dealer in horses and produce from Sydney; government contractor for roads, bridges, and railways; large pastoral interests Qld, NSW, Vic.; chairman of directors of Squatter Investment Co.; director of City of Melbourne Bank; grandmaster Loyal Orange Lodge. KB 1918.
MLA 1874–83. MLC Yarra Province 1886–1901. Minister without portfolio 1890–2.
Senator 1901–13.

HIGGINS, Henry Bournes: b. Ireland 1851, arr. Vic. 1870, d. 13 January 1929. Ed. St Stephen's Green, Dublin; Melbourne University. Primary-school teacher, Fitzroy; Vic. Bar 1876; councillor Melbourne University 1887–1924; justice High Court 1906–22; president Commonwealth Court of Conciliation and Arbitration 1907–20. KC 1903.
MLA Geelong 1894–1901.
MHR North Melbourne 1901–6. AG 1904.

ISAACS, Isaac Alfred: b. Melbourne 1855, d. 11 February 1948. Ed. Yackandandah State School; Beechworth Grammar School; Melbourne University. Teacher 1870–5; clerk in crown law department 1875–81; Vic. Bar 1880; justice High Court 1906–30, acting chief justice 1925, 1927, chief justice 1930; GG 1932. QC 1899. PC 1921. KCMG 1928. GCMG 1932, GCB 1937.
MLA Bogong 1892–3, 1893–1901. Solicitor-general 1893; AG 1894–9, 1900–1.
MHR Indi 1901–6. AG 1905–6.

PEACOCK, Alexander James: b. Creswick 1861, d. 7 October 1933. Ed. Creswick Grammar School. Teacher 1877–81; grocer; manager mining companies Creswick, Ballarat, Melbourne; grandmaster of Freemasons 1900–5. KCMG 1902.
MLA Clunes and Allendale 1889–1904, Allendale 1904–33. Minister without portfolio 1890–2; minister of public instruction 1894–9; chief sec. and minister of labour 1900–1; premier, treasurer, and minister of labour 1901–2; chief sec. and minister of labour 1907–8; minister of public instruction, vice-president board of land and works, and minister of labour 1913; minister of public instruction and minister of labour 1913–14; premier, treasurer, and minister of labour 1914–17; speaker 1928–33.

QUICK, John: b. Eng. 1852, arr. Vic. 1854, d. 17 June 1932. Elementary schooling until 10; later self-educated and Melbourne University. Employed at iron foundry; journalist with Bendigo newspapers and Melbourne *Age*; Vic. Bar 1878; solicitor Bendigo 1880; deputy-president Commonwealth Court of Conciliation and Arbitration 1922–30. LL.D. 1882. KB 1901.
MLA Sandhurst 1880–9.
MHR Bendigo 1901–13. Postmaster-general 1909–10.

TRENWITH, William Arthur: b. Launceston 1847, arr. Vic. *c.* 1867, d. 26 July 1925. Elementary schooling until 9. Bootmaker; union organizer and pioneer of labour movement; established Bootmakers Union 1879; president Melbourne Trades Hall Council 1886–7.
MLA Richmond 1889–1903. Minister of railways, commissioner of public works, and vice-president board of land and works 1900–1; chief sec., minister of railways, and vice-president board of land and works 1901–2.
Senator 1904–10.

TURNER, George: b. Melbourne 1851, d. 13 August 1916. Ed. Model School; Melbourne University. Solicitor's clerk; articled clerk 1875; admitted to practise 1881 and partner in legal firm; member St Kilda City Council 1885–1900, mayor 1887–8. PC 1897. KCMG 1897.
MLA St Kilda 1889–1901. Commissioner of trade and customs, minister of health 1891–3; solicitor-general 1892–3; premier and treasurer 1894–9; minister of defence, vice-president board of land and works 1894–5; premier and treasurer 1900–1; commissioner of trade and customs 1900.
MHR Balaclava 1901–6. Treasurer 1901–4, 1904–5.

ZEAL, William Austin: b. Eng. 1830, arr. Vic. 1852, d. 11 March 1912. Ed. Westbury and Clover House, Windsor. Railway engineer *c.* 1855–65; pastoralist Riverina 1866–70; director National Bank 1883–1912; chairman and director many companies; member Prahran City Council. KCMG 1895.
MLA Castlemaine 1864–5, 1871–4. MLC North West Province 1882–1901. Postmaster-general 1892; president LC 1893–1901. Senator 1901–6.

South Australia

BAKER: see appendix 1.

COCKBURN: see appendix 1.

DOWNER: see appendix 1.

GLYNN, Patrick McMahon: b. Ireland 1855, arr. Vic. 1880, arr. SA 1882, d. 28 October 1931. Ed. French College, Dublin; Trinity College, Dublin. Irish Bar 1879; Vic. Bar 1880; SA Bar 1883; leader writer for *Kapunda Herald*.
MHA Light 1887–90, North Adelaide 1895–6 (first member of parliament in Australia returned under adult suffrage), 1897–1901. AG 1899.
MHR Angus 1901–19. AG 1909–10; minister of external affairs 1913–14; minister of home and territories 1917–20.

GORDON: see appendix 1.

HOLDER, Frederick William: b. Happy Valley 1850, d. 23 July 1909. Ed. public schools and St Peter's College. Teacher; proprietor-editor *Burra-Record* newspaper and correspondent for *SAR*; Methodist lay preacher; captain in volunteer forces; mayor of Burra. KCMG 1902.
MHA Burra 1887–1901. Treasurer 1889–90; opposition leader 1890–2; premier and treasurer 1892; commissioner of public works 1893–4; treasurer 1894–9; premier and treasurer 1899–1901.
MHR Wakefield 1901–9. First speaker 1901–9.

HOWE, James Henderson: b. Scot. 1839, arr. SA 1856, d. 5 February 1920. Ed. Burns Academy, Forfar. Indentured merchant's apprentice 1852; police trooper; farmer and grazier.
MHA Stanley 1881–4, Gladstone 1884–96. MLC Northern District 1897–1918. Commissioner of crown lands and immigration 1885–7, 1890, 1892–3; commissioner of public works 1889–90.

KINGSTON: see appendix 1.

SOLOMON, Vaiben Louis: b. Adelaide 1853, d. 20 October 1908. Ed. J. L. Young's Educational Institute; Scotch College, Melbourne. Merchant in Northern Territory and Adelaide; editor *Northern Territory Times* 1873–90; mayor of Adelaide 1869–70. MHA Northern Territory 1890–1901, 1905–8. Government whip 1890–2, 1892–3; opposition leader 1899; premier and treasurer 1899. MHR 1901–3.

SYMON, Josiah Henry: b. Scot. 1846, arr. SA 1866, d. 29 March 1934. Ed. Stirling High School; Moray Training College, Edinburgh. Articled clerk at Mt Gambier 1866, Adelaide 1870; SA Bar 1871; partner in legal firm 1872; president SA Law Society 1898–1903, 1915–19; member Adelaide University Council 1897–1901; owner of Auldana vineyards, Adelaide. QC 1881. KCMG 1901. MHA Sturt 1881–7. AG 1881. Senator 1901–13. Senate opposition leader 1901–4; AG 1904–5.

Tasmania

BRADDON, Edward Nicholas Coventry: b. Eng. 1829, arr. Tas. 1878, d. 2 February 1904. Ed. privately and University College, London. Employed in cousin's mercantile firm, India, 1847-8 and later managed indigo factory; civil administrator, India, *c.* 1858–78; journalist with *Pioneer* newspaper; agent-general for Tas. 1889–93. PC 1897. KCMG 1891. MHA West Devon 1879–88, 1893–1901. Opposition leader 1886; minister of land and works 1887–8; premier 1894–8; premier and treasurer 1899. MHR Wilmot 1901–4. Occasional acting opposition leader 1901–4.

BROWN: see appendix 1.

CLARKE, Matthew John: b. Ireland 1863, arr. Tas. 1888, d. 13 April 1923. Ed. St Malachy's College, Belfast; University College, Dublin. Irish Bar 1886; Tas. Bar 1888. MHA Launceston 1897–1900.

DOBSON, Henry: b. Hobart 1841, d. 10 October 1918. Ed Hutchins School, Hobart. Tas. Bar 1864; partner in legal firm. MHA Brighton 1891–1900. Opposition leader 1891–2; premier 1892–4. Senate 1901–10. Temporary chairman of committees 1904–8, chairman 1908–9.

DOUGLAS: see appendix 1.

FYSH: see appendix 1.

GRANT, Charles Henry: b. Eng. 1831, arr. Tas. 1872, d. 30 September 1901. Ed. King's College, London. Indentured civil engineer in London office of Robert Stevenson to 1866; railway construction engineer Canada; constructing engineer of Hobart–Launceston railway 1872–6, manager 1876–90; constructing engineer of Hobart electric trams and Zeehan tramways; director of numerous companies, including Hobart Tramway Co., Zeehan Tramway Co., Hobart Coffee Palace Co., Parattah Hotel Co., G. M. and Quartz Crushing Co., Silver King, Silver Queen, Perpetual Trustees, Executors and Agency Co., Alliance Insurance Co. of London; chairman Cascade Brewery Co.; chairman Hobart Chamber of Commerce. MLC Hobart 1892–1901.

HENRY, John: b. Scot. 1834, arr. Vic. 1854, arr. Tas. *c.* 1870, d. 15 September 1912. Ed. Shetland; Normal School, Edinburgh. Grocer; gold miner Castlemaine; general merchant Ararat 1856–7; traveller for Blyth Bros, Castlemaine, 1857 established wholesale and retailers J. & W. Henry 1861 with branches in Ballarat and Melbourne; established trading company in Tasmania 1872; shareholder Mt Lyell and other mines; warden Mersey Marine Board 1878–86, 1889–92. CMG 1907.
MHA Devonport 1891–8. MLC 1901–2. Treasurer and postmaster-general 1892–4.

LEWIS, Neil Elliott: b. Hobart 1858, d. 22 September 1935. Ed. Hobart High School; Balliol College, Oxford. Inner Temple Bar 1883; Tas. Bar 1885; partner legal firm; director of several mining and commercial companies; captain in volunteer forces; a founder of Queensland University, member of first council, later vice-chancellor and chancellor; lt-governor of Tas. 1933–5. CMG 1901. KCMG 1902.
MHA Richmond 1886–1902, Denison 1902–3, 1909–22. AG 1892–4; opposition leader 1894–7; premier and AG 1899–1903; premier and treasurer 1909–12; treasurer and minister of mines 1916–22; chief sec. 1922.
Minister without portfolio (before first Commonwealth election), 1 January–23 April 1901.

MOORE: see appendix 1.

Western Australia

BRIGGS, Henry: b. Eng. 1844, arr. WA 1882, d. 8 June 1919. Ed. Leicester and St Mark's College, Chelsea. Teacher at College Gram-

mar School; headmaster Mottram Grammar School 1868–78; headmaster Fremantle Grammar School 1882–97; secretary Fremantle Chamber of Commerce 1883–95; JP 1895. KB 1916.
MLC West Province 1896–1919. Chairman of committees 1900–6; president LC 1906–19.

CROWDER, Frederick Thomas: b. near Adelaide 1856, arr. WA 1876, d. 2 May 1902. Manufacturer of aerated waters in father's firm; established aerated waters firm of Crowder & Letchford 1876; part owner of *Morning Herald* 1884–6; chairman of directors of publishers of *Daily News* and *Morning Herald* 1900–2; member Perth City Council; chairman Perth Gas Co.
MLC South-East Province 1894–1900, East Province 1901–2.

FORREST, John: see appendix 1.

HACKETT: see appendix 1.

HASSELL, Albert Young: b. Albany 1841, d. 20 September 1918. Ed. Albany. Station manager 1861–94; pastoralist 1894–1918; member Plantagenet and Albany Road Boards, often chairman; botanist; JP 1872.
MLC Albany 1871–4. MLA Plantagenet 1890–1904.

HENNING, Andrew Harriot: b. Adelaide 1863, arr. WA 1894, d. 2 December 1947. Ed. Prince Alfred College; Adelaide University. SA Bar 1887; practised Adelaide and Broken Hill 1887–94; WA Bar 1894; practised Coolgardie and founded firm with branches in Kalgoorlie and Perth; a founder of Coolgardie Chamber of Mines; pastoralist south-west WA 1905; established cattle-stud 1910.
MLC North-East Province 1897–8.

JAMES, Walter Hartwell: b. Perth 1863, d. 3 January 1943. Ed. state and high schools, Perth. Jackeroo north-west WA; articled clerk, Perth; WA Bar 1888; partner in various legal firms; member Perth Board of Education 1892–3; member Perth City Council 1891–6; director of West Australian Newspapers Ltd, agent-general for WA 1904–6; pro-chancellor University of WA 1929, chancellor 1930–6. KC 1902. KB 1907. KCMG 1931.
MLA East Perth 1894–1904. Minister without portfolio 1901; premier and AG 1902–4.

LEAKE, George: b. Perth 1856, d. 24 June 1902. Ed. Bishop Hale's School, Perth; St Peter's College, Adelaide. WA Bar 1880; partner in father's legal firm; acting crown solicitor and public prosecutor 1882–3, crown solicitor 1883–94.

MLA Roebourne 1890, Albany 1894–1900, West Perth 1901–2. Opposition leader 1895–1900; premier and AG 1901–2.

LEE STEERE: see appendix 1.

LOTON: see appendix 1.

PIESSE, Frederick Henry: b. Northam 1853, d. 29 June 1912. Ed. State schools, Guildford and Northam. Pearler 1872; postmaster and telegraphist, Williams, 1875–80; member Williams Road Board 1880–9, chairman 1886–9; JP 1889; senior partner in F. & C. Piesse, general merchants, millers, importers. CMG 1907.
MLA Williams 1890–4, Katanning 1904–9. Commissioner of railways and director of public works 1896–1900; acting premier 1900; opposition leader 1901.

SHOLL, Robert Frederick: b. Bunbury 1848, d. 8 December 1909. Ed. state school, Perth. Pearler in northwest 1868; large pastoral interests; members syndicate of Kimberley Pastoral Co., director Perth Ice Works Co. and Perth Brickworks Co.
MLC Gascoyne 1886–90, North Province 1904–9. MLA Gascoyne 1890–7.

TAYLOR, John Howard: b. Eng. 1861, arr. WA 1890, d. 1 October 1925. Ed. in England and Germany. Employed in sharebroker's office, London; goldminer South Africa and WA rushes of the 1890s; sharebroker Yilgarn fields 1891 and Coolgardie 1893–4; large mining interests and director many companies.
MLC East Province 1896–9.

VENN, Henry Whittal: b. SA 1844, arr. WA 1865, d. 8 March 1908. Ed. in SA. Business interests in Robe and Adelaide; large pastoral interests north-west WA, Maitland River 1866, Bunbury 1879.
MLC Wellington 1880–90. MLA Wellington 1890–6. Commissioner of railways and director of public works 1890–6.

APPENDIX 3

DICTATION TEST: THE 'OBJECTIONABLE' PASSAGES

All aboriginal inhabitants of Africa, Asia and Polynesia should be subjected to the test unless they come within the exceptions to Section 3, or are Pacific Island labourers or are otherwise exempted. In the case of White Races, the test will be applied only under special circumstances. The passage for dictation is to be one of the set forwarded herewith, and is to be changed according to the dates given.

The English Language will in general be adopted for the purpose of the test; but if in your opinion, the immigrant would, for reasons which you would be prepared to state, be an undesirable immigrant, it may be better to substitute for the English test, a passage from some other language. The choice of the language and of the passage will be left to your discretion. In every such case, a special report is to be furnished.

REFERENCES

1 *Federation: Designs, Expectations*

[1] *1898 MC*, II, pp.2466-7.
[2] Alfred Deakin, *The Federal Story* (ed. J. A. La Nauze), p. 50.
[3] *1898 MC*, II, p. 2508.
[4] Geoffrey Sawer, *Australian Federalism in the Courts*, p. 10.
[5] *1891 SC*, p. 22.
[6] Henry Parkes, *Fifty Years in the Making of Australian History*, pp. 604-5.
[7] See J. A. La Nauze, *The Making of the Australian Constitution*, pp. 35-7.
[8] *1891 SC*, pp. 60, 42, 82, 24.
[9] *1897 AC*, pp. 20, 17.
[10] *1890 MC*, pp. 17, 33.
[11] *1891 SC*, pp. 153, 413.
[12] *1897 AC*, p. 83.
[13] *1890 MC*, p. 12. Griffith had drafted the Federal Council Act.
[14] Sections 51 (ii) and (vi), 68, 69.
[15] The relationship between defence and federation is considered in detail in ch. 4.
[16] *1891 SC*, p. 672.
[17] Cockburn, *1891 SC*, p. 204. George Dibbs opposed a central defence power.
[18] *1898 MC*, II, p. 2425. The Braddon clause provided one-quarter of the net customs and excise duties as Commonwealth revenue. In 1899, at George Reid's insistence, application of the clause was in effect limited to ten years: it became section 87.
[19] *1891 SC*, pp. 675, 676, 677.
[20] Ibid., p. 113.
[21] *1897 AC*, pp. 318-19, 151, 767; *1897 SC*, pp. 1068-9.
[22] See *1897 SC*, pp. 1078-81. In the event some 60 years elapsed before federal legislation embraced the subject.
[23] *Australian National Government*, pp. 14-21.
[24] *1891 SC*, pp. 164, 688, 780, 784, 781, 782.
[25] *1898 MC*, I, pp. 194-5, 203.
[26] *1897 AC*, p. 355. Howe, a grazier, was elected to the SA Legislative Council as a candidate of the conservative National Defence League.
[27] *1898 MC*, I, p. 7.
[28] *1897 AC*, p. 355.

29 *1898 MC*, I, pp. 8, 9.
30 *1898 MC*, II, pp. 1995-6, 1993. The issue was clearly settled outside the Convention.
31 Ibid., pp. 1106-8. Bernhard Wise.
32 *1891 SC*, p. 683.
33 *1891 SC*, p. 663; *1898 MC*, I, p. 501; II, pp. 1302, 1314, 1456-60.
34 *1891 SC*, p. 526.
35 Ibid., pp. 525-6.
36 Ibid., p. 201.
37 See *1891 SC*, p. 383; *1897 AC*, pp. 298-9.
38 See *1897 AC*, p. 271; *1897 SC*, p. 651.
39 *1891 SC*, pp. 31, 111; *1890 MC*, p. 46; *1891 SC*, pp. 244, 26.
40 See *1891 SC*, pp. 56-60, 425; *1897 AC*, pp. 480, 484, 575.
41 NSW, SA, Vic., Tas. elected delegates. Parliament elected the WA delegates.
42 *1891 SC*, p. 707.
43 *1897 SC*, p. 423. See also *1897 AC*, pp. 684-6.
44 See *1897 AC*, p. 693; *1897 SC*, pp. 362, 372; *1898 MC*, II, pp. 1832, 1927.
45 *1891 SC*, p. 260.
46 For these views see *1897 AC*, pp. 160, 549; *1898 MC*, II, pp. 2127, 2176, 2483.
47 See *1897 AC*, pp. 110, 935, 940, 950.
48 *1897 AC*, p. 111; *1898 MC*, I, pp. 865, 1063, 898; II, pp. 2482-3; I, p. 979.
49 *1897 AC*, p. 67; *1898 MC*, I, p. 266; II, pp. 1489, 2350; *1897 AC*, p. 1032.
50 Briefly, these introduced an absolute majority at joint sittings of both Houses; limited operation of the Braddon clause; empowered federal parliament to grant financial assistance to States; made some provisions for siting the capital city; guaranteed existing State boundaries; altered provisions for constitutional amendments by referenda; enabled Queensland to create divisions for election of its Senators.
51 *SAR*, 21, 26 March; *Argus*, 3 June 1898.
52 *SMH*, 24 May 1898.
53 *Argus*, 31 May 1898.
54 *Age*, 25 May 1898.
55 Symon Papers, ANL, MS. 1736.
56 *The Federal Bill Analysed, Being an Examination of the Federal Bill as Amended by the Secret Conference of Premiers*, p. 10.
57 Tom Price, Labor MHA, *SAR*, 7 May 1898.
58 *Mercury*, 17 May; *SAR*, 4 May 1898.
59 *Argus*, 31, 30 May; *Orroroo Enterprise and Great Northern Advertiser*, 3 June 1898.
60 30 May 1898. Small colonies were more inclined to call the 'Braddon blot' the 'Braddon blessing'.
61 Barton to Holder, 5 May 1898, Barton Papers, ANL, MS. 51, series 1, item 148, copy. The Finance Committee consisted of J. R. French, manager of the Bank of NSW—a neutral on federation; Bruce Smith—a Billite nominee; Dr Normand MacLaurin—an anti-Billite nominee.
62 *Colonists' Anti-Convention Bill League*, 1899.
63 'Aspects of Campaigns in South-Eastern New South Wales at the Federation Referenda of 1898 and 1899', in A. W. Martin (ed.), *Essays in Australian Federation*, pp. 167-84. Parker–Blainey controversy in J. J. Eastwood and F. B. Smith (eds), *Historical Studies: Selected Articles*, pp. 152-98.
64 28 May 1898.
65 Deakin, *Federal Story*, p. 74.
66 *Advertiser*, 26 March; *Age*, 30, 31 May 1898.

[67] Wallaroo and Moonta Mining and Smelting Co. Ltd, General Minute Book, 1890-1923, 24 May 1898, p. 55, SA Archives. *Southern Yorke's Peninsula Pioneer*, 27 May 1898. A second director, W. H. Duncan, MHA, also campaigned for the Bill.

[68] *Kadina and Wallaroo Times*, 28 May 1898.

[69] C. M. Bagot, in Symon Papers, ANL, MS. 1736.

[70] *Advertiser*, 27 April 1898. There was a touching scene earlier in April at the Vintage Sports and Social in McLaren Vale. As Hardy watched the children playing he asked his manager 'What is to become of all these boys and girls?' He added, 'Dreams of federation . . . come as a consolation'.

[71] 30 May 1898.

[72] John Bastin, 'The West Australian Federation Movement', MA thesis, University of Melbourne (1951), pp. 37-8, 76-7.

[73] *NSW Parliamentary Debates*, LXXXIX, pp. 2620-35, 2731-6.

[74] See A. G. Lowndes (ed.), *South Pacific Enterprise: The Colonial Sugar Refining Company Limited*, pp. 49, 435-6.

[75] *Daily Telegraph*, 18 May, 3 June 1898.

[76] See *SAR*, 27, 28 April; *South Eastern Star*, 17, 27 May; *Kapunda Herald*, 3 June; *Advertiser*, 27 April, 6 May 1898.

[77] United Trades and Labor Council, Minute Book 1895-1899, 15 April 1898, SA Trades Hall.

[78] *Advertiser*, 10 May; *SAR*, 30 April 1898.

[79] Bastin, 'WA Federation Movement', pp. 39-41.

[80] See 'The First Federal Referendum: A Local Study', in *Royal Australian Historical Society: Journal and Proceedings*, vol. 46 (1960), pp. 69-82.

[81] See 'WA Federation Movement', pp. i, 37-8, 43, 54, 76-7, 113-17, 153-6.

[82] See R. Norris, 'Aspects of the 1898 South Australian Federation Referendum and the Parker–Blainey Controversy', BA thesis, University of Adelaide (1966), and Norris, 'Economic Influences on the 1898 South Australian Federation Referendum', in Martin, op. cit., pp. 137-66.

[83] C. G. Heydon, MLC, *Daily Telegraph*, 17 May 1898.

[84] Archdeacon Young, *South-Eastern Star*, 24 May 1898.

[85] See *SAR*, 2 June; *Daily Telegraph*, 18 May; *Mercury*, 13 May 1898.

[86] 8 August 1899.

[87] 5 September 1899, James Papers, ANL, MS. 296.

[88] *West Australian*, 30 July 1900.

[89] 30 May 1898.

[90] In 1898 the approximate percentage 'Yes' vote to formal votes was: Vic. 89, Tas. 81, SA 67, NSW 52.

[91] Percentage 'Yes' vote to formal votes: North 80, Centre 59, South 49.9, Brisbane 36. See G. C. Bolton, *A Thousand Miles Away*, p. 210.

[92] 8 August 1899.

[93] J. Quick and R. R. Garran, *The Annotated Constitution of the Australian Commonwealth*, p. 224.

[94] Bastin, 'WA Federation Movement', pp. i, 48. McMinn, 'First Federal Referendum', p. 81. Hewett, 'Campaigns in South-Eastern NSW', pp. 173-4. Also see B. K. De Garis, '1890-1900', in F. K. Crowley (ed.), *A New History of Australia*, pp. 249-55 for an account of federation and the referenda.

[95] *Age*, 31 May 1898. A reasonable statement about Victoria, an exaggeration elsewhere.

[96] Corowa Conference, *Official Report of the Federation Conference*, p. 24.

[97] 1 October 1894.

[98] 3 June 1898.

[99] The percentage of 'Yes' votes to qualified electors in the ten referenda was: NSW 23, 35; Vic. 40, 53; SA 26, 43; Tas. 37, 39; Qld 36; WA 47. R. S. Parker, 'Australian Federation: the Influence of Economic Interests and Political Pressures', in J. J. Eastwood and F. B. Smith (eds), *Historical Studies: Selected Articles*, p. 178.

[1] *The Constitution of the Commonwealth of Australia*, pp. 60-1.

[2] *SMH*, 19 May 1891.

[3] Sir Samuel Walker Griffith, *Notes on Australian Federation: Its Nature and Probable Effects*.

[4] Richard Chaffey Baker, *Federation*, p. 10.

[5] Sir John Forrest, *Speech by the Rt. Hon. Sir John Forrest on the Federation of Australia at St. Georges Hall*, Perth, pp. 6, 15.

[6] *Brisbane Courier*, 8, 2 August 1899.

[7] *1898 MC*, II, pp. 2483, 2500.

[8] Henry Bournes Higgins, *Essays and Addresses on the Australian Commonwealth Bill*, p. 118f.

[9] *1897 SC*, pp. 765, 335, 951.

[10] Rosa, *Federal Bill Analysed*, p. 4.

[11] *1897 AC*, p. 297.

[12] W. M. Hughes, *Labour in Power*.

[13] Symon's draft of an article 'United Australia', March 1900, Symon Papers, ANL, MS. 1736.

[14] Baker, *Federation*, p. 6.

[15] *Argus*, 30 May 1898.

[16] J. L. Purves, *Age*, 1 June 1898.

[17] *Argus*, 28 May 1898.

[18] 4 April 1898.

[19] *South-Eastern Star*, 24 May 1898.

[20] *Speech . . . at St. Georges Hall*, pp. 11, 16.

[21] *Argus*, 31 May 1898.

[22] Deakin, *Federal Story*, p. 93.

[23] *1898 MC*, I, p. 266. Glynn was a member of federal parliament for some 20 years.

[24] 19 October 1899, James Papers, ANL, MS. 296.

[25] Speech at Town Hall, 25 February 1901 (in Symon Papers, ANL).

[26] *The Times*, 3 October 1908.

[27] Holder, *1898 MC*, I, p. 828.

[28] 'United Australia', Symon Papers, ANL, MS. 1736.

2 *The Genesis of White Australia*

[1] *Asian Migration to Australia*, p. 1.

[2] *History of the White Australia Policy to 1920*, p. 119.

[3] *CPD*, IV, p. 4804; Willard's version is a slight misquote.

[4] *White Australia Policy*, pp. 119-20.

[5] 'The Commonwealth, 1900-1914', in J. Holland Rose (ed.), *The Cambridge History of the British Empire*, vol. VII, pt 1, p. 500.

[6] Marjorie Barnard, *A History of Australia*, pp. 442, 452.

[7] *1890 MC*, pp. 5, 84-5.

[8] Ibid., pp. 11, 12, 13, 23, 68.

[9] See *1891 SC*, pp. 23, 157, 274, 689.

[10] See *1897 AC*, pp. 17, 100, 310.

[11] *1897 SC*, p. 272.

[12] Special laws for people of any race—later section (xxvi)—concerned actual residents; immigration—section 51 (xxvii)—concerned potential residents. See *1898 MC*, I, pp. 227-55 for the debate.

[13] *1898 MC*, I, pp. 234-5.

[14] Ibid., p. 238.

[15] J. Quick and R. R. Garran, *The Annotated Constitution of the Australian Commonwealth*, p. 151.

[16] See Corowa Conference, *Official Report of the Federation Conference*.

[17] See Bathurst Convention, *Proceedings of the People's Federal Convention*. A letter from the Governor of Victoria and a paper from James Drake of Queensland—both printed at the back of the *Proceedings*—alluded to the admission of aliens.

[18] See *Daily Telegraph*, 31 May; *SMH*, 24, 30 May, 2 June 1898.

[19] See *Daily Telegraph*, 31 May; *SMH*, 2 June; *Bulletin*, 30 April, 4 June 1898.

[20] See *Age*, 25, 31 May, 1 June; *Argus*, 31 May 1898.

[21] See *Argus*, 30, 31 May, 2 June; *Age* 2 June 1898.

[22] 2 June 1898.

[23] See R. Norris, 'Economic Influences on the 1898 South Australian Federation Referendum', in A. W. Martin (ed.), *Essays in Australian Federation*, pp. 118-22, 165-6.

[24] See *Plain Dealer*, 23 April; *SAR*, 29 April; *Ororoo Enterprise*, 27 May 1898.

[25] *People's Weekly*, 4 June 1898.

[26] *Southern Argus*, 2 June 1898.

[27] See *Northern Territory Times*, 14 January 1888, 1, 8, 22, 29 April, 6 May, 3 June 1898; *SAR*, 26 April, 6, 12, 19, 28 May 1898.

[28] See *Weekly Herald*, 21 May; *Advertiser*, 14 May 1898; Norris, 'SA Federation Referendum', p. 151. Later it transpired that the 'leper' suffered only from the effects of a 'Chinese plaster'.

[29] See *Age*, 27 May; *Argus*, 28, 30 May 1898.

[30] 2 June 1898.

[31] 4 June 1898.

[32] *Daily Telegraph*, 8 June 1899.

[33] *SMH*, 8 June 1899.

[34] See *Daily Telegraph*, 14, 16, 20 June 1899; S. A. Rosa, *The Federal Bill Analysed*; *Worker*, 10 June 1899.

[35] *Brisbane Courier*, 3, 8, 14, 18 August 1899.

[36] *Australian Federation*: volume of handbills and cuttings issued in Queensland 1899, Mitchell Library.

[37] See *Patriot*, 24 June, 8 July, 9 September; *Brisbane Courier*, 3 August 1899.

[38] 26 August, 2 September 1899.

[39] Ibid., 12 August 1899.

[40] 15 February 1899, pp. 170-1.

[41] Ibid.

[42] Ibid., 15 June 1899, p. 267; 15 August 1899, p. 27.

[43] C. 8596, *Proceedings of a Conference Between the Secretary of State for the Colonies and the Premiers of the Self-Governing Colonies* in BPP, 1897, LIX, p. 14.

[44] *Vic. Parliamentary Debates*, vol. 88, 1898, pp. 245, 249, 251.

[45] Ibid., vol. 90, p. 3220.

[46] Ibid., vol. 89, p. 2265.

[47] See *Official Reports* of Intercolonial Trade Union Congresses from the first—1879—to the fifth—1888.

[48] *Official Report of the Sixth . . . Congress*, p. 62.

[40] *Official Report of the Seventh . . . Congress*, pp. 91-2.
[50] *Worker*, 2 February 1900.
[51] *Notes on Australian Federation.*
[52] Ibid.
[53] Griffith, *Australian Federation and the Draft Commonwealth Bill.*
[54] *Brisbane Courier*, 4 January 1901.
[55] Ibid., 26 January, 1 February 1901.
[56] *Annotated Constitution*, pp. 79-252.
[57] *Daily Telegraph*, 18 January 1901.
[58] 28 September 1900, Deakin Papers, ANL, MS. 1540, item 3335.
[59] To Deakin, 9 November 1900, ibid.
[60] 7 November 1901, Barton Papers, ANL, MS. 51, series 1, item 362.
[61] 14 November 1901, ibid., item 363.
[62] Barton Papers, series 5, item 977. The original draft read 'Next, it cannot be many years before the immigration of persons'. The words 'many years' were crossed out and 'long' substituted in a hand that does not seem to be Barton's.
[63] *Australian Federation*, p. 41.
[64] *SMH*, 27 January 1901.
[65] Ibid., 8 January 1901.
[66] *Mercury*, 27 February 1901.
[67] Ironically, Reid had done much to secure legislation on the question in NSW and he had shown some awareness of the potential dangers of any large Japanese population in Australia at the Colonial Conference of 1897.
[68] Section 19 of the Immigration Restriction Act, 1901, exempted Pacific Island labourers from its provisions.
[69] Correspondence on this issue between Barton, Philp, Forrest, Hobbs, and Drake is in CAO, CRS A6, file 01/117.
[70] 26 February 1901. Sydney date 22 January.
[71] 30 March 1901.
[72] See *Age*, 18 January 1901; *SMH*, 18, 19 January 1901.
[73] Quoted by *Brisbane Courier*, 23 January 1901.
[74] See *Brisbane Courier*, 1, 25 February 1901; *Bulletin*, 16 February 1901.
[75] *Brisbane Courier*, 27 February, 4 March 1901.
[76] John Arthur, *Brisbane Courier*, 12 March 1901.
[77] 9 March 1901.
[78] To Barton, 3 December 1901, CAO, CRS A8, file 01/272/1. This was a 24-foolscap-page typed protest.
[79] See *Brisbane Courier*, 8, 18, 19 March; *Bulletin*, 30 March 1901.
[80] Quoted by Philp to Barton, 1 August 1901, CAO, CRS A8, file 01/346/1. Chataway was also part proprietor, and probably editor, of the *Sugar Journal and Tropical Cultivator.*
[81] 24 June 1901, Littleton Groom Papers, ANL, MS. 236, series 1.
[82] 20 April 1901.
[83] W. Forrest to Symon, 5 April 1901, Symon Papers, ANL, MS. 1736.
[84] See *Brisbane Courier*, 1 April; *Bulletin*, 6 April 1901; *CPD*, I, p. 45.
[85] Federal Labor Party, Minute Book No. 1, 20 May 1901.
[86] Barton to Philp, 12 November 1901, CAO, CRS A8, file 01/272/1.
[87] See CAO, CRS A6, file 01/346.
[88] Barton to Philp, 20 November 1901, ibid., file 10/272/1.
[89] See *CPD*, III, p. 3502; IV, pp. 4634, 4805.
[90] See CAO, CRS A8, files 01/142/1 and 01/142/2.
[91] Notes by G. E. Flannery for O'Connor, ibid., file 01/142/2.
[92] Reverend J. B. Ronald, *CPD*, IV, p. 4666.

[93] Ibid., p. 4633.

[94] See ibid., pp. 4666, 4803; *Age*, 22 July 1899.

[95] *CPD*, III, p. 3504, and IV, p. 4804.

3   *Towards a Whiter Commonwealth*

[1] See Harry T. Easterby, *The Queensland Sugar Industry*, for an account of the pre-federation sugar industry.

[2] CAO, CRS A8, file 01/272/1.

[3] *Cane Sugar Industry of Australia*, in *CPP*, 1901-2, II, p. 975.

[4] See CAO, CRS A6, file 01/346.

[5] CAO, CRS A1, file 03/1714.

[6] *CPD*, XIII, pp. 80, 502.

[7] Ibid., pp. 1033, 1036, 1373-4.

[8] See *CPD*, XIV, pp. 1693-8, 2076, 2366, 2374, 2381, 2489.

[9] *CPD*, XV, pp. 2609-11.

[10] See *Sugar Bounty*, in *CPP*, 1904, II, pp. 1635-8.

[11] *Sugar Bonus (Report by Dr Maxwell)*, in *CPP*, 1905, II, pp. 1363-7.

[12] *CPD*, XXVIII, p. 4954; *CPD*, XXX, pp. 7373, 7376, 7378.

[13] *CPD*, XXX, pp. 7240-2.

[14] CAO, CRS A1, file 13/11647.

[15] Ibid.

[16] 9 August 1911, my italics.

[17] *Sugar Industry of Australia: Report by Dr Maxwell, 1910* in *CPP*, 1912, III, pp. 1019-33.

[18] See A. T. Yarwood, *Asian Migration to Australia*, pp. 22-41, for an account of the debates on the Immigration Restriction Bill.

[19] Pencilled notes in Barton's hand, 6 September 1901, CAO, CRS A8, file 02/51/-. Barton's reasons for proposing English, rather than a European language remain obscure.

[20] See attacks by Watson and McMillan, *CPD*, IV, pp. 4248, 4625-30, 4633-4.

[21] Federal Labor Party, Minute Book No. 1, 31 July, 27 September 1901.

[22] Pencilled notes, CAO, CRS A8, file 02/51/-.

[23] Yarwood, *Asian Immigration*, p. 36.

[24] Hopetoun to Chamberlain, 20 August 1901, Records of the Colonial Office, CO 418/10, ANL microfilm reel 2139.

[25] CAO, CP 78, series 1, file 65.

[26] CAO, CRS A8, file 01/203/1.

[27] CAO, CRS A8, file 02/52/-.

[28] CAO, CRS A8, file 02/108/3. See appendix C for the two passages.

[29] Symon to Lady Lugard, 29 June 1904, ANL, MS. 1736, copy. Symon, remember, had been president of both the Federation and Commonwealth Leagues.

[30] See Federal Labor Party, Minute Books Nos 1 and 2.

[31] *CPD*, IV, p. 5364.

[32] Goldfields Trades and Labor Council to F. G. Tudor, 14 March, 1902, copy, CAO, CRS A1, file 12/9287.

[33] *Intercolonial Conference of Ministers*, 4–5 March 1896 in *SA Parliamentary Papers*, 1896, II.

[34] *Admission of Japanese into Queensland* in *Qld Parliamentary Papers, Legislative Assembly*, 1901, IV, pp. 1121-52.

[35] 13 May 1901, CAO, CRS A8, file 01/203/1.

[36] CAO, CP 78, series 2, file 02/9.

[37] Garran to Wallington, undated letter, ibid. If Garran meant messages *to*

Hopetoun, this may have been an attempt to delay Hopetoun—and hence Chamberlain—knowledge of the protest until doubts about the date of assent were resolved.

[38] 31 December, ibid.
[39] 13 January 1902, CAO, CRS A1108, vol. 23.
[40] Deakin to Barton, 16 January 1902, ibid.
[41] CAO, CP 78, series 1, file 65.
[42] Philp to Barton, 25, 28 January 1902, telegrams, CAO, CRS A8, files 02/51/5, 02/51/6, 02/51/22.
[43] Telegram, copy., ibid., file 02/51/-.
[44] 18, 20 January 1902, telegrams, ibid., files 02/51/- and 02/51/4.
[45] CAO, CRS A1108, vol. 23.
[46] 30 January 1902, ibid.
[47] *Argus*, 14 February 1902.
[48] Eitaki to Barton, 15 February 1902; Barton to Eitaki, 21 February 1902, CAO, CRS A8, file 02/51/38.
[49] 3 June 1902, Barton Papers, ANL, MS. 51, series 1, item 513.
[50] *CPD*, I, p. 1247.
[51] Carruthers to Reid, 17 November, 20 December 1904, CAO, CRS A1108, vol. 23.
[52] Reid to Carruthers, 17 January 1905, ibid.
[53] 13 October 1905, 5 March 1906, ibid. See Yarwood, *Asian Migration*, pp. 86-90, for an account of the passport agreement between Australia and Japan.
[54] Deakin to Carruthers, 12 March 1906, copy, CAO, CRS A1108, vol. 23.
[55] Paper by H. V. Jackson in ibid.; *Conference of Commonwealth and State Premiers and Ministers* in *CPP*, 1906, II, p. 1390.
[56] Morgan to Deakin, 3 October 1905; Isaacs to Deakin, 11 April 1906, CAO, CRS A1108, vol. 23.
[57] Deakin to GG for S. of S., 1 May 1906, CAO, CP 78, series 1, file 1084.
[58] Elgin to GG for PM, 12 October 1906, cable, and 7 December 1906 with enclosure Hayashi to MacDonald, copies, ibid.
[59] See CAO, CRS A30, vol. IV, entries 06/7389 and 06/9050; Minute by Hunt, 23 January 1907, CAO, CRS A1108, vol. 23.
[60] See *CPD*, XXVIII, pp. 4089, 4121; *Argus*, 13 June 1906.
[61] *CPD*, XLI, pp. 5561, 5858, 5867-73.
[62] *Minutes and Proceedings of the Colonial Conference 1907* in *BPP*, 1907, LV, Cd 3523, p. 467.
[63] Minute, Groom to Deakin, 4 March 1907, Deakin Papers, ANL, MS. 1540. item 496.
[64] Elgin to GG for PM, 17 January 1908, CAO, CP 78, series 1, file 1084. See D. I. Wright, *Shadow of Dispute*, ch. 1, for the Vondel case and related issues.
[65] On 21 February 1908 Hunt passed a copy of Elgin's despatch—which Deakin received on 19 February—and commented 'it is proposed to give twelve months notice to terminate the Treaty'. CAO, CRS A1108, vol. 23.
[66] Deakin to GG for S. of S., 16 March 1908, CAO, CP 78, series 1, file 1084. Yarwood, *Asian Migration*, p. 91, stated Elgin gave the advice, which Deakin accepted, that notice of withdrawal should be given without delay: the despatch contains no such advice.
[67] Crewe to GG for PM, 25 April 1908, cable, CAO, CP 78, series 1, file 1084.
[68] Kidston to Deakin, 11 May 1908; Deakin to Barlow, 19 May 1908, CAO, CRS A1108, vol. 23.
[69] 28 May 1901, Deakin Papers, ANL, MS. 1540, item 498.
[70] See D. F. Nicholson, *Australia's Trade Relations*, pp. 4, 22, 26-7.

4 *Federation and Defence*

[1] The most detailed account is L. D. Atkinson, 'Australian Defence Policy: A Study of Empire and Nation', PhD thesis, Australian National University (1964). Also see J. A. La Nauze, *Alfred Deakin*, ch. 23.

[2] Quoted by G. L. Macandie, *The Genesis of the Royal Australian Navy*, p. 288.

[3] *The Times*, 24 March; *Saturday Evening Tribune*, February 1908, cutting in CAO, MP 84, series 1, file 1856/5/69.

[4] Copies of the memorandum and reports in C. 6188, *Correspondence Relating to the Inspection of the Military Forces of the Australasian Colonies by Major-General J. Bevan Edwards* in BPP, 1890, XLIX.

[5] Copy of telegram in NSW Government Archives, Col. Sec., 1890-1, 4/902.1; Tenterfield address in Parkes, *The Federal Government of Australasia*, pp. 1-6.

[6] Parkes, *Fifty Years in the Making of Australian History*, p. 585.

[7] La Nauze, *Deakin*, pp. 116-17; Geoffrey Serle, 'The Victorian Government's Campaign for Federation', in A. W. Martin (ed.), *Essays in Australian Federation*, p. 50.

[8] See *Northern Territory Times*, 22, 29 June. Edwards reached Sydney on 18 July.

[9] Copy in Parkes Correspondence, Mitchell Library, A916, vol. 46, pp. 158-9.

[10] *Proceedings of the Royal Colonial Institute*, 1890-1, XXII, p. 196.

[11] 30 November 1889, copy, NSW Government Archives, Col. Sec. 4/902.1.

[12] See Edwards to Parkes, 24 January 1890, Parkes Correspondence, A921; Gillies to Parkes, 6 March 1890, ibid., A885, vol. 15; Edwards to Parkes, 10 May 1890, ibid., A68.

[13] 24 January 1890, ibid., A921.

[14] Parkes, *Fifty Years*, p. 586.

[15] Parkes to Gillies, 30 March 1888, in *Inspection of Colonial Forces by an Imperial General Officer* in *Vic. Parliamentary Papers*, 1889, III, p. 617.

[16] See War Office to Colonial Office, 5 April 1889; Lord Knutsford to Governors of the Australasian Colonies, 17 June 1889, C. 6188, pp. 5, 36-7.

[17] 19 July 1889.

[18] C. 5091, *Proceedings of the Colonial Conference, 1887* in BPP, 1887, LVI, p. 6.

[19] Ibid., p. 37.

[20] For discussions on naval defence see ibid., pp. 28-49, 147-62, 298-310, 485-6, 489-511. For military defence, pp. 292, 293, 295, 362.

[21] Ibid., pp. 309, 485.

[22] See *Statistical Register of Victoria for 1899*, pt 1, p. 26; *Statistical Register of SA for 1890*, pt VI, no. 2, p. 6, and *1898*, pt VI, no. 2, p. 7.

[23] *SA Parliamentary Debates*, XL, p. 2561.

[24] Colonial Office, *Misc. No. 111. Confidential. Report . . .* , in CAO, CP 103, series 12, bundle 1.

[25] *1891 SC*, p. 281. See Thynne p. 17, Deakin p. 73, Jennings p. 126, Fitzgerald p. 169, Dibbs pp. 184-5, Cockburn p. 204, Moore p. 283, Cuthbert p. 289.

[26] Ibid., pp. 713-14.

[27] *1897 AC*, p. 888.

[28] See Corowa Conference, *Official Report . . .* , p. 21; Bathurst Convention, *Proceedings . . .* , pp. 38, 79, 84-5, 92.

[29] 25 May 1898.

[30] See *Argus, Daily Telegraph*, 31 May; *Ororoo Enterprise*, 27 May 1898.

[31] See *Weekly Herald*, 21, 28 May; *SAR*, 19 April 1898.

[32] The Anti-Commonwealth Bill League, undated circular, Symon Papers, ANL, MS. 1736.

[33] 25 March 1898.

[34] *Laura Standard*, 12 May 1898.

[35] *Southern Cross*, 3 June 1898.

[36] Parkes, *Federal Government*, p. 37.

[37] Ibid., pp. 39, 50.

[38] C. 6188, *Correspondence Relating to the Inspection of the Military Forces . . .*, in *BPP*, XLIX, p. 31.

[39] *1891 SC*, p. 316.

[40] *The Federal Defence of Australasia*, pp. 156-9.

[41] Ibid.

[42] S. A. Rosa, *Federation. An Exposure of the Federal Conspiracy*, p. 3.

[43] Colonial Office, *Misc. No. 111*, p. 70.

[44] Craig, *Federal Defence*, p. 151.

[45] *1897 AC*, p. 70.

[46] 30 April 1898.

[47] Barton Papers, ANL, MS. 51, series 5, item 977, my italics.

[48] 28 September 1900, Deakin Papers, ANL, MS. 1540, item 3335.

[49] *Port Augusta Despatch*, 3 June 1898.

[50] See Deakin, *Federal Story*, pp. 148-64.

[51] *SMH*, 18 January 1901.

[52] See Kingston to Deakin, 9, 10 November 1900, Deakin Papers, ANL, MS. 1540, items 3336, 3337; Deakin to Barton, 7 November 1900, Barton Papers, ANL, MS. 51, series 1, item 362.

[53] *SMH, Daily Telegraph*, 18 January 1901.

[54] See Forrest to NSW Minister of Defence, 27 February 1901; Barton to Forrest, 2 April 1901, CAO, CRS A6, file 01/886.

[55] 19 April 1904, ibid.

[56] Forrest to Military Commandant NSW, 27 February 1901, ibid.

[57] *CPD*, I, pp. 28-30, 37, 102.

[58] See *CPD*, III, pp. 2974, 2992, 3292. Atkinson, 'Australian Defence Policy', states that some 70 clauses depended on Queensland defence measures, and only 8 had no colonial precedent.

[59] 6 January 1900.

[60] 20 February 1901.

[61] *Advertiser*, 1 September 1902.

[62] *Military Forces of the Commonwealth: Minute Upon the Defence of Australia by Major-General Hutton, Commandant*, 7 April 1902, in *CPP*, 1901-2, pp. 53-60.

[63] 6 August 1902, CAO, MP 84, series 2, file 02/2688, copy.

[64] Hutton to Collins, 11 August 1902; Forrest to Collins, 24 June 1903, ibid.

[65] *Minute Upon the Defence of Australia . . .*, 7 April 1902, p. 59.

[66] See *CPD*, IX, pp. 12091, 12092, 12094-6, 12211.

[67] See Forrest to Collins, 2 May 1902; Collins to Hutton 3 May 1902; Philp to Forrest, 3 May 1902, telegram, CAO, MP 84, series 2, file 02/2441.

[68] Deakin to Barton, 14 May 1902, Barton Papers, ANL, MS. 51, series 1, item 504.

[69] 20 May, 17 June 1902, ibid., items 505, 518.

[70] See Minute by Collins, 11 June 1902, file 02/2441; Hutton to Forrest, 24 October 1902, file 02/2688; Forrest to Collins, 6 November 1902, file 02/2688; in CAO, MP 84, series 2.

[71] *Statement by the Minister of State for Defence on the Estimates of the Defence Department for the Financial Year 1903-4*, 30 July 1903, in *CPP*, 1903, II, pp. 129-47.

[72] 14 March 1904, CAO, MP 84, series 2, file 02/2688.

[73] See Hutton to Dawson, 7 July 1904, file 03/4592; Hutton to McCay, 29 August 1904, file 04/185; in CAO, MP 84, series 2.

[74] See *Proceedings of the Commonwealth Defence Committee*, 31 October 1904, file 04/185, ibid.; *Military Forces of the Commonwealth of Australia: Second Annual Report by Major-General Sir Edward Hutton*, 1 May 1904, in *CPP*, 1904, II, pp. 277-308.

[75] See CAO, MP 84, series 2, file 05/1678; Clarke to Deakin, 1 June 1906, Deakin Papers, ANL, MS. 1540, box 38, item 461.

[76] For the new Agreement see Cd 1299, *Papers Relating to a Conference Between the Secretary of State for the Colonies and the Prime Ministers of the Self-Governing Colonies* in *BPP*, 1906, LXVI. Mahan's works *The Influence of Sea Power in History* and *The Influence of Sea Power upon the French Revolution and the Empire*, were published in 1890 and 1892.

[77] See *Brisbane Courier*, 7 November 1902; Richard Jebb, *The Imperial Conference: A History and Study*, vol. I, p. 376.

[78] Undated, Jebb Papers, ANL, MS. 339.

[79] 'Some Aspects of Australian Attitudes to the Imperial Connection 1900-1919', MA thesis, University of Queensland (1958), pp. 132-3.

[80] See Macandie, *Genesis of the Royal Australian Navy*, pp. 58-60.

[81] 11 May 1901, CAO, MP 160, series 1, file 01/640.

[82] See *Age*, 20 December 1901; Deakin, *Federal Story*, p. 97.

[83] *CPD*, III, pp. 2964, 2975, 3106, 3196, 3293, 3520.

[84] Federal Labor Party, Minute Book No. 1, 30 April, 17 July 1902.

[85] Forrest to Barton, 31 May 1901; Beaumont to Hopetoun, 16 July 1901, CAO, MP 160, series 1, file 01/3890.

[86] Forrest to Barton, 5 October 1901, ibid.

[87] *Minute Forrest to Prime Minister as to Naval Defence*, 15 March 1902, in Cd 1299, pp. 9-14.

[88] Ibid.

[89] See Atkinson, 'Australian Defence Policy', pp. 93, 199-205.

[90] Barton Papers, ANL, MS. 51, series 5, item 977.

[91] 16 July 1902, cable, copy in Tennyson Papers, ANL, MS. 479, series 6.

[92] Grimshaw, 'Attitudes to the Imperial Connection', p. 132. See pp. 133-7 for a good summary of response to the Agreement.

[93] 28 September, 6 October 1899.

[94] See Arthur J. Marder, *From the Dreadnought to Scapa Flow*, vol. I, pp. 23-5.

[95] 'Australian Defence Policy', p. 158.

[96] Deakin Papers, ANL, MS. 1540, box 38, item 467.

[97] New series, XXXV, April to September 1907, p. 566. The 'Sydney Correspondent' was probably Jose or Deakin.

[98] *Morning Post*, 13 October 1909.

[99] 'The Naval Defence of Australia', 7 March 1904, CAO, MP 178, series 1, file 02/2688.

5 *Defending Australia and the Empire*

[1] *Morning Post*, 13 May 1911.

[2] 12 June 1905.

[3] See *CPD*, III, pp. 3292-9.

[4] See *Australian Workman*, 11 April 1891; *Worker*, 13 February 1897, 3 June 1899, 17 March 1900.

[5] J. C. Watson, 'The Labour Movement', in British Association for the Advancement of Science, *Handbook for New South Wales*, p. 136.

[6] Federal Labor Party, Minute Book No. 1, 20 May 1901, 30 April 1902.

[7] Commonwealth Political Labour Conference, *Official Report of the Fourth . . .* , pp. 16-20.

[8] See L. D. Atkinson, 'Australian Defence Policy', PhD thesis, Australian National University (1964), p. 329; D. C. S. Sissons, 'Attitudes to Japan and Defence, 1890-1923', MA thesis, University of Melbourne (1956), p. 329.

[9] 8 August 1906.

[10] *Morning Post*, 24 October 1905.

[11] November 1906.

[12] November 1906, May, August 1909, March 1910.

[13] Commonwealth Labour Conference, *Official Minutes of Proceedings, Sydney 1902*, p. 8.

[14] Creswell to Collins, 5 May 1904, CAO, MP 178, series 1, file 04/3436.

[15] Collins to Hunt, 20 June 1904, ibid.

[16] GG to Watson from S. of S., 17 July 1904, ibid.

[17] 9 February 1909, Jebb Papers, ANL, MS. 813.

[18] *The Times*, 31 July 1909, and Arthur W. Jose, *The Royal Australian Navy, 1914-18*, vol. IX of *The Official History of Australia in the War of 1914-18*, 4th ed., p. xxii.

[19] J. A. La Nauze, *Alfred Deakin*, p. 518.

[20] *Herald*, 12 June 1905.

[21] Deakin to GG for S. of S., 28 August 1905, CAO, CP 290, series 15, bundle 6.

[22] Deakin to GG for S. of S., 26 April 1906, ibid., bundle 1.

[23] 11 November 1905, 8 January 1906, Deakin Papers, ANL, box 38, item 461.

[24] *Report of the Committee of Imperial Defence Upon a General Scheme of Defence for Australia* in *CPP*, 1906, II, pp. 171, 177.

[25] 23 July 1906, Jebb Papers, ANL, MS. 339.

[26] 25 August 1906, Deakin Papers, ANL, box 10, item 1143.

[27] Cd 3523, *BPP*, 1907, LV, p. 131.

[28] See, for example, the *Age*, 8, 24 February 1906. For confirmation of Playford's 'indiscretion' see CAO, CP 290, series 15, bundle 1.

[29] *Sunday Times*, Johannesburg, 23 August 1908 and *Sun*, New York, 4, 26 October 1908: cuttings in Deakin Papers, ANL, box 41, folder 512.

[30] *Age*, 19 March; *Argus*, 24 March 1909.

[31] G. B. Simpson (NSW Government Administrator) to S. of S., 26 March 1909, CAO, CRS A2, file 14/4051.

[32] 30 March 1909, ibid.

[33] Symon to Bruce Smith, 21 June 1909, Symon Papers, MS. 1736, copy.

[34] See CAO, CRS A2, file 14/4051. La Nauze, *Deakin*, ch. 24, discusses the Dreadnought crisis and Fusion. He seems to imply—but stops short of a direct statement—that the crisis facilitated the merger of the two parties.

[35] Simpson to S. of S., 4 April 1909, CAO, CRS A2, file 14/4051.

[36] See Fisher to GG, 22 March 1909, file 09/2819; Hunt to GG for S. of S., 10 April 1909, cable, copy, file 12/577; Fisher to GG for S. of S., 29 April 1909, cable, copy, file 09/2819; CAO, CRS A2.

[37] *Age*, 29 May 1909.

[38] Deakin to GG for S. of S., 4 June 1909, CAO, CRS A2, file 14/4051.

[39] See Arthur J. Marder, *From the Dreadnought to Scapa Flow*, pp. 72, 77, 120. See also Marder, *British Naval Policy 1880-1905*.

[40] 15 July 1909, CAO, CRS A2, file 09/2819.

[41] See *Proceedings of the Imperial Conference on Naval and Military Defence*, p. 35, copy in Deakin Papers, ANL, box 38, item 470; Dominions No. 17, *Secret Imperial Conference on the Subject of the Defence of the Empire, 1909. Notes of Proceedings of Conferences at the Admiralty*, p. 5, in CAO, CP 103, series 12, bundle 8.

[42] Ibid., pp. 5-7.

[43] To Deakin, 13 August 1909, Deakin Papers, ANL, box 38, item 473.

[44] L. F. Fitzhardinge, *William Morris Hughes*, vol. 1, p. 140.

[45] Federal Labor Party, Minute Books Nos 1 and 2. Hughes was a member of the special defence committees of 1901, 1903, 1908, and the standing committee of 1909.

[46] CAO, MP 84, series 1, file 1856/6/3.

[47] 23 September 1907, Jebb Papers, ANL, MS. 813.

[48] See *The Times*, 27 December 1907, 25 August 1909.

[49] *Daily Telegraph*, 8 April 1909.

[50] *Age*, 29 June 1903.

[51] 30 July 1907, Jebb Papers, ANL, MS. 813.

[52] Deakin to Groom, 12 February 1909, Groom Papers, ANL, MS. 236, series 1, folder 9.

[53] *The Times*, 21 November 1910.

[54] See Sissons, 'Attitudes to Japan', p. 35 and C. Grimshaw, 'Some Aspects of Australian Attitudes to the Imperial Connection', MA thesis, University of Queensland (1958), p. 139ff., for other accounts of press reaction.

[55] 31 August, 2 September 1905.

[56] *Bulletin*, 18 February 1904.

[57] See *SMH*, 1, 2 September 1905; *West Australian*, 1 February 1907.

[58] See *Call*, 8 August 1906; *Morning Post*, 24 October 1905.

[59] *Call*, August 1908; Commonwealth Political Labour Conference, *Official Report of the Fourth . . .* , p. 19.

[60] *Sunday Times*, 23 August 1908, cutting in Deakin Papers, ANL, box 41, folder 512.

[61] *CPD*, XV, pp. 3094-7.

[62] *National Life and Character: A Forecast*, 2nd ed., pp. 147, 150, 154, 161, 168-70, 189.

[63] 20 February 1908, cutting in Deakin Papers, ANL, box 38, item 463.

[64] *The Times*, 26 April 1907.

[65] November 1907.

[66] 14 February 1906, Deakin Papers, ANL, box 38, item 463.

[67] *Report of the Committee of Naval Officers . . . to Consider the Memorandum of the Committee of Imperial Defence . . .* in *CPP*, 1906, II, p. 184.

[68] Memorandum, Creswell to Deakin: Considerations Affecting the Naval Defence of the Commonwealth, 6 March 1907, CAO, CP 103, series 12, bundle 6.

[69] Minute, Bridges to Ewing, 9 October 1908, CAO, MP 84, series 1, file 1856/1/4.

[70] Hunt to H. A. Gwynne (editor of the *Standard*), 3 September 1910, Hunt Papers, ANL, MS. 52, series 40, item 2203, copy.

[71] Deakin to GG for S. of S., 15 September 1909, CAO, CP 290, series 15, bundle 2.

[72] *SMH*, 6 January 1904, cited by Sissons, 'Attitudes to Japan', p. 25.

[73] 3 October 1905, Deakin Papers, ANL, box 38, item 461, copy.

[74] 4 June 1908, Jebb Papers, ANL, MS. 339.
[75] See Deakin to Jebb, 4 June 1908, 29 May 1907, 27 June 1911, ibid.; Deakin to Clarke, 3 October 1905, 8 January 1906, Deakin Papers, ANL, copies.
[76] Clarke to Deakin, 12 April 1906, Deakin Papers, ANL.
[77] *CPD*, XLII, p. 7512.
[78] *Age*, 5 July 1887.
[79] *CPD*, XLII, pp. 7510, 7526, 7531, 7509, 7535.
[80] *The Times*, 21 November 1910.
[81] Minute, Ewing to Bridges, 13 March 1907, CAO, MP 84, series 1, file 1856/4/4.
[82] *1891 SC*, p. 713.
[83] 1 September 1908, speech at Royal Yacht Club of Victoria, Deakin Papers, ANL, box 38, item 465. See F. K. Crowley, '1901-1914', in Crowley (ed.), *A New History of Australia*, pp. 260-4, for a discussion of the nature of nationalism.
[84] Fox to Jebb, 30 July 1907, Jebb Papers, ANL, MS. 813.
[85] *Brisbane Courier*, 1 January 1901.
[86] *SAR*, 31 March 1909.
[87] *West Australian*, 26 November 1910.
[88] Memorandum: Financial Problems of the Commonwealth: Proposed Scheme of Settlement, unsigned and undated, circulated March 1908, Groom Papers, ANL, MS. 236, folder 19.
[89] 12 September 1908.

6 The Development of Social Policies

[1] See *CPD*, XV, pp. 4750-1, 4785, 4788.
[2] See *CPD*, XIX, p. 1243; *CPD*, XX, p. 2689; *CPD*, XXI, p. 4029.
[3] *CPD*, I, pp. 106, 114.
[4] See T. H. Kewley, 'Commonwealth Old-Age and Invalid Pensions Schemes', *Royal Australian Historical Society, Journal and Proceedings*, vol. XXXIX (1953), part IV, pp. 155-8.
[5] Held invalid by the High Court (Griffith, Barton, O'Connor, with Isaacs and Higgins dissenting).
[6] Held invalid by the High Court (Griffith, Barton, O'Connor, with Isaacs and Higgins dissenting).
[7] W. K. Hancock, *Australia*, pp. 174, 189, first used the phrases 'party of movement' and 'parties of resistance'. For discussions of initiative and resistance see Henry Mayer, 'Some Conceptions of the Australian Party System 1910-1950', in Margot Beever and F. B. Smith (eds), *Historical Studies: Selected Articles*, pp. 217-40; D. W. Rawson, 'Another Look at "Initiative and Resistance"', in *Politics: The Journal of the Australasian Political Studies Association*, vol. III, no. 1 (May 1968), pp. 41-54.
[8] Brian Fitzpatrick, *The British Empire in Australia*, pp. 259-61.
[9] Childe, *How Labour Governs*, 2nd ed., p. 72.
[10] Ward, *Australia*, p. 91.
[11] *Australian Workman*, 11 April 1891.
[12] Australasian Federation League, *Report of the Inaugural Meeting in South Australia*, p. 5.
[13] 7 March 1896.
[14] 8 June 1899, Kirwan Papers, ANL, MS. 277, folder 8, item 16/2F.
[15] *The Labour Movement in Australasia*, pp. 92-3.
[16] Evatt, *Australian Labour Leader*, pp. 2, 97, 115. Statements from Black, see below.

[17] Crisp, *Australian National Government*, pp. 14, 16, 27, 29.

[18] *Federation: or, a Machiavellian Solution of the Australian Labour Position*, p. 12.

[19] See *Australian Workman*, 17 July 1897; *Worker*, Brisbane, 26 August 1899.

[20] Smith's personal manifesto appeared in advertisement columns of the *SMH* and *Daily Telegraph*, 13 February 1897.

[21] Black first quoted Moran and Smith in *A History of the N.S.W. Political Labor Party from Its Conception until 1917*, no. 4, p. 24. See earlier editions of his party history.

[22] 1 February, 7 March 1896.

[23] 6 March 1897.

[24] See Reid, *My Reminiscences*, pp. 179-80, for his problems with the Legislative Council's opposition to federation. Watson strongly supported Reid on this issue: see Bede Nairn, *Civilising Capitalism*, pp. 201-5.

[25] 24 March 1898.

[26] *NSW Parliamentary Debates*, LII, p. 127.

[27] Hancock, *Australia*, pp. 174, 192-3; Hancock, 'The Commonwealth, 1900-1914', pp. 492-4, 505-6.

[28] Maurice Blackburn, 'The Historical Development of Australian Political Parties', in W. G. K. Duncan (ed.), *Trends in Australian Politics*, pp. 2-3.

[29] See Calwell, *Labor's Role in Modern Society*, 2nd ed., p. 189; Fitzhardinge, 'Political and Public Life', in *Nation Building in Australia*, pp. 28, 35; Crisp, *The Australian Federal Labour Party 1901-1951*, p. 155; Crisp, *Australian National Government*, p. 156; Partridge, 'Political Institutions and Aspirations', in George Caiger (ed.), *The Australian Way of Life*, pp. 89-90; Greenwood, 'National Development and Social Experimentation, 1901-14', in Greenwood (ed.), *Australia*, pp. 200, 201-4, 213. Peter Loveday, 'Support in Return for Concessions', *Historical Studies*, vol. 14, no. 55 (October 1970), pp. 376-405, provides a critical account of the subject.

[30] *Labour Movement in Australasia*, pp. 96-7.

[31] *Australia's Awakening*, pp. 397, 380, 411.

[32] *Australian Socialism*, pp. 184-90.

[33] *The First Decade of the Australian Commonwealth*, p. 69.

[34] See *Worker*, 27 January 1900, and Federal Labor Party, Minute Book, No. 1, 20 May 1901.

[35] *CPD*, I, p. 143; *CPD*, VII, p. 8390.

[36] 15 January 1904, Groom Papers, ANL, MS. 236, series 1, folder 4.

[37] See Spence, *Australia's Awakening*, pp. 396-7, and compare Deakin's 1905 programme with reports of Deakin's 1903 policy in the *Age*, 30, 31 October 1903.

[38] Decided by caucus 6 June 1901, and confirmed 20 October 1904, 10 March 1908, Federal Labor Party, Minute Books, Nos 1 and 2.

[39] Ibid., 6 November 1901, 15 June, 17 September 1904.

[40] 31 May 1906, Watson Papers, ANL, MS. 451, series 1, item 7.

[41] 29 November 1906, Jebb Papers, ANL, MS. 813.

[42] To Deakin, 19 January 1907, Forrest Papers, ANL, microfilm reel G660.

[43] *Fourth Triennial Labour-in-Politics Convention 1905*, p. 9.

[44] Federal Labor Party, Minute Book No. 1, 23 April, 17 May, 1 June 1904.

[45] 17 December 1906, Watson Papers, ANL, MS. 451, series 1, item 90, copy.

[46] 9 March 1907, Forrest Papers, ANL, microfilm reel G660.

[47] 6, 19 March 1907, ibid., my italics.

[48] 26 July 1907, ibid.

[49] Federal Labor Party, Minute Book No. 1, 18 October 1905.

[50] See *CPD*, XX, pp. 3224, 3537-9, 3547; *CPD*, XXI, pp. 4010-16, 4131-6; *CPD*, XXIII, pp. 7282-6; *CPD*, XXIV, p. 7664; *CPD*, XXV, pp. 501-6, 584-7, 599; Federal Labor Party, Minute Book No. 1, 10 August 1904.

[51] *Morning Post*, 3 February 1906.

[52] *CPD*, XXV, p. 606.

[53] 'The Labour Movement', in British Association for the Advancement of Science, *Handbook for New South Wales*, p. 128.

[54] See Kingston to Deakin, 28 September, 9 November 1900, Deakin Papers, ANL, MS. 1540; Deakin to Barton, 7, 14 November 1900, Barton Papers, ANL, MS. 51, series 1, items 362, 363.

[55] *NSW Parliamentary Debates*, LXXIX, p. 858.

[56] *Australian Workman*, 1 February 1896.

[57] *Report of the Royal Commission on Old-Age Pensions* in *Vic. Parliamentary Papers*, 1898, III, pp. VI, 12, 14, 30, 34.

[58] *Report of the Royal Commission on the Aged Poor* in *SA Parliamentary Papers*, 1898-9, II, pp. V, VI, IX, X.

[59] *Censuses of NSW and Vic.* for 1861, 1901.

[60] *CPD*, I, p. 113.

[61] J. H. Symon, *The Commonwealth Election for the Senate*, p. 2, in Symon Papers, ANL, MS. 1736.

[62] *Mercury*, 14 March 1901.

[63] See *CPD*, I, pp. 42, 132, 143; *CPD*, III, pp. 3475-8, 3583; *CPD*, XXIII, pp. 7115-24.

[64] *Conference of Commonwealth and State Premiers . . .* , in *CPP*, 1906, II, p. 1316.

[65] *CPD*, XXXIX, p. 4574; *CPD*, XLIV, pp. 9303, 9306, 9310.

[66] 5 August 1908, Forrest Papers, ANL, microfilm reel G660.

[67] See J. T. Sutcliffe, *A History of Trade Unionism in Australia*, pp. 40-3, 37-8, 121.

[68] *CPD*, XV, pp. 2862-4, 3182.

[69] Commonwealth Political Labour Conference, *Official Report of the Second . . .* , p. 7; Commonwealth Trades Union Congress, *Official Report*, p. 20.

[70] 5 August 1902, Deakin Papers, ANL, MS. 1540, item 3347.

[71] *Age*, 13 June 1903. See Sutcliffe, *Trade Unionism in Australia*, p. 173; Lorraine Benham and John Rickard, 'Masters and Servants: The Victorian Railway Strike of 1903', in J. Iremonger, J. Merritt, and G. Osborne (eds.), *Strikes*, pp. 1-25.

[72] Federal Labor Party, Minute Book No. 1, 29 July 1903. Batchelor had been an apprentice and foreman at the SA railway workshops. He served four terms as president of the ASE and was president of the Railway Service Mutual Association for many years.

[73] CAO, CRS A6, file 01/1532. This is a notice paper with the two questions, Barton's query, and Kingston's reply.

[74] 5 April 1904, Hunt Papers, ANL, MS. 52, series 21, item 1258.

[75] *CPD*, II, pp. 1819-20.

[76] See *1898 MC*, I, p. 184; *CPD*, II, pp. 1821-3.

[77] Correspondence in CAO, CRS A8, file 01/46/-.

[78] Hancock, 'The Commonwealth, 1900-1914', p. 495; Federal Labor Party, Minute Book No. 1, 12 June 1901.

[79] National Anti-Sweating League, Minute Book No. 2, 24 July, 16 September 1901, Mauger Papers, ANL, MS. 403, item 15.

[80] Commonwealth Political Labour Conference, *Official Report of the*

Second . . . , p. 7; Federal Labor Party, Minute Book No. 1, 27 May 1903.
[81] *Argus,* 20 August 1901.
[82] Protectionist Association of Victoria, Minute Book, 25 July, 31 October 1904.
[83] 9 August 1911.
[84] Commonwealth Political Labour Conference, *Official Report of the Third* . . . , pp.14-18.
[85] *CPD,* XXXVI, p. 207.
[86] *Age,* 31 October 1903. See J. A. La Nauze, *Alfred Deakin,* pp. 83-4, 140, 412-14.
[87] Protectionist Association, Minute Book, November 1901.
[88] Ibid., 2 November 1902.
[89] Anti-Sweating League, Minute Book No. 2, 25 September 1903.
[90] *Royal Commission on Customs and Excise Tariffs: Progress Report No. 5* in *CPP,* 1906, IV, p. 85.
[91] *CPD,* V, p. 6033; *CPD,* XIV, p. 1487.
[92] *CPD,* XXXIV, pp. 3997, 4115, 4118.

7　Prosper the Commonwealth

[1] *1891 SC,* p. 544.
[2] Sidney and Beatrice Webb, *The Webb's Australian Diary 1898* (ed. A. G. Austin), p. 106.
[3] *The Government of Victoria,* p. 373.
[4] A. C. Onslow to Symon, 30 March 1897, Symon Papers, ANL, MS. 1736.
[5] *Brisbane Courier,* 1 January 1901.
[6] *CPD,* III, p. 3294. Hughes somehow overlooked uniform immigration control.
[7] *NSW Parliamentary Debates,* LXXXIX, p. 2632.
[8] H. A. Grainger (SA Agent-General) to Symon, 9 December 1904, Symon Papers, ANL, MS. 1736.
[9] Higgins' appointment to the High Court—and hence his famous judgment—came about adventitiously. Deakin first offered the seat to Sir Samuel Way, who rejected it on the grounds of age and inconvenience. Privately Way was disinclined to take 'fifth place in any tribunal' and preferred to be 'first in a small city [rather] than fifth in Rome'. Way to Sir Cyprian Bridges, 16 October 1906, Way Papers, SA Archives.
[10] National Anti-Sweating League, Minute Book No. 2, 16 September 1901, Mauger Papers, ANL, MS. 403.
[11] See Conrad Joyner, *Holman Versus Hughes: Extension of Australian Commonwealth Powers,* for a monograph on the dispute.
[12] 14, 28 May 1902, Barton Papers, ANL, MS. 51, series 1, items 506, 508.
[13] 24 June 1902, ibid., item 520. The evolution of procedures, precedents, and principles, however, was a two-way process similar to that described by Oliver MacDonagh, *A Pattern of Government Growth 1800-1860.*
[14] Gerald E. Caiden, *Career Service,* pp. 451-60.
[15] See *Official Year Book of the Commonwealth,* No. 1, pp. 652-3; No. 3, p. 805; No. 5, pp. 802-3.
[16] Downer to Barton, 3 June 1902, Barton Papers, ANL, MS. 51, series 1, item 514.
[17] 24 August 1907.
[18] 9 June 1908.
[19] *The First Decade of the Australian Commonwealth,* p. 259.
[20] Election poster, 12 December 1912, Symon Papers, ANL, MS. 1736.

[21] Price to Governor of SA for S. of S., 12 December 1906, in Cd 3340, *Correspondence Relating to the Colonial Conference 1907*, p. 24.

[22] *Brisbane Courier*, 28 February 1901.

[23] Barton to GG for S. of S., 12 March 1902, copy in Records of the Colonial Office CO 418/18, ANL, microfilm reel 2150. A CO minute of 22 April commented: 'It was apprehended that the Commonwealth might claim a quasi-national & international status, but . . . Mr Bartons minute does not bear out that apprehension. Presumably such status will be claimed if at all only in instances where it is convenient to do so'.

[24] Chamberlain to GG for PM, 27 May 1902, CAO, CP 78, series 1, file 192, copy.

[25] A. T. Yarwood, *Asian Migration to Australia*, pp. 90, 183.

[26] Watson to Editor of *Daily Citizen*, 1915, Watson Papers, ANL, MS. 451, series 1, item 125.

[27] *Report of the Royal Commission on the Sugar Industry*, CPP, 1912, III, pp. viii, ix.

[28] *Report of the Proceedings of a Conference Between Ministers of the Commonwealth and Ministers of the States*, Melbourne, November 1901, p. 46, in CAO, CRS A571, file 04/608.

[29] Marginal note by Forrest on a memorandum by Playford, 10 October 1905, Deakin Papers, ANL, MS. 1540, box 36, item 435.

BIBLIOGRAPHY

The bibliography lists material cited in footnotes and a few general reference books.

I. OFFICIAL SOURCES

A. Manuscript

(i) In the Australian National Library, Canberra

Records of the Colonial Office, CO 418/10 and 418/18 (Australian joint copying project microfilm reels 2139 and 2150), despatches to and from the State Governors and Governor-General and the Secretary of State for Colonies, with office minutes.

(ii) In the Commonwealth Archives Office, Canberra

Department of External Affairs:
CRS A6, correspondence files 1901.
——— A8, correspondence files (folio system) 1901-2.
——— A10, number registers and indices to A6 and A8.
——— A1, general correspondence files 1903-.
——— A30, number registers (record books) for A1.
——— A1108, collected papers relating to External Affairs assembled by the Director, Pacific Branch.

Governor-General's Office:
CP 78, series 1, correspondence relating mainly to imperial matters 1901-11.
———, series 2, correspondence relating mainly to local matters 1901-11.
CP 290, series 15, special bundles of papers extracted from the Governor-General's files, 1903-.

Prime Minister's Office:

CRS A2, correspondence files 1904-.

———— A48, registers and indices for A2.

CP 103, series 2, minutes, proceedings, and papers laid before the Imperial Conference 1911.

————, series 12, records of Imperial Conferences 1897-1933.

Treasury:

CRS A571, correspondence file 1901-.

———— A572, registers and indices for A571.

(iii) In the Commonwealth Archives Office, Melbourne

Department of Defence:

MP 160, series 1, correspondence Victorian Dept Defence 1879-1901.

MP 178, series 1, general correspondence (naval) 1901-6.

————, series 2, general correspondence (naval) 1906-13.

MP 84, series 2, general correspondence (military) 1901-6.

————, series 1, general correspondence (military) 1906-13.

(iv) In New South Wales Government Archives

Colonial Secretary, 4/902.1, Federation bundle, 1890-1.

B. Printed

(i) Australia

Censuses of New South Wales, South Australia, Victoria, 1861-1901.

Commonwealth Parliamentary Debates, 1901-.

Commonwealth Parliamentary Papers, particularly:

Cane Sugar Industry of Australia, 1901-2, II.

Military Forces of the Commonwealth: Minute upon the Defence of Australia by Major-General Hutton, 1901-2, II.

Statement by the Minister of State for Defence on the Estimates of the Defence Department for . . . 1903-4, 1903, II.

Coloured Persons (Numbers in Various States . . .), 1903, II.

Military Forces of the Commonwealth of Australia: Second Annual Report by . . . Hutton, 1904, II.

Sugar Bounty, 1904, II.

The Defence of Australia (Statement by . . . Deakin), 1905, II.

Sugar Bonus (Report by Dr Maxwell), 1905, II.

Report of the Committee of Imperial Defence Upon a General Scheme of Defence for Australia, 1906, II.

Report of the Committee of Naval Officers . . . to consider the Memorandum of the Committee of Imperial Defence . . . , 1906, II.

Conference of Commonwealth and State Premiers . . . , 1906, II.
Royal Commission on Customs and Excise Tariffs: Progress Report No. 5, 1906, IV.
Report of the Royal Commission on the Sugar Industry, 1912, III.
Sugar Industry of Australia: Report by Dr Maxwell, 1912, III.
New South Wales Parliamentary Debates.
Official Record of the Proceedings and Debates of the Australasian Federation Conference 1890. Melbourne, 1890.
Official Record of the Proceedings and Debates of the National Australasian Convention 1891. Sydney, 1891.
Official Record of the National Australasian Convention Debates. Adelaide, 1897.
Official Record of the Debates of the Australasian Federal Convention. Sydney, 1897.
Official Record of the Debates of the Australasian Federal Convention. 2 vols. Melbourne, 1898.
Official Year Books of the Commonwealth, 1907-.
Queensland Parliamentary Papers, Legislative Assembly, particularly: *Admission of Japanese into Queensland*, 1901, IV.
South Australian Parliamentary Debates.
South Australian Parliamentary Papers, particularly: *Intercolonial Conference of Ministers, 4-5 March 1896*, 1896, II.
Report of the Royal Commission on the Aged Poor, 1898-9, II.
Statistical Registers of South Australia and Victoria for 1890, 1898, 1899.
Victorian Parliamentary Debates.
Victorian Parliamentary Papers, particularly: *Inspection of Colonial Forces by an Imperial General Officer*, 1889, III.
Report of the Royal Commission on Old-Age Pensions, 1898, III.

(ii) Great Britain

British Parliamentary Papers, particularly:
    C. 5091, *Proceedings of the Colonial Conference 1887*, 1887, LVI.
    C. 6188, *Correspondence Relating to the Inspection of the Military Forces of the Australasian Colonies by Major-General J. Bevan Edwards*, 1890, XLIX.
    C. 8596, *Proceedings of a Conference Between the Secretary of State for the Colonies and the Premiers of the Self-Governing Colonies, London 1897*, 1897, LIX.
    Cd 1299, *Papers Relating to a Conference Between the Secretary of State for the Colonies and the Prime Ministers of the Self-Governing Colonies*, 1902, LXVI.
    Cd 3340, *Correspondence Relating to the Colonial Conference, 1907*, 1907, LIV.

Cd 3523, *Minutes and Proceedings of the Colonial Conference 1907*, 1907, LV.

Colonial Office, Confidential Prints:

Misc. No. *111*. *Confidential*. *Report of a Conference Between the Rt Hon. Joseph Chamberlain and the Premiers of the Self-Governing Colonies of the Empire, 1897* (in CAO, CP 103, series 12, bundle 1).

Misc. No. *144*. *Confidential*. *Conference Between the Secretary of State for the Colonies and the Premiers of the Self-Governing Colonies. Minutes of the Proceedings and Papers Laid Before the Colonial Conference 1902* (in Menzies Library, Australian National University).

II. OTHER SOURCES

A. Manuscript

Barton, (Sir) Edmund. Papers, ANL, MS. 51.

Cook, J. Hume. Papers, ANL, MS. 610.

Deakin, Alfred. Papers, ANL, MS. 1540.

Federal Labor Party. Minute Books, Nos 1 and 2, 1901-10 (consulted with the permission of Mr E. G. Whitlam, leader of the Federal Parliamentary Labor Party, at Parliament House, Canberra).

Forrest, John (Baron). Papers, ANL, microfilm reel G660.

Groom, (Sir) Littleton. Papers, ANL, MS. 236.

Hunt, Atlee. Papers, ANL, MS. 52.

———. Diaries, ANL, MS. 1100.

James, (Sir) Walter. Correspondence, ANL, MS. 296.

Jebb, Richard. Letters from Deakin 1906-14, ANL, MS. 339.

———. Letters 1905-19, ANL, MS. 813.

Kirwan, (Sir) John Waters. Papers, ANL, MS. 277.

Mauger, Samuel. Papers, ANL, MS. 403.

National Anti-Sweating League. Minute Book No. 2 (in Mauger Papers).

Parkes, Henry. Correspondence, A63, A68, A885, A916, A921, Mitchell Library.

Pearce, (Sir) George F. Papers, ANL, MS. 1827.

Protectionist Association of Victoria. Minute Book (in Mauger Papers).

Symon, (Sir) Josiah. Papers, ANL, MS. 1736.

Tennyson, Hallam (Baron). Papers, ANL, MS. 479.

United Trades and Labor Council. Minute Book 1895-1899, SA Trades Hall, Adelaide.

Wallaroo and Moonta Mining & Smelting Co. Ltd. General Minutes Book, 1890-1923, SA Archives.

Watson, J. C. Papers, ANL, MS. 451.

Way, (Sir) Samuel. Papers, Private Record Group 30, SA Archives.

B. Newspapers and Periodicals

The following were consulted for relevant periods or appropriate dates:

Advertiser, Adelaide
Age, Melbourne
Argus, Melbourne
Australasian, Melbourne
Australian Workman, Sydney
Brisbane Courier, Brisbane
British Empire Review, London
Bulletin, Sydney
Call, Sydney
Commonwealth, Sydney
Daily Telegraph, Sydney
Herald, Melbourne
Kadina and Wallaroo Times, Kadina
Kapunda Herald, Kapunda
Launceston Examiner, Launceston
Laura Standard, Laura
Mercury, Hobart
Morning Post, London
Mount Barker Courier, Mount Barker
Northern Territory Times, Palmerston and Port Darwin
Orroroo Enterprise and Great Northern Advertiser, Orroroo
Patriot, Bundaberg
People's Weekly, Moonta
Plain Dealer, Kadina
Port Augusta Dispatch, Port Augusta
Review of Reviews, Melbourne
Royal Colonial Institute: Proceedings, London
South Australian Register, Adelaide
South-Eastern Star, Mount Gambier
Southern Argus, Strathalbyn
Southern Cross, Adelaide
Southern Yorke's Peninsular Pioneer, Yorketown
Sugar Journal and Tropical Cultivator, Mackay
Sydney Morning Herald, Sydney
Times, The, London
Tocsin, Melbourne
United Service Magazine, new series, London
Weekly Herald, Adelaide
West Australian, Perth
Worker, Brisbane
Worker, Sydney

C. Some Contemporary Books, Pamphlets, Reports

Australian Federation: volume of handbills and cuttings issued in Queensland, 1899. Mitchell Library.

Australasian Federation League, *Report of the Inaugural Meeting in South Australia*. Adelaide, 1895.

Baker, R. C., *Federation*. Adelaide, 1897.

Bathurst Convention, *Proceedings of the People's Federal Convention*. Sydney, 1897.

Black, George, *A History of the N.S.W. Political Labor Party from its Conception until 1917*, no. 4. Sydney, n.d.

———, *The Labor Party in New South Wales: A History from its Formation in 1891 until . . .*, various editions. Sydney, n.d.

Clark, Victor S., *The Labour Movement in Australasia*. New York, 1906.

Cockburn, John A., *Australian Federation*. London, 1901.

Colonial Sugar Refining Co. Ltd, *Reports and Speeches*, January 1885 to October 1908.

Colonists' Anti-Convention Bill League. Sydney, 1899.

Colonists' Anti-Convention Bill League, *Manifesto*. Sydney, n.d. [1898-9].

Commonwealth Political Labour Conference, *Official Report of the Second*, held at Sydney 1902. Brisbane 1902.

———, *Third*, held at Melbourne 1905. Brisbane 1905.

———, *Fourth*, held at Brisbane 1908. Brisbane 1908.

Commonwealth Trades Union Congress, *Official Report*. Sydney, 1902.

Corowa Conference, *Official Report of the Federation Conference*. Corowa 1893.

Craig, George Cathcart, *The Federal Defence of Australasia*. Sydney, 1897.

Cyclopedia of Tasmania. 2 vols. Hobart, 1900.

Deakin, Alfred, *The Federal Story* (ed. J. A. La Nauze). Melbourne, 1963.

Forrest, John, *Speech by the Rt. Hon. Sir John Forrest on the Federation of Australia at St. Georges Hall Perth*. Perth, 1898.

Fourth Triennial Labour-in-Politics Convention, 1905. Brisbane, 1905.

Garran, Robert Randolph, *The Coming Commonwealth*. Sydney, 1897.

Griffith, Samuel Walker, *Notes on Australian Federation: Its Nature and Probable Effects*. Brisbane, 1896.

———, *Australian Federation and the Draft Commonwealth Bill*. Brisbane, 1899.

Haynes, H. Valentine, *Federation: or, a Machiavellian Solution of the Australian Labour Position*. Sydney, 1891.

Herald, The, *A White Australia*. Melbourne, 1901.

Higgins, Henry Bournes, *Essays and Addresses on the Australian Commonwealth Bill*. Melbourne, 1900.

Hughes, W. M., *The Case for Labor*. Sydney, 1910.

———, *Labour in Power*. Melbourne, 1913.

Intercolonial Trades Union Congress, *Official Report of the First*. Sydney, 1879.
——, *Second*. Melbourne, 1884.
——, *Third*. Sydney, 1885.
——, *Fourth*. Adelaide, 1886.
——, *Fifth*. Brisbane, 1888.
——, *Sixth*. Hobart, 1889.
——, *Seventh*. Ballarat, 1891.
Jebb, Richard, *The Imperial Conference: A History and Study*, vol. I. London, 1911.
Jenks, Edward, *The Government of Victoria*. London, 1891.
Johns, Fred, *Notable Australians*. Adelaide, 1906.
——, *Fred Johns's Annual*. Adelaide, 1912, and London, 1914.
Kimberly, W. B., *History of West Australia*. Melbourne, 1897.
Mennell, P., *Dictionary of Australasian Biography*. London, 1892.
Moore, W. Harrison, *The Constitution of the Commonwealth of Australia*. London, 1902.
Parkes, Henry, *The Federal Government of Australasia*. Sydney, 1890.
——, *Fifty Years in the Making of Australian History*. London, 1892.
Pearson, Charles H., *National Life and Character: A Forecast*, 2nd ed. London, 1894.
Quick, John and Garran, Robert Randolph, *The Annotated Constitution of the Australian Commonwealth*. Sydney, 1901.
Reid, George Houstoun, *My Reminiscences*. London, 1917.
Rosa, S. A., *Federation. An Exposure of the Federal Conspiracy*. Sydney, 1898.
——, *The Federal Bill Analysed, Being an Examination of the Federal Bill as Amended by the Secret Conference of Premiers*. Sydney, 1899.
Spence, William Guthrie, *Australia's Awakening*. Sydney, 1909.
St Ledger, A., *Australian Socialism*. London, 1909.
Symon, J. H., *The Commonwealth Election for the Senate*. Adelaide, 1901 (in Symon Papers).
Turner, Henry Gyles, *The First Decade of the Australian Commonwealth*. Melbourne, 1911.
Watson, J. C., 'The Labour Movement', in British Association for the Advancement of Science, *Handbook for New South Wales*. Sydney, 1914.
Webb, Sidney and Beatrice, *The Webbs' Australian Diary 1898* (ed. A. G. Austin). Melbourne, 1965.
Wise, B. R., *The Making of the Australian Commonwealth 1889-1900*. London, 1913.

D. Some Later Books and Articles

Barnard, Marjorie, *A History of Australia*. Sydney, 1962.

Benham, Lorraine and Rickard, John, 'Masters and Servants: The Victorian Railway Strike of 1903', in John Iremonger, John Merritt, and Graeme Osborne (eds), *Strikes*. Sydney, 1973.

Blackburn, Maurice, 'The Historical Development of Australian Political Parties', in W. G. K. Duncan (ed.), *Trends in Australian Politics*. Sydney, 1935.

Blainey, Geoffrey, 'The Role of Economic Interests in Australian Federation', in J. J. Eastwood and F. B. Smith (eds), *Historical Studies: Selected Articles*. Melbourne, 1964.

Bolton, G. C., *A Thousand Miles Away*. Brisbane, 1963.

—— and Mozley, Ann, *The Western Australian Legislature 1870-1930*. Canberra, 1961.

Caiden, Gerald E., *Career Service*. Melbourne, 1965.

Calwell, A. A., *Labor's Role in Modern Society*, 2nd ed. Melbourne, 1963.

Childe, Vere Gordon, *How Labour Governs*, 2nd ed. Melbourne, 1964.

Crisp, L. F., *The Australian Federal Labour Party 1901-1951*. London, 1955.

——, *Australian National Government*. Melbourne, 1965.

Crowley, F. K., '1901-1914', in Crowley (ed.), *A New History of Australia*. Melbourne, 1974.

de Garis, B. K., '1890-1900', in ibid.

Easterby, Harry T, *The Queensland Sugar Industry*. Brisbane, n.d.

Evatt, Herbert Vere, *Australian Labour Leader*. Sydney, 1940.

Fitzhardinge, L. F., 'Political and Public Life', in *Nation Building in Australia: The Life and Work of Sir Littleton Groom*. Sydney, 1941.

——, *William Morris Hughes: A Political Biography*, vol. I, Sydney, 1964.

Fitzpatrick, Brian, *The British Empire in Australia*, 2nd ed. Melbourne, 1949.

Gollan, R. A., 'Nationalism, the Labour Movement and the Commonwealth 1880-1900', in Gordon Greenwood (ed.), *Australia: A Social and Political History*. Sydney, 1955.

——, *Radical and Working Class Politics: A Study of Eastern Australia, 1850-1910*. Melbourne, 1960.

Greenwood, Gordon, 'National Development and Social Experimentation, 1901-14', in Greenwood (ed.), *Australia: A Social and Political History*. Sydney, 1955.

Hancock, W. K., *Australia*. Brisbane, 1961 [first published 1930].

——, 'The Commonwealth, 1900-1914', in J. Holland Rose (ed.), *The Cambridge History of the British Empire*, vol. VII, pt 1. Cambridge, 1933.

Hewett, Patricia, 'Aspects of Campaigns in South-Eastern New South Wales at the Federation Referenda of 1898 and 1899', in A. W. Martin (ed.), *Essays in Australian Federation*. Melbourne, 1969.

Hughes, Colin A. and Graham, B. D., *A Handbook of Australian Government and Politics 1890-1964*. Canberra, 1968.

Jose, Arthur W., *The Royal Australian Navy 1914-18*, vol. IX of *The Official History of Australia in the War of 1914-18*, 4th ed. Sydney, 1937.

Joyner, Conrad, *Holman Versus Hughes: Extension of Australian Commonwealth Powers*. University of Florida Monographs, Gainesville, 1961.

Kewley, T. H., 'Commonwealth Old-Age and Invalid Pensions Schemes', in *Royal Australian Historical Society, Journal and Proceedings*, vol. XXXIX, pt IV (1953).

La Nauze, J. A., *Alfred Deakin: A Biography*. Melbourne, 1965.

———, *The Making of the Australian Constitution*. Melbourne, 1972.

Loveday, Peter, 'Support in Return for Concessions', *Historical Studies*, vol. 14, no. 55 (October 1970).

Lowndes, A. G. (ed.), *South Pacific Enterprise: The Colonial Sugar Refining Company Limited*. Sydney, 1956.

Macandie, G. L., *The Genesis of the Royal Australian Navy: A Compilation*. Sydney, 1949.

MacDonagh, Oliver, *A Pattern of Government Growth 1800-1860*. London, 1961.

McMinn, W. G., 'The First Federal Referendum: A Local Study', in *Royal Australian Historical Society: Journal and Proceedings*, vol. 46, pt 4 (1960).

Marder, Arthur J., *British Naval Policy 1880-1905*. London, 1940.

———, *From the Dreadnought to Scapa Flow*. London, 1961.

Mayer, Henry, 'Some Conceptions of the Australian Party System 1910-1950', in Margot Beever and F. B. Smith (eds), *Historical Studies: Selected Articles* second series. Melbourne, 1967.

Morrison, A. A., 'Some Lesser Members of the Queensland Parliament', in *Journal of the Royal Historical Society Queensland*, vol. VI, no. III (1960-1).

Nairn, Bede, *Civilising Capitalism: The Labor Movement in New South Wales 1870-1900*. Canberra, 1973.

Nicholson, D. F., *Australia's Trade Relations*. Melbourne, 1965.

Norris, R., 'Economic Influences on the 1898 South Australian Federation Referendum' in A. W. Martin (ed.), *Essays in Australian Federation*. Melbourne, 1969.

Parker, R. S., 'Australian Federation: the Influence of Economic Interests and Political Pressures', and 'Some Comments on the Role of Economic

Interests in Australian Federation', in J. J. Eastwood and F. B. Smith (eds), *Historical Studies: Selected Articles*. Melbourne, 1964.

Partridge, P. H., 'Political Institutions and Aspirations', in George Caiger (ed.), *The Australian Way of Life*. Melbourne, 1953.

Rawson, D. W., 'Another Look at "Initiative and Resistance"', in *Politics: The Journal of the Australasian Political Studies Association*, vol. III, no. 1 (May 1968).

Sawer, Geoffrey, *Australian Federal Politics and Law 1901-1929*. Melbourne, 1956.

————, *Australian Federalism in the Courts*. Melbourne, 1967.

Scholefield, G. H. (ed.), *Dictionary of New Zealand Biography*. Wellington, 1940.

Serle, Geoffrey, 'The Victorian Government's Campaign for Federation, 1883-1889', in A. W. Martin (ed.), *Essays in Australian Federation*. Melbourne, 1969.

Sutcliffe, J. T., *A History of Trade Unionism in Australia*. Melbourne, 1921.

Thomas, Kathleen, and Serle, Geoffrey, *A Biographical Register of the Victorian Parliament 1859-1900*. Canberra, 1972.

Ward, Russel, *Australia*. Sydney, 1965.

Waterson, D. B., *A Biographical Register of the Queensland Parliament 1860-1929*. Canberra, 1972.

Willard, M., *History of the White Australia Policy to 1920*, 2nd ed. Melbourne, 1967 [first published 1923].

Wright, D. I., *Shadow of Dispute: Aspects of Commonwealth-State Relations, 1901-10*. Canberra, 1970.

Yarwood, A. T., *Asian Migration to Australia*. Melbourne, 1964.

E. Theses

Atkinson, L. D., 'Australian Defence Policy: A Study of Empire and Nation 1897-1910'. PhD, Australian National University (1964).

Bastin, John, 'The West Australian Federation Movement'. MA, University of Melbourne (1951).

Grimshaw, C., 'Some Aspects of Australian Attitudes to the Imperial Connection 1900-1919'. MA, University of Queensland (1958).

Norris, R., 'Aspects of the 1898 South Australian Federation Referendum and the Parker–Blainey Controversy'. BA, University of Adelaide (1966).

Sissons, D. C. S., 'Attitudes to Japan and Defence 1890-1923'. MA, University of Melbourne (1956).

INDEX

Abbott, Sir Joseph P., 8, 12, 211
Administration of justice, *see* Justice, administration of
Admiralty, 113, 129, 132-5, 137, 141, 143-5, 147-9, 151, 159
Adult suffrage, *see* Parliament
Advertiser, 17, 23, 54
Afghans in Australia, 60; *see also* Immigration
Age, 22-4, 29, 31, 51, 55, 72, 88, 115, 130, 134-5, 146, 151, 183, 194
Agricultural machinery, 164, 196
Agriculture, tropical, 56, 73
Albany (W.A.), 26
Alexander, F., 30
Anglo-Dutch Convention, 104
Anglo-Japanese Alliance (1902), 98; (1905), 149, 153; (1911), 203
Anglo-Japanese Treaty of Commerce and Navigation (1894), 95-106, 203, 205, 207; (1911), 203
Annotated Constitution of the Australian Commonwealth (J. Quick and R. R. Garran), 65
Anstey, F., 154
Anti-Chinese League, 61
Anti-Commonwealth Bill Leagues, 17, 20, 24, 31
Anti-Sweating League, *see* National Anti-Sweating League
Appropriations, 10, 12, 121; *see also* Finance, public
Arbitration, 7-8, 67, 162-5, 169, 180, 183, 187-90, 202-3
Arbitration Court (Cwlth), 163
Argus, 20, 52, 55, 98, 102, 135, 146, 184

Asian immigration, 44-6, 53-4, 56-60, 62, 64-6, 69-70, 74-5, 77, 89-90, 92, 94; *see also* Immigration; *under national groups*
Atkinson, Sir Harry A., 220
Atkinson, L., 133, 135
Australasian, 69, 73
Australasian Federal Convention (1897-8): election of delegates to, 32, 37, 181; membership of, 2, 13, 16, 46-7, 120, 168-70, 181, 222-30; moves and resolutions at, 1, 3-14, 19, 46-7, 49, 62, 64, 78-9, 117, 152, 190
Australasian Federation Conference (1890), 4, 45-6, 49-50, 78, 170
Australasian Federation League, 31, 49, 51, 115
Australasian National League, 52
Australia (battle-cruiser), 107
Australian Federation Enabling Bill (N.S.W.), 24, 202; (Qld), 16, 63
Australian Federation League, *see* Australasian Federation League
Australian Industries Preservation Act (Cwlth), 164
Australian National Defence League, *see* National Defence League
Australian Natives Association, 18, 30-2, 40, 49, 52, 130
Australian Order of Industry, 50
Australian Workman, 167, 170

Baker, Sir Richard C., 5-6, 12-15, 17, 22-3, 25, 35-6, 85, 171, 199-200, 205, 214
Bankruptcy, 37
Banks and banking, 37, 182